CARPET SAHIB
A Life of Jim Corbett

Carpet Sahib

A LIFE OF JIM CORBETT

MARTIN BOOTH

Oxford   New York

OXFORD UNIVERSITY PRESS

1991

Oxford University Press, Walton Street, Oxford OX2 6DP
Oxford New York Toronto
Delhi Bombay Calcutta Madras Karachi
Petaling Jaya Singapore Hong Kong Tokyo
Nairobi Dar es Salaam Cape Town
Melbourne Auckland
and associated companies in
Berlin Ibadan

Oxford is a trade mark of Oxford University Press

First published 1986 by Constable & Company Ltd
First issued as an Oxford University Press paperback 1991

British Library Cataloguing in Publication Data
Data available
ISBN 0–19–282859–2

Library of Congress Cataloging in Publication Data
Booth, Martin.
Carpet Sahib: a life of Jim Corbett / Martin Booth.
p.   cm.—(Oxford lives)
Includes index.
1. Corbett, Jim, 1875–1955.   2. Hunters—India—Biography.
3. Conservationists—India—Biography.   I. Title.   II. Series.
799.2'6'092—dc20   SK17.C6B66   1991   91–16758
[B]
ISBN 0–19–282859–2

Printed in Great Britain by
Biddles Ltd.
Guildford and King's Lynn

this book is dedicated
to
the hillfolk of Kumaon,
Uttar Pradesh,
India

CONTENTS

ACKNOWLEDGEMENTS

A great number of people have assisted me in a good many ways with the writing of this biography; they have trusted me with the loan of their possessions, presented to me mementoes or documents, passed on to me their memories and memoirs, provided me with facilities for research, afforded me the hospitality of their homes (or their country), and have given generously of their time, advice and support. I owe a very great debt of gratitude to Audrey and Robert Baylis, Norah Vivian, Dorothy Lincoln-Gordon, Mr and Mrs Ray Nestor, Lord and Lady Glendevon, Mrs Vera Cumberlege, Nancy Fortescue, David and Eileen Woodward, Peter Jones and the staff of 'The Natural World' Unit (BBC TV Bristol), Mr Ramesh Chandra (Add. Director General, Department of Tourism, the Government of India), Mr A. S. Sawhney (Assistant Director: Government of India Tourist Office, New Delhi), Raj Mittal, The Project Tiger officers and staff at Ramnagar and Dhikala/Corbett National Park, Brijendra Singh, Mr and Mrs Francis Ford-Robertson, Dr and Mrs P. Ball, Brig. Geoffrey Beyts, B. S. Negi, Col. Patrick Hearn, John Elliot, Joan Davis, Giri Raj Singh, Lady Muriel Measures, Lord Dalhousie, the Marquess of Linlithgow, Sir Michael Blundell, the Countess of Feversham, Lady Betty Clay, Lady Chrystal Champion, D. C. Kala, R. E. Hawkins, Brian Stutchbury, Col. A. W. Buchanan, Brig. Michael Calvert, David Lincoln-Gordon, Alan and Tessa MacGregor, Pru Palmes, Jan Hemsing, Malcolm A. Freshney, R. J. Prickett (senior hunter, Treetops), Elizabeth Knight and Will Sulkin of Oxford University Press, the Librarian and staff of the India Office Library (London), Eric Risley, Nigel Champion, Barbara Donaldson, Philip Mason, Lt.-Col. Hilary Hook, Mrs Creina Stephens, Mrs June Koot, H. E. Corbett-Marshall, Maurice Nestor, G. A. Haig, Phil Berry, Jerry A. Jaleel, Mahout Sharafat Hussein (and his elephant 'Molly') and Gil, my Indian driver.

Without the kindness of these people this book could not have been written.

Introduction

When I was twelve or thirteen years old, I borrowed a book from my school library simply because of the picture on the cover and the title. The dust jacket illustration was a drawing of the face of a snarling tiger and the title was *Man-Eaters of Kumaon*. I had been unable to borrow a book about man-eating lions attacking construction workers on the Nairobi to Mombasa railway at a place called Tsavo and this seemed a similar sort of book promising similar excitement, gory scenes and accurate shooting. It matched my expectations, but that was not all it offered by a long measure.

By the time I had finished reading the book, I was addicted not so much to the man-eater stories but to the life and thoughts of the extraordinary man who had written them.

Jim Corbett was a domiciled member of the British Raj. He lived in northern India for most of his life and became an expert *shikari* – the Hindi word for a hunter – especially where tigers and leopards were concerned. He tracked them, stalked them, drove or beat for them and shot them from elephant back, from platforms in trees and on foot for sport. He also shot deer, bears, peafowl and jungle-fowl and was a keen sport fisherman. In his early thirties, he turned his hand to shooting not only trophy tigers and leopards but also man-eaters.

In Jim Corbett was every attribute I demanded of a hero. He was knowledgeable, brave and a crack shot. He was unmarried, tall and dressed – according to the photographs in his books – only in bush clothing. He skinned his own animals with his own knife. Yet what really impressed me were his attitudes towards hunting for, in middle age, he changed from being a killer to being a conservationist.

He did not undergo this drastic metamorphosis suddenly. There was no lightning conversion. Instead, he gradually saw the error of his ways and the ways of men. He still hunted for sport, though only very moderately, and continued to shoot man-eaters when so asked, but he reacted against the mass butchery of wildlife.

Instead of shooting with a .275 Rigby or a .450 or .500 rifle, he shot with a Leica still or with a Bell & Howell cine camera. His photographs and movies, he maintained, were better trophies than a stuffed corpse or a furry rug. They showed the vitality of the living creature and it took just as much skill to achieve a full-frame portrait as it did to place a well-aimed bullet.

'Conservation', as we understand it to mean today, was not a word in everyday usage thirty years ago when I was a schoolboy. It was certainly not in common parlance when Jim Corbett was criticising his fellow sportsmen sixty years ago. Yet the conservation movement was beginning and Jim Corbett was one of its first champions.

From Jim Corbett's books I obtained or was educated in a way of thinking, of natural philosophy, that has never left me. His doctrine of the sanctity of wildlife is one that has deeply affected and guided me.

For many years, I thought to write Jim Corbett's biography but held back because I was afraid that what I might find would be contrary to the vision I had of him: either he would turn out to be a charlatan or else I would discover him to be too pietistic and sanctimonious for comfort. Finally, I accepted the task, fearful of uncovering a hero and finding a sham.

What has emerged is the picture of a shy, gentle and immensely courageous man who was generous and kind, just and loving. He was also at times opinionated, stubborn, jealous and patronising. Additionally, he was a shrewd and quietly thrusting businessman. In other words, like ordinary mortals, he was fallible and had his faults all of which, as his biographer, I have welcomed.

If anything, I have lost a boyhood hero and found a rare, true man.

MARTIN BOOTH
Drayton, Somerset: 1986

Those Who Went East

At the end of the eighteenth century, Ireland was a harsh country in which to live. Its agriculture was largely subsistence farming and the Industrial Revolution that was transforming England appeared to be missing Ireland by. Poverty, without the enriching promise of industrialisation, was somehow more cruel in the Emerald Isle than in the rest of Britain and for those who had the financial wherewithal or the sheer guts and courage there was only one reasonable alternative. They emigrated.

It was at this time that the great exodus west to the new world of America commenced, to gather momentum in earnest over a period of forty years. For those who did not, for one cause or another, want to sail towards the sunset, there lay open to them the expanding vistas of the British Empire of which Ireland herself was at that time a fragment, for the land was under the rule of the British monarchy.

The possibilities hidden in the distant corners of the Empire were seemingly endless. Trade was burgeoning and required its nation of shopkeepers and traders to use and then administer it. Natural resources were there for the picking and taking, for anyone with an axe to fell forests or a shovel with which to dig. The native hordes were waiting for exploitation, for government, for civilisation and for the accompanying firm hand of the laws of Man and God, both of whom were white. Overseas, in the colonies, a white man was like a king, or so the rumour had it. He had servants and authority, he had a position in life and he had the responsibility of ruling. Above all, he had the opportunity for a very much better if very different way of life. Many took the chance and signed on with the army, with trading organisations or with their own consciences and went east. Amongst these emigrants from Great Britain were the ancestors and future relatives of Edward James Corbett.

The first to go left Dublin in 1794 aboard the *William Pitt*. He was Thomas Nestor from Limerick and what he originally went to India to do is lost although, in 1814, he enlisted in the army. Quite possibly, he was at some time in the employ of the East India Company for his son, William Richard Nestor, was a Company official fifty years later when he married Harriet Mary Dwyer in the garrison church in Calcutta.

Their lives, like those of all foreigners in India, were soon to be cast into turmoil by the Indian Mutiny, but the family survived the unrest and William Nestor left the East India Company to become a civil servant in the secretariat for the North-West Province. His office had two head-quarters as was common in the British communities: the cooler winter months were spent down on the plains at Allahabad and the summers, unbearably hot and sultry below two thousand feet, were passed in the newly developing Kumaon hill resort of Naini Tal.

In the early 1860s, after the upheaval caused by the Indian Mutiny and in the new concentration of white settlement that followed the vanquishing of the mutineers, Nestor purchased a plot of land at Kaladhungi, fifteen miles or so to the south-west of Naini Tal where the hills ceased and the plains of India began. He was a generous man to a fault and, as a result of his generosity, was to soon lose the land having put it up as surety for the debt of a friend who broke his bond.

William Nestor died in 1880, but by then his family path had crossed in Naini Tal and Kaladhungi with that of the Corbetts.

The next to leave the old country were James Prussia, born in North Belfast, and his wife Mary Oliver, born of an Anglo-Irish family from the Isle of Man. Whether or not they were married before they embarked for India is not known but they soon had three children, one of whom was Mary Jane, born in Calcutta on 12 March 1837 and baptised four months later at St Andrew's Church. The father's occupation at the time was given as being with the Ishapore gun carriage factory in which he was a sort of craftsman-supervisor: he was subsequently to move to a post with the Serampore paper mill north of Calcutta.

While the children were still young, James Prussia died and his widow, seeking the security of her own family, left Calcutta to settle in the Punjab at Ferozepore (today Ferozpur) where her brother lived. She took with her Mary Jane, the two elder sons being sent to boarding school either in India or back in the British Isles with her parents.

To travel across India in those days was hazardous and difficult. For a European woman to do this with an infant and unaccompanied by an escort of any sort was to make the one thousand mile journey even more dangerous and risky. The railways had yet to be built and the road system was, for the most part, unmapped. India was a series of states with wild countryside inhabited by bandits and natural obstacles. They took some months over the journey, travelling by cart, river boat and dandy, finally arriving in Ferozepore tired but undaunted. It was a journey the like of which baby Mary Jane was to make twenty years later under far more dangerous circumstances.

Others arrived: there were the Morrisons from the Borough of Chelsea in London and Corsham in Wiltshire who owned land in Naini Tal and were not expatriates but lived in Britain and only visited India from time to time throughout the nineteenth century; the Malins from the Midlands and Hamburg who can be traced back to 1691 and include in their ranks Sir Richard Malins, vice-chancellor of England; and there were the Deases and the Doyles.

On 7 February 1815, Joseph and Harriet Corbett disembarked from the *Royal George* to set foot in India, a voyage that they had begun in Ireland on 26 July the year before. They had with them their first child, one year old Eliza.

Corbett is a common surname in the West Midlands and the family name of the barons Rowallan. The name derives from the Old French for a raven and implies the characteristics of that bird – a raucosity of voice and a black complexion. The family line, if Joseph could have traced the relationship, would show the Corbetts to be of ancient French lineage with their predecessors arriving in England with William the Conqueror: they would be entitled to a crest of three ravens.

Joseph and Harriet Corbett, their possible family heritage apart, had just as interesting an immediate past. Joseph had been born in the parish of St Peter's in Belfast in 1796 and when he set sail for India, he gave his profession as a gilder and carver on the army recruitment documents which he had signed on 15 June 1814: he had put himself down for unlimited service as an infantry private. In truth, gilding and carving might well have been his most proficient skills for he had previously been a monk. Harriet had been a novice in a nearby convent. How this young couple had met and improbably fallen in love is anybody's guess but the fact was that they both broke their holy vows and eloped, if one can from a monastery and a nunnery, to be married.

In 1817, Joseph was posted from the infantry to the horse artillery and served with them until his death on 28 March 1830, at the age of 33, rising to the rank of sergeant. He was buried in Meerut. According to his military record, Joseph Corbett was a short man of 5′ 4″ with a long face, sallow colouring, hazel eyes and black hair.

Harriet Corbett bore Joseph nine children. Eliza, the eldest, was born in Belfast on 18 May 1812 and she was followed by Mary (born 1814) who married Patrick Dease on 7 July 1831, John (1816), Joseph (1818), Catherine (1820), Christopher William (1822), Richard Henry (1824), Harriet (1826) and Thomas Bartholomew (1828). Only three of them can be traced: Mary's husband became consultant engineer to the Government of Bombay and she bore him eight children; Thomas Bartholomew became the family hero after whom sons were named for two generations, for he was captured by mutineers at the siege of the Red Fort in Delhi, roped to a stake and burned alive just before the relieving force arrived; Christopher William, who also took part in the fighting at Delhi and who saw his younger brother's awful death, entered the army. One of his many children was Edward James.

Christopher William was born on 11 September 1822 at Meerut, the sixth child of Joseph and Harriet: Joseph had by now risen to the rank of corporal in the horse artillery. Where Christopher William was educated is unknown but it is most likely that he attended school either in Meerut or, after his father's death, in Mussoorie. When he took the Queen's shilling and joined the army is unknown too, but he was soon to see active service as a junior medical officer. At the age of twenty, he held the rank of assistant apothecary with the 3rd Troop of the 1st Brigade: Horse Artillery, possibly following in his father's footsteps into the same unit. He was in action on the North-West Frontier, in the First Afghan War and received a medal for service at 'Cabul'.

The rank of assistant apothecary approximated to assistant surgeon and led on to promotion to apothecary lieutenant and captain. In truth, the job was not what it seems. The duties of the apothecary officer were to act as druggist-cum-chemist and sawbones rather than doctor in the modern sense. However, it does show a degree of skill and knowledge in Christopher William that was to pass on, increased, into his children.

Returning from the North-West Frontier, Christopher William was posted to Dehra Dun and, on 19 December 1845, he married Mary

Anne Morrow at Landour, Mussoorie, which was a military cantonment at the time. No sooner was the honeymoon over – and it was but a brief one extending over the Christmas festivities – than he was posted to the Army of the Sutlej for the Sikh wars and, serving with it in the same rank as before, was awarded the Aliwal medal for 1846: he fought in the battle of Aliwal as well as those at Sobraon and Chilianwala.

Nothing can be found of Mary Anne Morrow's background except that she was 18 when she married and she bore Christopher William two sons and a daughter before her death in her early twenties.

By 1849, Christopher William was in the Army of The Punjab as a hospital steward to the Bengal Army where he was once again decorated, his award bearing the Gujerat bar. The final medal of his military career was the Mutiny Medal with the Delhi bar, presented to Apothecary Christopher William Corbett of the 2nd Bengal Fusiliers.

Returning to his posting at Mussoorie and the cantonment at Landour in the summer of 1859, he met and married on 13 October, Mary Jane Doyle, the widow of Dr Charles James Doyle of Agra.

Mary Jane Doyle (*née* Prussia) had married her first husband at Ferozepore in 1851, at the age of 14. He was 21. Shortly after their marriage, they moved to Agra, south-east of Delhi, where Doyle established a practice. She was to bear him four children: Charles, George, Evangeline and Eugene Mary. Three survived infancy, Evangeline having died of smallpox and been buried in the Tota Talao cemetery at Agra.

When the Indian Mutiny erupted, Mary Jane and her children, along with all the other women and children in the European community of Agra, were sent for safety into the fort and suffered the terrible privations brought on there by the mutineers' siege. Charles Doyle remained on the outside fighting as a civilian volunteer with the army.

During the Mutiny, he rose to a command consisting of what remnants of the Etawah Light Horse and the 13th Troop of Police Cavalry survived the various battles. In late November 1858, a force of Oudh rebels attacked Etawah, halfway between Agra and Kanpur, plundering and murdering whoever they could catch. Doyle's unit engaged these mutineers at what became known as the battle of Harchandpore and resoundingly defeated them. However, on 8 December in the course of the fighting and having killed two mutineers by sword from horseback, he was pulled from his saddle and hacked to death. He lies buried in the cemetery at Etawah and, in the church there, there is a plaque in his honour which reads,

> 'Sacred to the memory of Charles James Doyle who fell leading a small band against overwhelming numbers of savage foes at the battle of Harchandpore . . . Truehearted, generous and gentle as he was brave. His companions in arms have erected this tablet in remembrance of their lost friend; fighting only in his country's cause, beloved and respected by all his comrades and at peace with God.'

Mary Jane Doyle was widowed at 21, with three children and only a very small pension given to her by the army as her husband had died as a civilian in active service. She moved from Agra to Mussoorie, a journey that was not unlike that taken by her mother when her father had died. Indeed, there is a chance that the journey was even more hazardous, courageous and exciting for there is an account of her having escaped before the siege of the fort at Agra was lifted by climbing over the walls on a rope, dressed in a sari and with baby Eugene Mary swaddled up in a basket: she was then said to have made her way through the rebel lines and off to safety down (or up) the River Jumna. How much credence can be placed in this possibly apocryphal tale is doubtful, but it would have been in character for she was a remarkably resourceful and powerful woman as time was to tell.

In Mussoorie, she met and married Christopher William Corbett after a very brief courtship. For Christopher William, as with so many of his countrymen, the Indian Mutiny had been a shocking and horrendous experience and, when it was all over and a degree of normality in every day life was re-establishing itself, he either bought his way out of the army or was by now of such an age that he could legitimately retire with a military pension. Whichever was the case, in 1858, he quit military service and joined the government-run civilian post office. He was employed as a postmaster on a salary that was grossly inadequate when one considers his family responsibilities – he brought to his second marriage two sons and a daughter whilst Mary Jane brought a similarly constructed trio. From their wedding day, they started married life with six children ranging from an infant to two teenagers. It was heavy going even in an age when large families were the norm.

The first two years of their married life were spent at Mussoorie and Mathura until, in the early summer of 1862, Christopher William was transferred to the postmastership of Naini Tal. They made the journey of about two hundred miles with Mary Jane and the children being carried in a doolie whilst her husband and their older children rode ponies or walked. The trip took the hill routes and those on the edge of the plains, in those days little more than pathways and bridle tracks: it was an eventful month or so during which tigers had to be scared off the way by being approached with lighted, torn sheets soaked in kerosene or pine oil and dacoits (Indian bandits) were continually to be watched for and feared. At Kaladhungi, before the ascent to Naini Tal, the doolie was abandoned and replaced by a dandy.

Neither form of transport was at all comfortable: the doolie was a sedan-chair-like contraption without the seat, padded sides or silk trimmings. Indeed, it was spartan. The passenger – or passengers, for the doolie could carry several adults at a time – settled into the box and the whole thing was lifted on shoulder poles and carried by eight bearers with a back-up team to take over every half hour. The dandy was equally uncomfortable, especially over long periods. It consisted of a hammock-like cloth made of a light cotton, carpet-like material (a dhurrie) suspended from a pole. The passenger sat on the carpet, was lifted up by two or, on occasion, four bearers and carried, keeping upright by grasping on to the pole. The dandy was modified in time to a less awkward, deep stretcher-like affair but it was still just as uncomfortable a mode of transport. In the early 1860s, it was even more primitive than its successors. Going uphill was particularly strenuous as the passenger had to grip on to the pole in order not to slide down the hammock. Those using these methods of transport were required to be familiar with them. The bearers had to be expert, too: those carrying the doolie had to walk in step for the comfort of the passengers whilst those with the dandy had preferably to walk out of step.

Naini Tal, to which the eight Corbetts were going, had been dis-covered by Europeans only twenty years before. It was to be their family home until India gained her independence from colonial rule after the Second World War.

A sacred Hindu lake, first mention of it was made by a Mr Barron of Shahjahanpur. He had been travelling with two companions through the Kumaon region and they had made camp in the Kossila River valley twenty-five miles south of Almora. Barron claimed that one other European had visited the lake a few years previously – he believed Traill, the Commissioner of Kumaon, had found the place – but certainly he was the first to publish the fact of the existence of the hidden valley. On 18 November 1841, having succeeded in persuading their guide to take them to the sacred valley only by forcing the unfortunate servant to stand in the midday sun holding a large stone over his head, they reached the shores of the lake (the *tal*) and beheld a sight of such exquisite beauty that Barron instantly saw in it a setting for a hill station and a sanatorium for those suffering from illness on the hot plains five and a half thousand feet below. He and one of his companions, Captain Weller, an army engineer and the executive officer of Public Works in the Kumaon region, camped on the lake shore for one night and then left with plans already formulating in their minds.

In the summer of 1842, the whole valley was officially surveyed and the results published: the obscurity of the lake was dissolved. Its secret, so long well guarded from Europeans, was out and the glass-clear, emerald-green waters of the lake and the teeming wildlife were ready for exploitation and development.

A year after his discovery, in December 1842, Barron returned to Naini Tal with Captain Weller. Already the valley was marked out with a number of plots and Mr Lushington, the Commissioner, had begun building a house. The site for a native bazaar was surveyed and the land rent fixed at twelve annas per acre. On this second visit and in true pioneering spirit, Barron brought a twenty-foot boat up the mountain-side and sailed it upon the lake. This act of blasphemy against the Hindu pantheon, compounded by the fact that Barron used the event to force a local headman into renouncing his claim on Naini Tal, was to bring about a curse upon all Europeans settled in Naini Tal: annually, a European must drown in the lake to assuage the anger of Vishnu. The curse, it seems, has been particularly effective ever since.

On his third visit in late 1843, Barron found Naini Tal to have become a thriving, embryonic settlement. Barron had built himself a house, ironically called 'Pilgrim Lodge', and a Christmas party there that year was attended by Lushington the Commissioner, Messrs Saunders and Maclean of Shahjahanpur and a Dr Colquhoun.

The Indian Mutiny virtually left Naini Tal unaffected. Refugees, particularly from Rampur, Moradabad and Bareilly, arrived in order to avoid the pillaging that dacoits were conducting on the plains, but other than that there was little upheaval. The nearest mutineers got to Naini Tal was eleven miles away and five thousand feet down the precipitous mountainsides. According to a military report, the greatest hardship was occasioned by the lack of beer. For the local residents, the Mutiny was almost a godsend. As in other hill stations, Naini Tal rents soared and the house owners made a killing on the market. By the time the Corbetts arrived, Naini Tal was a flourishing hive of colonial endeavour, well established but with plenty of opportunity for expansion that had yet to be achieved. That promised land for which Joseph and Harriet had left their native Ireland was being visited upon their son and his second wife.

The post office for which Christopher William Corbett was responsible was situated at the upper end of the lake, on the outskirts of the thriving bazaar that catered to the needs of the local populace. At first, the family rented a house and lived in a building opposite the treasury in Malli Tal where the bazaar existed. Whether or not the family purchased this house is unknown but certainly it was not their intention to remain as tenants for any longer than was necessary. Naini Tal was growing by the month and the aim was to buy property and live either in it or off the proceeds from seasonal letting.

There was another factor working in their favour. Christopher William not only held a position of some civilian importance, but he was also an ex-soldier; this, on top of his approachable and charming manner, put him in contact and friendship with many of the Europeans in the area, not only his equals on the social ladder but many of his superiors as well. Indeed, Christopher William Corbett was to become a leading local figure.

One of his acquaintances was Sir Henry Ramsay, the district commissioner for Kumaon, a taciturn but generous and fair-minded man cast very much in the mould of the colonial local ruler. He saw fit to suggest to the Corbetts that they seek to obtain a second home down on the plains, to which to withdraw in the winters: Naini Tal can be bitterly cold from December to February and it is often under deep snow for weeks at a time. He arranged for a grant of land to be deeded in the name of Christopher William Corbett, the plot being just outside the small village of Choti Haldwani at the point where the road from Naini Tal joined that running along the rim of the plains at Kaladhungi.

In the early 1860s, Kaladhungi was not a particularly inviting spot, although it had, amongst other things, the importance of being the junction for travellers to the hill station. It was, in fact, notorious as a sort of white man's graveyard, for the forests and the swampy plains surrounding it were a vast breeding ground for malarial mosquitoes of the most virulent variety. Nevertheless, Ramsay's land grant was accepted with considerable gratitude for Kaladhungi was not only a terminus for the *dak gharry* service from Moradabad to Naini Tal, the very loosely approximate equivalent of the English counties' mail coach, but also a thriving little industrial centre with a rich open-cast iron ore workings, run by Davis & Co., and an active native charcoal manufacturing complex drawing its raw materials from the surrounding forests. Additionally, there was a market there which operated upon the produce of local farms which were beginning to extend themselves into the gradually cleared and drained countryside. There was even a hotel, the Murray Hotel, which was a staging post much used by travellers. In short, for all its drawbacks on the grounds of health, Kaladhungi, like Naini Tal, was a place to make a bit of money.

Upon his plot of land, Christopher William erected a substantial, colonial-style stone house which he nostalgically named Arundel: the ruined shell still exists and shows that the house was not only well-built but, for the times, was quite comfortable to say the least. It had a large living room, several bedrooms, assorted servants' outhouses and the usual offices. The privy was separate and properly drained to a soak-away, no doubt a sign of the apothecarial knowledge of the owner.

Being only ten acres in size, the plot did not at that time lend itself to profitable agriculture and Christopher William and his wife put most of the acreage down to mango and other fruit trees and soft fruit bushes, some of the former of which still stand. The whole area was irrigated from a canal, one of the achievements of Ramsay's administration. This ran along the northern end of the property, drawing water from a nearby river and taking it to the Kaladhungi bazaar. The house, too, drew upon this water supply.

It was quite a little country estate in its own way, not grand but comfortable and secure, surrounded by the forests and with its back to the hills. The Corbetts were inordinately proud of it. After years of itinerant army movement, the horrors and rigours of the Mutiny and generally struggling against the odds, they now had a home in which to raise their family and bear more children. What was more, not only were they settled, but they were settled in an area in which there were other Europeans with whom they could relate and build friendships.

The other main resident Kaladhungi European family was that of the Nestors. Quite what they did for a living is uncertain now. Possibly, they were employed in the iron workings: a tumbled ruin near to 'Arundel' is said to be a smelter owned by the Nestors, though others say it was in the possession of the Morrisons who had purchased a good deal of property in the area long before the Mutiny – perhaps as early as the 1830s – and whose family ghost is said still to haunt the road through Kaladhungi, from Ramnagar to Haldwani. Some claim the Nestors owned the hotel. It is of no importance.

The Corbetts' life formed itself into the mould of the domiciled English civilian. The summers were spent in Naini Tal and the winters down at Kaladhungi. Christopher William became a councillor in Naini Tal. His wife bore him children. She was a good, shrewd, resilient and loving woman and he was a kind, just and loving husband. They were contented.

They had neither the necessity nor the desire to return 'Home': the generation that separated them from the shores of Britain had somehow cured their blood of the emotional ties by which the old world might have held on to them. India was their country now, affording them whatever they wanted and it embraced them into its social order which they, as a part of it, helped to shape. They were blessed with the position of colonial superiority, though it is doubtful if they ever saw it in such stark terms, and they worked for themselves and the land and its people. In all but blood, they were Indians – the new Indians, the white Indians.

2

The Postmaster of Naini Tal

Edward James Corbett was born on 25 July 1875 in Naini Tal. His was, not surprisingly, an easy birth for his mother had had much experience in bearing children. Jim, as he was affectionately called by the family, was the twelfth child Mary Jane Corbett had carried – four by her first husband and, with baby Jim's arrival, eight by Christopher William Corbett. Her surviving daughter from her first marriage, Eugene Mary Doyle, acted as midwife to the local doctor. Despite the fact that the mother was 38 years of age, there was relatively little concern for her health. In fact, Jim was to be her penultimate child for, in 1879, she again bore a son, Archibald d'Arcy.

The family at the time Jim arrived into it was very large indeed, even by the standards of the day. All seven of the Corbett children were living at home although the firstborn, Thomas Bartholomew, who was the first to be named after the Mutiny hero, was old enough to be employed and was working in the post office, having entered the job as a junior under his father as postmaster: in time, he became the postmaster of Naini Tal, too. What was more, there were the children of relatives living with the family as well. Aunt Mary, Christopher William's elder sister, who had married Patrick Dease in 1831, was dead: both she and her husband had died and Christopher William had agreed to bring up the last four of their eight children: Patrick Paget, Robert, Stephen and Carly Thomas. It is apparent that Christopher and Mary were good parents, both natural and adoptive: just before her death in 1940, Eugene Mary (who lived much of her life with the family) felt strongly enough about their goodness as to write to that effect to a distant relation. Be that as it may, they seem to have done their nephews proud for both Patrick and Robert grew up to be eminent engineers, Stephen became first a medical practitioner and then a doctor of divinity and Carly Thomas (again the hero's name cropped up) was to become a superintendent of the post office and was awarded the CIE medal for 'Frontier Services'.

Jim's brothers and sisters were various and mixed. The eldest, for whom he would show hero-worship through his childhood, was Thomas Bartholomew. After that came Harriet who was to marry Richard Nestor from Kaladhungi and Naini Tal and who, in turn, had her two children, Ray and Vivian, brought up under the Corbett roof by Mary Jane. Next was Christopher Edward who subsequently married Richard Nestor's sister, Helen Mary. The next down was John Quinton (who married one of the Morrisons from Kaladhungi in due course): he was to be a childhood companion of Jim's even though there was eight years difference between them. Younger still were Edith, Maurice and Margaret Winifred, who was but a year older than Jim. Maggie, as Margaret Winifred was called, was the third of a triumvirate of chummery formed by herself, Jim and John: so close were they that their mother always referred to them as the 'Jam Sandwich' – two bits of boyish bread with the sweetness of their sister in between. In such a huge family, such companionship amongst approximate peers was common and the friendship between Jim and Maggie, strengthened after John left home, was to be the most important relationship for both of them. Their love for each other was the precious bond that was to be the backbone of Jim's life.

Quite how the parents managed to feed, clothe and house such a veritable tribe of children is a semi-mystery. Certainly a good part of the problem was overcome by Mary Jane's astute housekeeping, but the income the family had to rely upon was not vast. Christopher William's salary was not geared to such a large family. What was more, when he retired from the position of postmaster he received a pension which, though adequate for a pensioner, was hardly sufficient to support such a sizeable family. It is likely that the Deases left some money in kind or in trust for the upbringing of their children. Certainly, the two Nestor children's parents contributed towards their offspring's keep. The latter and any necessary money was received a little gracelessly: Richard Nestor was disapproved of by Mary Corbett and her husband who had opposed the match. Even so, this would have meant a degree of tight budgeting. In truth, the family had a second income of sorts, due to Mary Jane's cool-headed business acumen and determination to succeed in life. They owned property.

This sounds quite grand, but it is not all that it seems. With the growth of Naini Tal in the 1860s, the Corbetts had bought pockets of land on the hill slopes about the town and lake. Upon some of these plots they had built houses ranging in size from small chalet-type structures to bungalows and, in a few instances, larger houses. These they had sold judiciously from time to time, reinvesting in other plots as they became available or accessible by bridle track or road. Those properties they retained they rented in the summer. This was not to bring them amassed wealth, but it did afford a steady income. Additionally, they invested modestly in such local enterprises as stores and the town brewery. Mary Jane, who operated the real estate side of the Corbett family, was also shrewd enough to see an opportunity when it arose and she grabbed at one that was to be the saving of herself and her extended family.

Naini Tal was, by the year of Jim's birth, a bustling and successful centre of trade. It was a point to which the hill-folk came to barter and sell their wares and to purchase supplies. Being an important religious centre gave it a substantial if not large pilgrim traffic: it was not too difficult for those pilgrims who were making for the holy sources of the Ganges at Badrinath and Kedarnath to make their journey by way of Naini Tal. When the railway reached Haldwani, twelve miles or so below Naini Tal, and was followed not long after by a new road (so causing Kaladhungi to become the backwater which it remains to this day), the flow of goods and people increased considerably. The acceptance of Naini Tal as the summer administrative centre for the provincial government again boosted the town's importance. The fine climate and exceptional natural beauty of the amphitheatre of mountains about the town attracted visitors who were travellers, those on leave, those who needed a safer, healthier climate and those who wanted to educate their children in better air and away from the discomforts of the plains – not to mention the risks of living to the south: another mutiny might come to pass and the memories of the deaths of wives and children stayed long in the minds of the Europeans. Naini Tal seemed an ideal spot. Government offices, schools, a hospital and barracks were quickly constructed.

The influx of people, many of them well-heeled businessmen and government officers, needed places to live. A few owned houses. Others owned houses they did not need. Mary Jane, with intuitive foresight, saw the chance. She began operations as an agent handling the letting of houses and taking a commission on the rent.

She was ideal for the job, locally respected and respectable, a staunch member of the congregation at the Naini Tal church of St John-in-the-Wilderness, wife of the postmaster and a mother. She was a Mutiny survivor, lived in the locality all the time and was domiciled. She was on the right rung of the social ladder: European and so to be trusted, but not so high as to be unable to accept the position of tradesperson. Mary Jane became, in effect, Naini Tal's first estate agent in the modern sense of the word.

For the first few years of his life, Jim lived in the style of any European child in India. He was looked after by an ayah, a female servant appointed to be his nanny-cum-nurse. He learnt the local tongue from her, from visitors to the house and from his family. Everyone in the household spoke at least two Indian dialects and to be fluent in two or three, as well as Hindi, was commonplace. The round of summers in Naini Tal and winters in Kaladhungi was adhered to with strict and practical regularity.

It was a privileged childhood for any European, no matter what their place in the hierarchy of expatriate society. Servants were plentiful, incredibly loyal and cheap to the point of the ridiculous. It was quite normal for the servants to adore the children of their employers and, in the case of the Corbett's staff, this was just as true. Additionally, servants of domiciled or long resident Europeans were very important in the development of their young charges. Although Mary Jane Corbett was an active mother, not a semi-absentee one, as was not rare in European circles where parents were known to rely upon the servants for most of their children's upbringing, she did leave her children in the care of servants for most of the time. This led to the servants 'educating' the children in local tongues, etiquette and, for want of a better term, 'native knowledge' which covered every topic of Indian life from religion to superstition.

From the servants, Jim learnt much that was to shape him as an adult. He picked up the language easily and could speak the Kumaoni dialect as readily as he could English. He understood the basis of the religion and philosophy of the Indian hillfolk and was to become far more familiar with and sympathetic to Hinduism than ever he was to Christianity. He came under the influence of their superstitions, too: for the rest of his life, regardless of his immense knowledge of natural history, he abhorred snakes, be they dangerous, poisonous or harmless to him and he believed that the killing of a snake was auspicious for the immediate future. It certainly was on a number of occasions. Paradoxically, though, he did for a while keep a pet Indian python.

From his mother and half-sister, Eugene Mary, he learnt to read, write, add up and subtract. They taught him the manners of the European and – above all else – they taught him the basis of his own culture. Although a domiciled family not one immediate member of which had so far returned to Britain, they were nevertheless fiercely patriotic and very keen on their cultural heritage. Mary Jane was exceptionally well-read and an accomplished pianist. She obtained the latest books, where they were deemed suitable, and their home was certainly not devoid of reading matter: nineteenth century fiction and poetry, religious tracts and medical books, various books on hunting and sport and the classics – Shakespeare and curiously, for neither of the parents had had a lasting formal academic education, Chaucer's *Canterbury Tales* in the original Middle English.

The medical books were the biggest non-fiction section. The Corbetts were a distinctly medical family in some respects. Christopher William had been a doctor of sorts as an apothecary. Mary Jane's two sons by her first husband, who had been a doctor, went on to become quite eminent in their chosen medical fields.

Charles and George Doyle were living in Britain by the time Jim was born, having probably been sent 'home' to school at the time of or just before the Mutiny. They both became doctors in the present day sense: Charles, the elder of the two, gained his degree from Aberdeen University in the year of Jim's birth, having served internships at Guy's Hospital: London, the Royal Infirmary: Edinburgh and the Royal Infirmary: Aberdeen, and a dispensary in Edinburgh. He took up a practice in Magdalen Street, Norwich in 1878 and rose to become a surgeon in the town with a brief period away during the Great War. In later life, he emigrated to California and, upon retirement, became an author.

George also graduated in medicine from Aberdeen, six years after his brother. He settled in a practice in Hawkhurst in Sussex and became a member of his university's general council: after a period as a public health officer, a ship's doctor and inspecting doctor for a large life insurance company, he was appointed colonial surgeon at St Lucia in the West Indies. He moved to this post for his own health and died there.

Eugene Mary, by means of practical experience and through training briefly in Britain and at Lahore in India, but no formal qualification as such, became a competent and much-respected nurse and unqualified missionary doctor in India. She was a short woman and dumpy even when young, reminding acquaintances of the typical vision of an English village lass with bright blue eyes, pink cheeks and her mousy hair always tied in a bun. For many years, she worked on the medical staff of St Catherine's Hospital at Amritsar and, being conversant with a good number of Indian dialects as well as a fluent speaker of Punjabi, she was much respected. In her years in the Punjab, she established and maintained a travelling clinic throughout a wide geographical range, becoming loved, respected and feared by the local population for her dedication, strength of personality and distinctly no-nonsense approach to the heathens, whose bodies she sought first to heal before getting to work, usually ineffectively, upon their souls. To hope to convert Sikhs in the homeland of their own religion was not a little ambitious. The teachings of Christ, however, were Eugene Mary's driving motivation in life and were, in time, to be her undoing in no uncertain and undignified terms.

After medical books, volumes on Christian theology were the next largest category. Mary Jane Corbett was an ardent and pious Anglican, a pillar of the Christian community in Naini Tal and the family home was run along strictly Christian lines. She and Eugene Mary kept alive the faith throughout the area. The day was begun with a family prayer and ended with a small service of prayers and a hymn in the evenings, Mary Jane accompanying her children and husband on the piano. So highly regarded by the church was Mary Jane Corbett that, when she died in her late eighties, the graveyard of St John-in-the-Wilderness, which had been filled to capacity by the turn of the century and superseded by a new cemetery outside the town, was reopened especially for her burial.

For his first three years, Jim lived the life of any child, his days filled with the discoveries and explorations of life. And yet, even in the environment of India, his was an exceptional upbringing from the start. Most European children lived within the boundaries of security imposed by their parents or the servants *in loco parentis*. They did not run risks with their children in what was, even for the domiciled Englishman, a strange and still somewhat inscrutable land. It was uncommon for a child of foreign parents to be left to its own devices, even more rare that it should be given enough rein to wander as it would and to explore without restriction. Yet for Jim, this was an everyday occurrence.

Mary Jane was not an uncaring mother: quite the opposite, she was a firm woman with set and rigid ideas on motherhood. Yet she also had a huge brood over which to govern and it was impossible for her, even with the help of her eldest daughter and the servants, to watch all of the children all of the time. There were, therefore, many opportunities for the children to get away from the apron strings, if only temporarily.

As an infant, Jim was guided by John Quinton. When in Naini Tal, with his brother and Maggie, he would explore the surroundings to their home. The bazaar was not far and the holy shrine of Nanda Devi only a few hundred yards distant. The lake was close and the wooded hills around teemed with wildlife. In the winters, down at Arundel, he had the run of the gardens and an area of forest behind the house which was to play an immensely important part in his development as a lad. Wildlife was again to the fore and Jim lived alongside nature from his earliest moments of recognition. The birdlife was stunning in its beauty and comprehensivity. The streams held fish in abundance, the insect life was raucous by night and fascinating by day. Tigers were frequent, wary visitors to the grounds of the house and wild elephants wandered in family groups through the adjacent forests. For a small child with even a slight degree of curiosity it was a paradise of experiences. For Jim, with an inate sense of wonderment and a childish desire to know things, it was sheer heaven.

This happy childhood, however, was to receive a severe blow that affected the whole family to a very great extent.

Christopher William retired from the postmastership of Naini Tal in 1878. His retirement was not a time of idleness for he had been, since 1872, one of the city fathers of Naini Tal, a prominent member of the town council and one who recognised the need, now that the town was established but still expanding rapidly, for an organised sewage system. Lessons learned in the service of the Queen and applied in Arundel at Kaladhungi were now to be considered for the town and it is to his initial promptings that the town has, ever since, had an adequate foul water drainage system. He advocated a clean water drainage system, too, but this was not taken on with such determination, to the town's considerable – and Mary Jane's – future cost.

On the morning of Easter Sunday, 1881, Christopher William was preparing to attend the festival service with his wife when he suffered sharp chest pains and took to his bed. For a few weeks, he lingered in pain and discomfort and died on 21 April at the age of 58. A post mortem showed that he died of a 'fatty degeneration of the heart' and, as was common in the tropical colonies, he was buried the next day by the local priest, the Revd Mr Olton, in the graveyard to St John-in-the-Wilderness.

The church stands on a wooded hillock above the lake, behind the bazaar and surrounded by the horseshoe of steep mountains that protects the town. The graveyard is on the south side of the church and consists of a series of terraces cut into the slope and shaded by conifers. Christopher William was laid to rest on one of the upper terraces, near to the public gate. The family mourners gathered around the graveside whilst the rest of the congregation stood above, behind a low stone wall that marked off the graveyard from the church ground.

For Mary Jane, not to mention her children, Christopher William's death was a shock but not one for which she was unprepared. His health had not been solid for several years and, besides, life expectancy was comparatively short even amongst those who were domiciled and thereby somewhat toughened against the rigours of India. Against the day of his death, she had made a few wise investments.

In 1875, the family had moved from the centre of town, near the Treasury and the bazaar, to live in a two storey house below Alma, the second lowest of the hills around the town: they also owned a single storey cottage nearby. However, the year before Christopher William's death, tragedy struck Naini Tal and the Corbetts' financial security.

What happened is best described by a local government officer in the *Kumaun Gazetteer*:

'The rain commenced to fall steadily and without cessation from Thursday the 16th September, 1880 until Sunday evening, the 19th. During Friday and Saturday, 33 inches of rain fell, of which 20 to 25 inches had fallen in the 40 hours preceeding Saturday evening. The rain was accompanied by violent gusts of wind from the east; the roads were injuired, the water-courses choked, and there was a general saturation of the soil in all places where the loose debris of rotten shale, of which the northern ridge is composed, allowed the water to penetrate. There was much clearing of new sites during the previous year, and the builders did not always provide for the derangement of natural drainage channels. In many places the water was allowed to sink into crevices in the hill and find new outlets for itself, and this it did with a vengeance . . . About 10 a.m. on Saturday morning, the first slip occurred in a part of the hillside immediately behind the Victoria Hotel, carrying away a portion of the outhouses and of the western wing of the hotel, and burying in the ruin an English child and its nurse, and some native servants. Working parties were called for, and Mr. Leonard Taylor, CS, Mr. Morgan, Overseer, and a party of soldiers and officers from the depot set to work to dig out those that were buried . . .

'. . . and about twenty minutes past one I passed from the hotel to the bazar and, whilst passing with Mr. Wright, heard a noise, and saw a large boulder falling from the cliff above towards the hotel. I thought nothing of it and went on. In another ten minutes the landslip took place.

'The whole hillside was one mass of semi-fluid matter, and required little to set it in motion. The state of the hill has been described as in dry weather a mass of the consistence of oatmeal, which, when mixed with water, spread out like porridge. The motive power was a shock of earthquake, a very common occurrence in these hills, and which was felt on that day by competent observers in the Bhabar below and in Naini Tal itself.'

The landslip was terrifying and catastrophic. From where the Corbetts lived they could see quite clearly what was happening and they must have thought that they too would soon be cannoned into the valley below for their houses were but two to three hundred yards or so to the west of the slip site.

Another eyewitness reported:

'A rumbling noise, similar to that occasioned by the falling of large masses of earth, was heard by many in the station; and such as had an opportunity of looking towards the direction of the crash could plainly see vast clouds of dust rising from the situation described above. It was apparent that a large portion of the hill behind the hotel, from the Upper Mall (a road that ran just below the ridge above), disunited, had descended with enormous velocity and violence, had completely buried the hotel and had dashed together into an unrecognizable heap, the orderly room, the shop and the Assembly Rooms. The wave of earth and water, making a clean sweep of the extensive hotel premises, had apparently driven the shop on to the Assembly Rooms, carrying forward the massive building over 50 yards onto the public rooms, a portion of which was hurled into the lake and the remainder reduced to a heap of ruins. The catastrophe, as far as can be ascertained, was the work of a few seconds only; so that escape on the part of any who happened to be in the course of the avalanche was practically impossible.'

The first sign of the impending disaster was the cracking of oak trees on the ridge 400 feet above the hotel, from which not all residents had been evacuated after the minor morning slip. Cries of alarm were heard but the last stone hit the lake in less than half a minute. The death toll was 151 including 43 Eurasians or Europeans. During the night of that Saturday, fissures began to appear in the still comparatively unstable hillside but no second slip occurred. Sir Henry Ramsay, the commissioner, was quick to institute a totally new drainage scheme and no similar disaster has occurred since.

Not only European property was destroyed: so too were the pilgrimage temple dedicated to Narayani, or Naini Debi, and the *dharmsala* of the local holy man or fakir, Parambar Baba. Such was the force of the landslide that the temple bell was hurled and carried across the head of the *tal* to rest on the opposite shore where, today, the new temple stands that was constructed and completed in early 1881.

No doubt, Mary Jane was relieved that her family had not been dropped into the lake. However, what did plummet was property prices on the slopes where the Corbett houses were and this hit hard at the family finances. The two storey house was sold in a panic within weeks of the disaster and went for a song: it no longer stands, but another building occupies the site. The cottage was left empty until after Christopher William's death, when it was dismantled.

In 1871, as an act of speculation, Christopher and Mary Jane had purchased a building plot on Ayarpata Hill, the slope facing the landslip from across the waters of the lake. It was not a fashionable site at the time for the sunset fell over it and the better houses were on the west-facing hill. Additionally, the view was not as spectacular: from Ayarpata Hill, one sees the slopes of Cheena (the highest of the peaks) and Alma, and the upper reaches of the town whereas, from the opposite hill, one sees the panorama of the lake and the drop to the Indian plains below.

The site was taxed at two rupees per acre and was 1.7 acres in size.

Originally, Mary Jane had bought it to speculate with but she now realised that it was perhaps better to use it herself. The chance of a landslide there was minimal in the extreme.

Shortly after, or about the time of, her husband's death, the dismantled cottage was carried across the valley and reconstructed, with additions, in an oak copse. Another section of the site was self-contained and a house called Clifton was built there and rented to summer visitors.

The reconstructed building was named Gurney House. It was to be the Corbetts' home and, later, Jim and Maggie's home for almost the rest of their lives.

3

A Jungle Childhood

As soon as he could walk and be independent, Jim wandered. He was at times the bane of his ayah's life, sneaking off when her eye was averted to satisfy his wonderment at whatever he saw. In India, that was not always safe. Wherever there was habitation there was rubbish and where there was rubbish there were rats, and where there were rats there were snakes to prey upon them. Cobras were commonplace and poisonous snakes were very much to be feared for antidotes were virtually non-existent and, if they were known, they were seldom at hand for medical treatment was scarce even in a household with a medical background. On more than one occasion, the toddling Jim came face to face with a snake and luckily for him the snake, as they usually will, simply turned aside.

Snakes were not the only threat to children, native or European, for fatal diseases were rife. Malaria was the scourge of Kaladhungi, typhoid and cholera visited the north of India with seasonal regularity, rabies was endemic and leprosy widespread. On top of snakes and these unseen dangers to an infant there was also the wildlife.

The jungles around Naini Tal and Kaladhungi were teeming with game of all sorts. There were two totally different sorts of jungle with their own fauna. Below Naini Tal was what was termed the *bharbar*, a mountainous tree jungle that in summer was filled with an impenetrable undergrowth up to eight feet high but which, in the winter months, died back so that the forest became more like an English or temperate climate woodland with open glades beneath the canopy and occasional thickets of thorn, hill bamboo (known as ringal bamboo and about as thick as garden canes), lantana or clerodendron. The trees were of a wide variety of species but most prominent were the sal and mountain oak. There was no autumnal leaf fall as such but, in the winter, the trees shed some of their foliage to give the ground a rich carpet of humus covered with golden and brown dead leaves.

Around Kaladhungi was an utterly different terrain – known as the *terai* – and its accompanying flora. At the Corbetts' winter home commenced the flat plains of northern India and the forests here were more scrubby, if possible even more impenetrable all the year round and, worst of all, very swampy especially in the rainy seasons, with vast areas of twelve-foot high grasses, bamboos and similar cover. The standing water was infested with disease and mosquitoes rose in whining clouds at the slightest disturbance.

Each type of vegetation had its own miracles however and Jim, from his earliest comprehending age, appreciated it, was fascinated by it, began to understand it and allowed it to embrace him with its aura of sights, smells and sounds. Living as he did from birth surrounded by jungle of one sort or the other, having to travel through it from winter to summer homes and being guarded, served upon and communing with the local people who themselves lived in the jungle, it followed as a natural progression that he would become at one with his environment. That he was not packed off to school in England, as some of his elder siblings had been, added to his indoctrination with the ways of the natural world.

Jim's first jungle was his own backyard – quite literally. Across Ramsay's irrigation canal from Arundel there was a triangular section of jungle bounded on two sides by watercourses that were, except in the monsoon, almost dry *nullahs* or water-cut river beds. It was into this patch, nicknamed 'The Farm Yard', that Corbett as a young lad first experienced the jungle for himself and it was here that he overcame his fear of wild animals and started on his lifelong acquisition of jungle lore.

The Farm Yard was to be a stamping ground for Corbett throughout his childhood and the later years of his life. It still exists though it is much reduced in size, for when Corbett first took his boyhood steps into it, it was shaped like an equilateral triangle a mile wide at the base, four hundred yards wide at the apex and two miles long. He had only to cross the canal by way of a fallen tree to be enveloped by it.

The presence of water all the year through, and the heavy cover the

Farm Yard contained, made it a homing beacon for all the wildlife of the area. Deer drank there, bears visited it, monkeys of various sorts preened and chattered and swung through it. The birdlife, which to this day is stunning in its range and beauty, was drawn to it as were wild elephants, from time to time. Wherever monkeys and deer go then so too appear leopards and tigers. And so it was here, in the Farm Yard, that Corbett first saw a tiger and it was here, as an old man in his seventies, that he reluctantly and sorrowfully shot his last, one that had supposedly been taking local cattle.

There were, in the early 1880s, fifteen European children living in Kaladhungi. Jim was the youngest of the eight boys, not counting his brother Archie who was a babe-in-arms. As the youngest and seemingly the most innocent or naïve, he was set a daily task by his mother which at first he found onerous in the extreme. Every morning, he was obliged to accompany the seven girls to the canal to act as lookout whilst they swam, bathed and played: he was also entrusted to look after their clothes and carry their towels and the night-dresses which decorum demanded they wear in the water. He was, furthermore, instructed to prevent the girls from being drowned in a deep part of the stone-clad channel and to look the other way as they entered the water, for their cotton night-dresses would float up and this was to be the moment for him to avert his face. His primary task, however, was to warn of approaching males: the path by the canal was a thoroughfare used by woodcutters, dak runners, pilgrims and others heading for the bazaar in Kaladhungi.

Whether or not Jim was an efficient sentry is open to question. He seems to have spent most of his time looking away from the girls not so much as an act of polite indifference but as one of ornithological fascination. He was envious of the other boys being able to go off hunting or fishing but this jealousy was tempered by the permanent show of birds that paraded themselves before him – rose-headed parakeets, golden orioles, rosy pastors, pied kingfishers, horned owls, hoopoes and drongos, king-crows which are not crows at all but creatures related to the birds of paradise and shrikes. On occasion, he was chastised by the girls for allowing men to come near unannounced.

Whilst Jim kept cave, the other boys would swim or fish or shoot at birds with catapults. Hunting was an everyday part of life.

In northern India as throughout the country in the second half of the nineteenth century, hunting or shooting was an accepted pastime at every level of society. Royalty, the maharajas, the viceroys, the senior army officers and those high in commerce attended massive shoots at which up to three dozen tigers would be shot in a day. More junior officers in the army and others regularly shot for sport. Tigers and leopards (sometimes confusingly called panthers) were common trophies as were head of deer or smaller game. Pig-sticking, the killing of wild boar from horseback with a lance, was a more exacting and dangerous sport. Birds were shot for sport much as pheasant or partridge or grouse are to this day in Britain but in enormous, immeasurable numbers. It occurred to no one that this heavy seasonal slaughter would do very much to diminish the population of wildlife: as soon as one tiger was killed, another moved in from the inaccessible mountains of Nepal or the higher foothills of the Himalayas and took its place. Game seemed to be in universal, continual abundance.

The animal life of Kumaon was a naturalist's dream. The variety and sheer numbers overawed those who first visited the region.

Deer were abundant not only in quantity but also in species. The most often spied (and shot) were sambhar and cheetal, both stock diet items of tigers. The sambhar is a big deer about as large as a small-sized cow. It is greyish-russet brown in colour with a whitish chin and coarse hair, the mature stags bearing a mane of sorts. It is deliberate but not clumsy in its movements. It has a short, tufted tail which it flicks to and fro and, in common with the cheetal, it has large ears and an inquisitive nose that continually sniffs the air for danger. The cheetal, or spotted deer, is smaller and dainty, looking a little like a European fallow deer, with short horns and a brown coat mottled with white flecks, the belly and innermost side of the tail and legs being off-white. Its forest camouflage is perfect and it can remain unseen until within a few feet. Both graze largely by night and in the early and late day, resting up in the hot hours. The sambhar and the cheetal were hunted for their meat and the trophy of their antlers: the liver and tongue of the former were considered a delicacy.

In addition to these two common species there were a number of other deer, as numerous but less visible. The shy and delicate muntjac, kakar or barking deer, incongruously nicknamed the 'jungle sheep', was a frequent visitor to the gardens of Arundel. These tiny beasts are a deep browny-grey with a whitish throat and belly and a pair of Bambi-like horns: they call to each other or show alarm by barking like a dog and, when chased, they roar and click their teeth like castanets. Four-horned antelope and the nilgai (also called the Blue Bull) were infrequently discovered in the area, whilst at higher altitudes were found goral, a form of mountain goat.

Bears were commonplace, six foot tall or more on their hind legs with black fur, brown muzzles and white chest markings. Wild dogs, wild boar, striped hyenas, jackals and a variety of smaller jungle cats complemented the stock of elephants which roamed, for the best part, peaceably through the forests and hills browsing on the undergrowth, keeping themselves to themselves and generally avoiding human contact unless threatened, confronted whilst guarding young or going rogue when they could be exceptionally dangerous to all the forest dwellers, be they two- or four-legged.

At the head of the hierarchy were the leopards and the tiger itself. They were shot in vast numbers for their pelts and much competition took place amongst the well-to-do Indians and Europeans as to who could bag the biggest. When shot, the animals were measured with a tape in one of two ways: either the tape was run over the curves of the prone body, lying on its side, from the nose to the tip of the tail or the measurement was taken 'between the pegs' – that is, measured in a straight line from the nose to the end of the tail. The latter was deemed to be the correct way. Tigers over nine feet long were considered excellent and those over ten feet exceptional. The ratification of records was a hit-and-miss affair often but the record for a tiger seems to be in the region of 10 feet 4 inches.

Trophies, when treated by being rubbed with saltpetre and pegged to dry, were mounted and preserved. Heads of deer were either stuffed or the flesh boiled away and the horns mounted on the skull: tigers and leopards were either stuffed and mounted or more usually skinned and spread out as a carpet or wall hanging, the head occasionally being mounted to stand proud of the pelt.

It was at the hands of a former school friend of his brother Tom that Jim had his first experience of firing a gun when he was five years old and, as with any small boy, the memory and effects upon him were profound and lasting.

Dansay was, as Jim put it himself, the disinherited son of a general who had been dismissed from a job in the forest service and was staying in Kaladhungi as a guest of the Morrisons whilst hoping for a posting to the political service. Apart from loafing about the European community and seeking to court the older of the Corbett, Morrison and Nestor girls, Dansay spent his time as most young men at a loose end did in those times. He hunted. The profusion of game made this an easy recreation.

Irish by birth and therefore finding himself akin by national blood if nothing else to the Corbetts, Dansay mixed with the family, amusing the children with ghost stories and games, teaching them to read under the shade of the trees in the grounds of Arundel and being the butt of their good-natured if sometimes dangerous pranks. Indeed, it was just such a prank that probably suggested to Dansay that he might have his own back. The girls, teasing him in a wooing manner, had contrived to sew him into a bearskin in which he was nearly shot and killed by another young man, Neil Fleming, brother Tom's assistant postmaster in Naini Tal. The plot was, in Dansay's mind, partly Jim's responsibility for he knew the boy was party to the girls' plans because he had guessed that Jim had known of them from listening to their chatter whilst bathing. In truth, it was Tom who had connived in the prank. Additionally, it had been the small boy's idea that had caused him to be sewn into the bearskin with stout waxed twine rather than double cotton thread.

Whatever the motive, however, Dansay invited Jim to accompany him into the forest where the young man promised he would initiate Jim into the shooting of a tiger. Armed with a muzzle-loading rifle and a muzzle-loaded shotgun, the man and boy headed into the forests around Kaladhungi. It was winter and the undergrowth was thin, the ground dry. For several hours, they traversed the woodland but, although they frequently discovered the spoor of tigers, they did not actually come close to one.

On the way home, accepting that no tigers would be forthcoming, they entered a forest glade at the far end of which a flock of white-crested laughing thrushes was feeding on termites in the leaf litter. These birds are quite large, about eight inches long and exquisitely beautiful in the manner of plainly-coloured birds: they have a grey-olive back with a pure white breast and throat, lead-grey legs and a bright yellow mouth. When alarmed or disturbed they holler out a garrulous, screaming cacophony of noise. When in flight, their white fronts flicker and their body feathers shimmer with reflected light.

Seeing the birds, the two stopped and Dansay unslung his shotgun and gave it to Jim. There followed a quietly whispered preliminary lesson in the firing of such a weapon – left foot forward slightly, right foot out at a slight angle, lean a little forward, press the butt into the shoulder, hold the gun steady, aim over the barrel and, holding the breath, gently squeeze the trigger. Jim, with childish eagerness, obeyed. The gun exploded into sound. In later years, Jim pondered over whether or not it was overcharged as a lesson to him in retaliation for the bearskin episode or whether perhaps Dansay, being a strong man, simply usually charged the gun in such a fashion. It seems that the latter is more likely: few would risk handing an overloaded gun to a child. Whichever is the truth, the result was the same. Jim was bowled over backwards, spread-eagled on the ground. The shotgun fell from his hands. Dansay rushed for it to inspect the damage as it had fallen on some rocks.

There was not a single laughing thrush dead on the ground. The flock had melted raucously into the trees. In their place, on the dry leaves, was a tiny flycatcher. It was unmarked and had presumably expired of sheer fright.

A few weeks later Tom, who had assumed the position of head of the family upon Christopher William's death and prompted by Dansay's actions, decided it was the moment to accept his paternal responsibility and take Jim into the jungle for a serious introduction to hunting. Much to Mary Jane's alarm, Tom announced that he was taking Jim with him to hunt a bear and, eventually, the mother agreed.

So it was that that evening Tom, carrying two guns, left the house and took Jim along a mountain path that cut across the steep hill that rises from the rear of the Arundel estate. Upon reaching a rock-strewn and precipitous ravine, Tom stopped and instructed his most junior brother to sit on a rock by the track whilst he traversed the ravine and positioned himself in an oak tree half a mile away. If Jim saw a bear that was not in Tom's vision, he was told to walk to the oak and report the fact. He placed in Jim's hands one of the two guns, with two ball cartridges, and set off, abandoning Jim to his fate, or so it seemed.

An evening breeze rose and Jim was terrified at being left on his own in the alien jungle.

After some time, as the light was fading, Jim saw a bear on the hillside above the oak tree and, timorously, he set off to inform his brother of the fact. En route, he was greatly shaken by a falling tree bough, dislodged by bears scavenging for acorns upon which they fed in the winter months, and this drove off what little courage he had: he slunk back to his rock and remained there until, in the early evening darkness, Tom returned and together they went home empty handed.

In one of his books, *Jungle Lore*, Jim wrote of this event and ended by saying that, if a healthy human could die of fright, he would have died that night and upon many an occasion afterwards, throughout his life.

This first real visit to the jungle was to scare him but it was also to lay a foundation of experience in Jim. He was soon to realise that boundless imagination, based upon fancy rather than fact, had no place in the Indian forests.

The first real lesson Jim had in shooting was also learnt at the side of Tom. He hero-worshipped his elder brother and what he was taught was to remain with him. Not long after the fruitless bear hunt, Tom took Jim shooting for peafowl.

The peafowl is common in India and indigenous there. It is the most magnificent of birds, the peacock being a gaudy, iridescent creature weighing up to twelve pounds and much sought after in the days of Jim's childhood for the table: the peacock makes a fine dish roasted. The hen, on the other hand, is dully coloured and half the size of the male, but just as tasty.

In an area of the forest near Garuppu, seven miles from Kaladhungi and thick with wild plum trees, Jim received his first true guidance in shooting. A number of peafowl were brought up from cover and, alarming, roosted in some trees. Jim was handed a primed 12-bore breach-loading hammer shotgun and told to advance to shoot one of the perching hens. He made for the birds through waist-high, dew-sodden grass and halted to cock the gun. Tom, whistling quietly, drew his attention and beckoned him back. Jim, thinking his brother had assumed he was about to fire, stated that he knew he was out of range and had only paused to draw the hammers back. Tom's reply was to warn him about moving with a cocked gun in his hands. Once more, Jim headed for the birds, using (at his brother's suggestion) a bush as cover. He got within easy range of a peacock in his finest plumage but his excitement and the cold of the morning froze his fingers so that he had not the strength now to pull the hammers back against the spring. The peacock, in the meantime, flew away. Disappointed at his failure, Jim went home with his brother who had shot three peafowl and a brilliantly coloured red jungle cock, the wild forerunner of the domestic chicken.

So it was that the great *shikari*-to-be, as he was to put it, opened his account with the bank of nature.

Within a few months, his account was nearly foreclosed. Jim contracted pneumonia.

In the days before antibiotics, pneumonia was a dreaded killer. It struck at children, the vulnerable and the elderly, and the chances of survival were very slim indeed. The attack the disease made on Jim was determined. He was in a coma for days, weakened to the point of death and his sisters, mother and Mary Doyle fought to keep him alive. In some respects, it was easier for him that he caught the disease in the winter months. Had he been struck down in the summer, even in Naini Tal where the weather was cooler, he would have found it even more difficult to breathe and would almost certainly have succumbed.

When the disease had run its course and the family were seeking to interest Jim once more in living, and instilling into him the will to live, Tom came to his bedside one evening with a catapult with which he bribed the invalid to drink beef tea which he detested but which was the staple food of the convalescent. Lying in his sick-bed, Jim listened to Tom's talk of the jungle.

He explained that there were closed seasons on the hunting of animals, allowing them the chance to procreate – they should never be killed with young or whilst hatching eggs; animals and birds should not be shot willy-nilly but with a purpose in mind – one killed them for food or for trophies but not wantonly. Sitting up in bed, he was shown how to skin and mount a bird and he was given a skinning knife and some arsenical soap to aid him. Gradually, he gained in strength until finally the day came for him to quit his sick-bed and try out his catapult, his first intentions being to collect specimens for Stephen Dease, a cousin who was compiling a dictionary of all the birds of northern India. Whether or not this volume was eventually published is not known now but Jim kept the manuscript copy all of his life and it gave him the incentive to get out and start hunting seriously. It was the start of the main activity of his life.

Soon proficient with the catapult, Jim felt confident enough to go into the Farm Yard with it and here he started to hunt and study the jungle in earnest: throughout his childhood and teenage years, he would go off alone into the forests, sometimes for days on end, much to the consternation and worry of his mother and sisters, all the while learning the ways of the wild.

In the first days of his exploration of the area, he was taught some important lessons not by humans but by the family pet dogs. Tom owned two dogs, a pye dog (a stray) he had found starving in the streets of Kabul during the Second Afghan War and a liver and white spaniel called Magog. The dogs' company gave Jim the confidence to range wider afield than he might otherwise have done and it was the junglewise Magog who gave him one of his first real encounters with wild animals.

Hunting one day with his catapult, seeking to bring down a scarlet sunbird for the Dease collection, he met Dansay who was out walking his own dog, a Scots terrier called Thistle. The terrier incautiously entered some thick brush, which Jim noticed Magog was careful enough to avoid, putting up a porcupine and the two dogs, ecstatic with joy, raced after it leaving Jim and Dansay not only behind but without giving the latter a clear shot at the arched, quill-covered back. Porcupines are notoriously fierce when they need to be and their method of defence and attack is not only surprising but skilful and cruelly effective. Instead of charging at their foe, they run from it, then halt and – as quickly – run backwards with quills puffed out. They do not shoot their spines, but contact with one is both painful and risky. Each quill has tiny barbs on its blade and, once embedded in the enemy, they either come loose from the porcupine or break off in the attacker.

After a half a mile of chasing, the porcupine was cornered in a gully and Magog got hold of it by the nose whilst Thistle gripped its throat. By the time Jim and Dansay arrived, the fight was virtually over and the porcupine was put out of its misery with a load of shot. Both dogs were badly quilled and covered with their own and the porcupine's blood. Immediate freeing of the quills prevented them from working their way deeper into the dogs' flesh. Magog, however, had a six inch long section of quill rammed up his nostril and, that night, it was removed against the barbs with a pair of pliers. The dog bled so profusely it was expected to die but it pulled through to join in two other exciting jungle apprenticeship lessons with Jim a year or so later.

After the catapult came a pellet bow which was awkward to use and, though stronger than a catapult, was less accurate: Jim, however, succeeded in becoming accurate enough with it to beat the champion Gurkha pellet-bowman who was one of a contingent which guarded the town Treasury opposite the Corbetts' summer home in Naini Tal. Jim's next weapon was a bow and arrow. It was a boyish quirk that caused Jim to make one for he had started to read and, the household library being rich, he discovered Fenimore Cooper's American Indian stories. He failed to hit any animal at all with an arrow but his continued wandering into the jungle increased his knowledge of the natural world.

Always conscious that a catapult or a bow and arrow were slight defence against some of the creatures he was likely to meet in the jungle

– and on their terms rather than his own – Jim walked with caution when he was out alone. He admits to having had a considerable fear of the animals he knew might well be watching him whilst he was oblivious of the fact and it is a credit to him that he accepted this fear and learnt to assimilate it. In due course, it left him, but that was much later on.

His desire to know the jungles and yet his justified fear caused Jim to be not only careful but also ingenious. He quickly learnt – though he preferred to use the word 'absorbed' – how to stalk by using cover, how to utilise the wind direction to mask his scent, how to walk silently and preferably barefoot for his shoes were still leather and noisy: rubber or canvas shoes had yet to be invented. In a watercourse that ran through the Farm Yard, he studied and understood the spoor left by those animals who used the shallow, often dry gully as a highway. With Magog as guide and scout, he discovered all the places to be avoided, saw how a tiger's pugmarks going in to the cover, but not out of it, suggested the presence of the beast. Different tracks told different stories and it was gradually, by trial and error and acute observation, that the young boy picked up the means to read them.

It was at this time that Jim, aged about seven, started to think seriously about the world of nature. With the dedication common in a child, he sought not only to understand his environment but to appreciate it and it was then that he classified, in a childish but soundly philosophic manner, the animals he saw every day. His philosophy remained with him all of his life.

He took all the animals he knew and set them into groups according to their natural function as he saw it. His list reads as follows:

Birds

a) Birds that beautified nature's garden. In this group I put minivets, orioles, and sunbirds.
b) Birds that filled the garden with melody: thrushes, robins and, shamas.
c) Birds that regenerated the garden: barbets, hornbills, and bulbuls.
d) Birds that warned of danger: drongos, red jungle-fowl, and babblers.
e) Birds that maintained the balance of nature: eagles, hawks, and owls.

f) Birds that performed the duty of scavengers: vultures, kites, and crows.

Animals

g) Animals that beautified nature's garden. In this group I put deer, antelope, and monkeys.
h) Animals that helped to regenerate the garden by opening up and aerating the soil: bears, pigs, and porcupines.
i) Animals that warned of danger: deer, monkeys, and squirrels.
j) Animals that maintained the balance in nature: tigers, leopards, and wild dogs.
k) Animals that acted as scavengers: hyaenas, jackals, and pigs.

Crawling creatures

l) Poisonous snakes. In this group I put cobras, kraits, and vipers.
m) Non-poisonous snakes: python, grass-snakes, and dhamin.

There are few scientific criteria that could be applied to such a random method of classification but the fact remains that this was a good working division of animal life for the student of jungle lore. By arranging the animals according to their functions, Jim was able to assess them in their own surroundings and accept them for what they were – additionally, he had to keep clear of the balancers of nature whilst not worrying too much about the beautifiers: the warners of danger were friends and the scavengers not . . . and so on. The science of natural labour was more useful to him than that of evolution or form.

Having sorted out the animals to his own ends, the next task was to set about studying them in depth. It was to involve him for the rest of his life for he was never without finding something new to add to his store of knowledge and, as with any true naturalist, the continual curiosity he exercised was part of his joy of living.

His primary concern, after tracking, was to understand the calls of the animals. These he set to studying and imitating.

The realisation that animals have a language common to their own species and appreciated if not understood by others came to him from watching a racket-tailed drongo. A spectacular bird, the drongo is common across India; it is about a foot long but with a pair of outer tail feathers that can double its body length and which are quite bare of feathering until the final four inches when they fan out in a wide display. Entirely glossy blue-black in colour, the bird also sports a plumed crest above its only coloured part – a sharp, crimson eye. With the malignant humour of the parrot, the drongo can imitate other creatures and use their 'words' to its own ends.

Jim saw a drongo perched above a clearing in which ground-feeding birds were scratching over the humus in search of grubs and seeds. The bird was acting as a look-out for those on the ground but it expected to be paid for its job. Its crimson eye missing little, the drongo waited until it saw a bird scratch up a grub at which point the drongo, screeching as one of the feeding birds might when attacked by a hawk, swooped down. The feeding birds took to terrified flight and the drongo picked up the grub and any others that were abandoned in the escape.

Not only birds had languages of their own. So had most of the forest dwellers. Cheetal hinds issued a sharp bark to regroup the herd or sneezed and barked curtly in alarm. Sambhar 'belled' when alarmed, a noise something like an asthmatic factory hooter. Tigers hissed or sneezed, roared or growled or 'purred' according to their mood or the function of their conversation – to find a mate, show enjoyment, dispute territory or threaten.

It was important to know what was being said by the animals but it was also necessary to know why they were saying what they did. A cheetal, for example, makes a different noise when seeing a tiger feeding (and therefore of no immediate threat) from that which it makes on spying the tiger out for a stroll or, again, lying in cover. Langur monkeys also show alarm at big cats and by knowing their voices as well as their actions, it is possible to not only know what the monkey, from his high vantage point in a sal tree, has seen but also how far away the unseen object is and what it is doing: the langur always faces a leopard so wherever the monkey faces then that is where the leopard is or was when last noted. A cheetal, on the other hand, runs from it.

It was not long before Jim himself had his own senses so primed that he too could hear the slightest noise and know what it meant. Lying in bed in Arundel, he could listen through the window and tell exactly what was where and what it was up to: in the morning, his tracking would more often than not verify his assumptions.

It also occurred to Jim that if birds could imitate the sounds of other animals, then so could he within the limitations of the human voice-box. It was an art at which he was to become a grandmaster.

Tracking was a large and vital part of his jungle education and he was quick to realise that the expert tracker was not so much an observer as an interpreter of all he saw. At first, he found following and understanding spoor to be very difficult, but this was overcome by his watching certain animals cross the dried winter watercourses in the Farm Yard and then, having seen what they were doing, going forward to see what imprint this made on the sandy soil.

Sambhar and pig confused him until he worked out that the rudimentary hoof on the pig's foot is longer than that of the deer: tiger cub and leopard pugs he differentiated by noting that the tiger's toes are out of proportion compared to those of the leopard. Gradually, as he had with the animal inhabitants of the jungle, he classified tracks: for example, animals that run down their prey have big toes compared to their pads whilst those that stalk them have small ones and the claws of the chasers show up in the dust but the claws of the stalkers do not.

With snakes, Jim had to be more exacting and study the nap on the sand to see in which way the grains that stood proud of the dirt had been pressed. Poisonous snakes leave a lot of wriggles in the dirt, for they move slowly whereas non-poisonous varieties have to travel at speed and so are straighter in their tracks, which are uneven in depth as the snake does not touch the whole ground at once with the entire length of its body.

Always cautious of snakes, which he regarded in adult life with a superstitious eye, Jim also came to understand that there were exceptions to any rule and that one had to be ready for this, for an error in appreciating an exception could cost the hunter his life. In the instance of snakes, the hamadryad was the exception for it is highly poisonous and yet can also travel across ground at a high speed. Legend has it that it can keep up with a cantering horse.

With a good background knowledge of jungle signs and sounds and an embryonic ability to reproduce noises to such an extent that he could cause some creatures to come to or follow him, Jim was now ready to become the *shikari* himself.

A *shikari* is an expert hunter. The word implies not merely a crack shot with a gun but is extended to mean a person who is at one with the environment in which he hunts and with the hunted. For Jim, that was to be the forests of northern India and the region of the Kumaon hills in particular.

A hunter without a gun, however, is hardly a hunter at all. A catapult, pellet bow and bow and arrow are hardly appropriate, no matter how accurate the user. Jim needed a gun and he was given one.

4

The Young Shikari

It was Stephen Dease who presented Jim with his first firearm, a double-barrelled, muzzle-loading shotgun the right barrel of which was unusable, it having been split lengthways by an over-zealous load of powder at some time in its long and chequered history. The same discharge as had split the barrel had also cracked the stock, which was now married to the barrels by a stout strapping of brass wire. Thus armed with a left barrel and a very limited supply of powder and shot, Jim entered upon a lifetime of hunting. He was just eight and a half years old.

The derelict shotgun gave him much sport for two years, during the course of which, not unnaturally, Jim continued to learn about the forests and their ways. He shot almost entirely birds for the larder – peafowl and jungle fowl – but he was quick to admit that these were all shot whilst sitting rather than in the more sportsmanlike state of flight. He was never ashamed of this for he justified his every shot with a kill and his ammunition was scarce. On one occasion, he stalked a cheetal and drew close enough to it to kill it with a charge of No. 4 shot, more usually used for bringing down small birds such as pigeon. He hit it in the head from a range of not more than twenty feet and was inordinately proud though, in adulthood, he regretted the shot as would any true sportsman. It was risky in that he might merely have seriously wounded the animal and to shoot a deer with a shotgun loaded with pellets rather than a rifle carrying a single bullet was not the done thing.

His wanderings with this gun, albeit hardly an effective weapon against the larger game he was likely to encounter, gave him fresh confidence and it was at this age of eight to nine that he was to learn his most important lesson of the forest – to control or rationalise fear.

For an uninitiated adult to enter Indian jungle is a terrifying action. The mind fills to the brim with the possibilities of imagination: snakes (always poisonous), tigers and leopards, scorpions, rogue elephants all crowd into the brain and, as Jim knew, in time clouded both logic and acute awareness. The more fear played upon the hunter, the less efficient and, proportionately, the more at risk he was: mistakes are made by those who do not pin their full attention on the task at hand. For a child, even one who lived all his winter months on the edge of the jungle and his summers in the mountain forests, the jungle is doubly awesome.

It was, indirectly, Dansay who helped Jim to overcome his fear. He had told the children, one night around a picnic fire, a horror story about the banshees of his – and their – native Ireland. In northern India, there is a local banshee, known as the *churail*. It is so feared by the natives that, if they hear its nocturnal scrawling and whining and survive, they pretend not to have heard it and they never ever speak of it: to do so is to invite death.

One day, returning from a hunting trip and carrying several shot birds, Jim was caught in fairly open country ahead of a hailstorm. Eager to protect himself from the hail, which in the Kumaon can flatten acres of standing crops in less than a minute and kill not only birds but also men with the size of the stones and their ferocity, he ran for cover through a copse of trees. As he sprinted through the trees, the wind began to gust as it will ahead of a tropical storm. Suddenly, above him in the trees and slightly behind him, there was a rending scream that jerked him into running as hard as he could. The skies were thundering, lightning was playing in the plumbous clouds and the first hailstones were hitting the ground. He arrived home scared stiff and just ahead of the ensuing storm. However, he survived hearing the *churail* and, several weeks later, found himself again in the area of woodland where he had heard it.

Curiosity getting the better of him, he edged into the cover, his heart in his mouth. He found the *churail*. It was nothing more than one tree rubbing a huge fallen bough against another and, climbing into the tree, Jim sat next to the polished worn wood whilst it made its noise. From then onward, Jim investigated the unknown and usually – but not always – unearthed the truth. (In his forties, he found out what the real *churail* was. Seated on the veranda of his own house in Kaladhungi one March evening in the 1920s, he heard once more the blood-chilling scream. It was issuing from a bird the like of which he had not seen before or would ever see again: it was perching in a haldu tree in the right hand corner of the compound to the house, by the side of the Kaladhungi-Ramnagar road. Grabbing a pair of field-glasses, he focused them on a bird he assumed to be a migrant rather than a resident species. It was brown or black and slightly smaller than an eagle, with a short tail and long legs. It called by throwing its head back and raising its beak. He thought to shoot it but it was out of shotgun range and to use a rifle in moonlight would be to greatly reduce the chances of a hit. He reasoned that the village folk – who had been noisily busy in a post-harvest rush but had stopped all activity at the first screech – would assume it was an evil spirit unharmed by bullets if he failed to bring it down. To have attempted a shot would have brought fear to the villagers so he desisted. After a short time, it glided away into the night.)

The muzzle-loader presented Jim with other more exciting and naturally rather than supernaturally related adventures. Magog featured in many of them for Jim was often accompanied by the dog, using him as a companion, teacher and guide as much as a pet: from Magog stemmed Jim's early ability to relate to animals on their own level and to see the world through their instinct-governed eyes as well as his reasoning own pair.

Naya Gaon was a village several miles from Kaladhungi and it was famous for the wide variety of game that inhabited the nearby jungle. It was also infamous in the area for the amount of crop damage suffered at the beak and tooth of the wildlife. In order to enter the farmlands, the game – pea- and jungle-fowl, cheetal, wild pig and sambhur – had to traverse a trackway running between the cover and the fields and Jim knew that this afforded him a chance of a good shot. In later life, it afforded him very many good shots but of a completely different variety: the verb *to shoot* had taken on a totally different connotation by then.

At dawn one morning, he and Magog set out to shoot peafowl, making sure that they walked in the centre of the road as the light was sparse and the area was a common haunt of both tigers and leopards. Reaching the point where the track made off from the road, Jim stopped to load the good barrel, half-cock the hammer and insert a cap on to the percussion nipple. Half a mile later, the pair came upon a glade at the far end of which were a number of birds all crossing the open space in single file.

Once the peafowl were out of sight, and creeping towards their last known position, Jim sent the dog ahead to bring the birds up: they would settle upon boughs from which a sitting shot would be easy. Upon hearing the dog after them, the birds had run through the cover, taking Magog after them. Suddenly, Jim was regaled with a cacophony of bird alarms; Magog's yelping was ominously followed by the roar of a tiger. The dog had come upon a tiger sleeping in the early sunlight. Always one for a bit of sport, the dog had begun to bark after its initial shock and run towards Jim, the irate tiger following it. The boy, with more alacrity than he believed himself capable of, took to his heels along the game track. Magog soon reached and overtook his master. The tiger, fortunately, withdrew from the race and instead roared its disapproval in the increasing distance.

On another occasion, Jim made his own error without the assistance of Magog. Whilst stalking a peacock, he stepped unwarily into a grass-filled depression in the ground to discover his bare foot pressing down upon a coiled python. He leapt clear and aimlessy fired the gun into the snake before fleeing without awaiting the result of his shot.

When out with Magog, Jim encountered his first leopard. This happened in the hill forests around Naini Tal, where leopards were common and to be feared, for the leopard, unlike the tiger, jumps from tree foliage upon its victims and an escape from a leopard is rare.

They were walking down the road from Naini Tal to Kaladhungi and had stopped at a smaller lake hidden in the valley. On the shore of the lake below the road, known as Sarya Tal, Jim shot a pheasant. This task accomplished, he was making back for the road when he and the dog came upon a grassy clearing across which a number of pheasants were jumping up to a clump of balsam to snatch the berries. Unable to hit a moving bird, Jim sat on the ground, Magog at his side, to wait until they stopped their antics. A brace of birds for the crowded family dinner table would have been thankfully received.

After a while, some carters passed by on the road, their milk churns and cans rattling and banging. Just as they passed above the spot in which Jim was sitting, he heard them start to holler and bellow and bang their tin milk cans and assumed, correctly, that they were driving an animal off the road in front of them. The undergrowth threshed about with activity, nearing the glade all the time. Quite suddenly, a large leopard sprang into the clearing spying, as he was in mid-air, the boy and his dog. Upon landing, the big cat instantly flattened itself on to the ground and froze. It was thirty feet away.

The situation was at an impasse. The leopard didn't want to move and risk being shot: the boy did not want to move for fear of what the leopard might do. The muzzle-loader was redundant against such an animal. With astute forethought, Jim had lifted his left hand from the all but useless gun and restrained Magog with it, feeling as he did so the electricity of excitement quivering in the dog's neck muscles.

Sharing the dog's thrill and, like him, not feeling immediately threatened by the leopard, he just sat quite still and marvelled at the beauty of it. For his part, the leopard just as accurately assessed the situation and realised that the boy and the dog were of no threat to him. He jumped up from his crouch and bounded out of sight down the hillside. As soon as he was gone and the wind, rising from the valley floor, carried his scent to the dog, Magog was up on his feet, growling and priming his hackles. It was lucky for Magog that he had been restrained. Leopards are not only capable of easily despatching a fair-sized dog but also relish the act: dogs are a favoured meal of leopards.

Life was not always as boyishly idyllic as these episodes might imply. When he was nearly eight, a new intrusion impinged itself upon Jim's life: school.

Naini Tal, since it was a centre for provincial government as well as a place permanently free of the scorching, dry heat of the plains, was well-supplied with schools which catered for children of both native and European background. These were run by the government, by religious organisations and by individuals who operated them as businesses. All the hill stations of India were favoured spots for the establishment of schools and they were, because of their social as much as their geographical location, able to draw upon the whole of northern India for their pupils. Not only those lower down the social ladder attended but so too did the sons of the Indian princes and maharajas. The standard of education was almost as good as that to be purchased in the public schools of Britain upon which, inevitably, many of the expatriate schools were modelled.

Jim's first school was called Oak Openings. Situated just below the summit of Sher Ka Danda, the most easterly of the peaks surrounding Naini Tal and just above St Asaph Road, it commanded a stunning panoramic view of the town, the *tal* and the drop to the plains of India.

The magnificent view – at just below 7500 feet, the renamed and now much expanded school claims to be the highest in India, possibly in the world, with Jim's original school surviving as a house close to the main buildings – was not overly appreciated by the boys for the school was operated and co-owned by a ruthless and cruel ex-Indian Army officer who was known to his seventy pupils as 'Dead Eye Dick' for his aim with both a rifle and a bamboo cane was exceedingly accurate. It was said that his accuracy was such that he could place his cane exactly upon the weal left by the previous beating and he taught not by example or by deft academic manipulation but by fear. The academic education offered by this man was basic in the extreme and modelled upon that to be anticipated in an English preparatory school: mathematics, writing, reading, grammar and a smattering of Latin and other, general knowledge-type subjects. His two main aims in life appear to have been to prepare boys for entry into public schools and to have under his command the best cadet company in the region and certainly in Naini Tal.

It became a favourite memory of Jim's, in his later years, to remark how Oak Openings was the site of the shooting of the last mountain quail, driving it into extinction. As far as he was concerned, he was not pushed to the brink of extinction by 'The Captain', as he was addressed. In fact, he was unknowingly to be an important figure in Jim's jungle life.

All the pupils above the most junior classes were forced to be members of the cadet corps and Jim, at the age of ten, became the youngest recruit.

The Captain was fiercely proud of his unit and to say that he was a stickler for drill, presentation and the minutiae which sergeant-majors throughout the history of the British Army have existed to instil is a gross understatement: he was brutally scathing to those whose uniforms showed but a speck of dust or a hint of unpolished brass. To be found lacking was to incur severe punishment involving endlessly repetitive cleaning of kit, stripping and oiling and reassembling of rifles and hopping Russian-dancer-like around the school house with a rifle held overhead and a pack on the back. In the sun of the Siwalik foothills, this was verging on physical and mental torture and, at that oxygen-thinner altitude, no mean feat for a boy to accomplish who was used to life lower down in the world. Jim, with his mountain upbringing, found this less difficult and he was frequently given such penance to pay.

The uniforms they were obliged to wear were a torture in themselves which Jim remembered with stoic dislike for the rest of his life. They were made of dark blue serge and, being hand-me-downs through the ranks, were worn rough and chafed in the armpits and groin. Being dark in colour they also not only showed every mark of dirt or blanco, the military brass polish, that slipped over the metal buckles or buttons but they also exaggerated the heat. The helmets were worse still. Constructed of leather and compacted papier mâché, rather like modern riding helmets, they bore on the top a four-inch spike which screwed down into the head cavity. To stop this from denting the wearer's skull, the top of the hat had to be stuffed with paper or rags and the whole assembly was held in place by a tight leather chin strap. Wearing such a uniform for three hours of drill twice a week gave the boys continuous migraine headaches and naturally affected their learning. Jim records how the cane was more frequently used on drill days than on others.

One day, after musketry drill and formation parading before a visiting regular Army officer, the Naini Tal battalion, which was named the Voluntary Rifles and included boys from all the schools in the town as well as local adults, was marched up through the town to Sukha Tal. This was a dry lake, save in the monsoons, used by the townsfolk in later decades as a sometime sports field, practice polo ground or picnic area. When Jim was a boy, it was also a rifle range.

The cadets were seated on the low banks of the lake whilst their adult superiors shot as a demonstration for the visiting dignitary. This done, the cadets were instructed to line up at the firing point where the best four in each unit would shoot to display the quality of their training. The remainder stacked their rifles in the traditional cones and sat down on the ground. Jim and his peers treated the event as a sort of inter-school sports day and excitement ran high as the various teams took to the firing point and loosed off at the target that was hung before a butt of corrugated iron sheeting. Jim's team came a creditable second.

Whilst they were chattering amongst themselves at this comparative success, the much-feared and therefore respected battalion Sergeant-Major approached and, unexpectedly, singled out Cadet Corbett to shoot. In his haste and fear, Jim tugged his carbine clear of the piled pyramid of weapons: his was the locking gun: the whole array fell down. The Sergeant-Major, none too pleased at this act of military folly, bellowed for him to come to the two hundred yard firing point, whispering on the way that Cadet Corbett had best not disgrace himself, the Sergeant-Major and the human race in general.

The visiting officer, finding out that Jim was the youngest cadet in the company, smiled at the lad and benignly asked him to shoot. Corbett duly loaded his .450 Martini carbine.

After the muzzle-loading shotgun, the Martini was a shocker. Standard issue to the various armies of the Queen, it was a powerful gun with an accuracy matched only by a Remington or a Winchester. It had a high velocity for its time and had a recoil to match that could do justice to a bee-stung mule.

His shoulder tender and bruised from a session on the rifle range earlier in the week, Jim was nervous of pulling the trigger. As soon as he fired, he knew that he would be once again punching his already sore flesh. On the command, he loaded five rounds into the magazine, took what aim his nervousness allowed and squeezed the trigger. To be sure of a hit on the target, one had to be able to hear the metal 'ping' as the bullet hit the target backing. No 'ping' resulted from the shot. All the listeners could discern was an earthy plug as the bullet hit the soil behind.

No doubt anticipating the Sergeant-Major's wrathful scorn, the visiting dignitary took over. To Cadet Corbett's surprise and subsequent gratitude, the visitor – in his smart parade-ground uniform – lay down on the oily and dusty tarpaulin next to the boy and asked to see his carbine. Taking it, the officer looked it over, adjusted the back sight to the correct range, recommended a slower shot and returned the gun. Jim, in his flustered state of mind, had overlooked the sighting of the rifle.

The next four shots hit the target and produced a score of ten out of a maximum of twenty, the first shot recorded as a miss. The visitor praised the cadet warmly and the cadet's peers scorned him, on his retaking his seat on the ground, for letting down their side.

The episode was not wasted on the future hunter. Whenever, in later life, he was tempted to rush a shot or make a snap decision, he paused to recall the visiting officer advising him to bide his time and the advice was never to prove false. The officer was, in due course, to become Field Marshal Earl Roberts.

The Sergeant-Major, a professional soldier posted in Naini Tal, was impressed by the youngster who had displayed at least ten out of twenty in front of the assembled 'brass' and, at the end of that school term, he took Cadet Corbett aside to make him an offer no boy would be able to refuse and which, in Corbett's case, was to immeasurably alter his life.

Perhaps the Sergeant-Major felt a soft spot for the boy from the huge, domiciled family of an ex-comrade and assumed that he deserved a treat: perhaps he saw the potential inherent in Cadet Corbett. Whichever it was, he offered to lend the boy a rifle from the Naini Tal armoury with as much ammunition as he wanted, the only stipulations being that he must look after the gun, keep it clean and return the empty shell cases, the brass from which was recycled.

With alacrity, Jim agreed to the terms and accepted.

At the age of ten and a half, Jim was to find himself in the jungles around Kaladhungi armed with a .450 Martini rifle, a set of sights especially calibrated for him by the Sergeant-Major and a never-ending supply of bullets. It was, in fact, not the most appropriate rifle for a young boy to train on. The bullet for the Martini was heavy and could do immense damage to its target: the charge was also heavy and the rifle, as mentioned, had a vicious recoil far more powerful (and painful) than any other contemporary small arms weapon. The rifle itself was no lightweight. However, in its favour, it had an accuracy that was rarely equalled.

Armed with the military rifle, Jim now had what he most wanted and needed for his career as a hunter. He had a gun which gave him great confidence. The old one-barrelled shotgun bound with brass wire was unsuitable for anything larger than a barking deer and even killing a kakar with it would have been as much luck as expertise. The Martini, on the other hand, could bring down an elephant with a skilful eye shot and the gun was more than capable of placing its bullet on such a small target.

He was quick not to condemn his bow and arrow, catapult or Stephen Dease's gift. With such poor weapons, he had had to be all the more wary and understanding of the forest environment. His fear honed his wits and powers of observation, his hearing and his sense of smell to such an extent that he was, by the time he acquired the Martini, as at home in some parts of the jungles around Kaladhungi as the animals themselves who inhabited it. He also developed what mother nature provides for most animals by placing their eyes in the sides of their heads rather than in front – he purposely exercised his awareness of his eyesight so that his peripheral vision registered as clearly in his mind as his forward. The old shotgun had also taught him not to waste ammunition and to be sure of every shot before taking it. With the Martini, he kept up his deliberate policy of making every shot count and he continued to bring in birds for the pot, priding himself that he rarely ruined a bird for the table. The Martini, with a body hit on a bird the size of a peacock, would mangle the carcass: the gun was intended for much larger prey and its makers did not worry too much about the state of the bodies of the men it had killed. With the gun's considerable accuracy, not to mention his own growing expertise, Jim was able to shoot the heads off the birds and so provide good flesh for the Corbett family's cook.

The confidence the Martini brought to him allowed Jim to wander further into the jungles, less fearful than he had been with his inferior gun. With the greater range now offered to him, he stepped out buoyed up with excitement and natural curiosity and into the first of his great hunting experiences and adventures.

5

From the Farm Yard to the Railways

The Farm Yard had been Jim's jungle classroom already for some years and he had a better than good knowledge of its outskirts but he had never dared to venture too far into the centre of it, preferring to keep to the edges where he could work the cover with the safety of the more open ground as a retreat. He went into the central areas of the Farm Yard only when travelling through it on the road from Kaladhungi to the village of Kota which, for part of its length, cut across the area. It was a road much used by local people and a *dak* (postal) runner route so it was fairly busy, by forest standards, and comparatively secure from attack. Jim learnt early on in his life that animals did not attack unless provoked in some way: they preferred, being wise to the ways of humans, to keep themselves to themselves whenever possible.

The forest of the Farm Yard was of the typical *terai*-foothill sort: trees up to fifty feet in height with occasional thick undergrowth that thickened or thinned according to the season. Being on the hinterland of both the jungle and the swampy plains, it was filled with a vast population of birds, such as Jim claimed never to have seen the likes of again in his life. The birdlife also travelled through the forest on a number of well-defined aerial roadways and one of the most popular of these was a narrow but deep ravine that cut through the area. It was here that Jim often sat to shoot a junglefowl or peacock for the pot and, not long after obtaining the use of the Martini rifle, he went out late one afternoon to bag a bird or two. He positioned himself behind a boulder brought down the ravine by monsoon rains and chose a large cock-bird at which to shoot. He did not fire immediately, wanting a solid background to the bird before firing. A Martini-projected round can travel with a degree of accuracy for half a mile or more and, since the road was in the area and the forest was a place in which women gathered firewood and kindling, Jim always made it a rule not to fire if the bullet could carry on into the distance and possibly do untold harm.

Waiting with his finger on the trigger and the safety catch off, he was suddenly distracted by a large animal of some sort coming towards him at a good pace from higher up the slope of the land, where the road ran across the face of the hill. It was obvious to Jim that the animal had been disturbed by something on the road. Whatever it was, it was making a good deal of noise on its way as it broke through the undergrowth and, inevitably, it put the peacock, his hens and some junglefowl to flight. In fright as well as through sound judgement, Jim spun sideways to look at the oncomer and discovered himself face to face with a leopard. For his part the leopard, in the confusion of crashing through the jungle and the rapid alarming of the junglefowl, failed to see Jim.

At the point where the encounter took place, the ravine was fifteen feet wide, twelve feet high on the left bank and eight on the right. Jim was seated on a rock two feet under the lower side.

As he reached the ravine, the leopard, still oblivious of the boy hunter, halted and looked over his shoulder to ensure that he was not being followed. Jim, unseen by the leopard, raised the rifle to his shoulder, aimed at the leopard's chest and fired. It was a very stupidly conceived and risky shot.

The gun roared and Jim's view was instantly obscured by the smoke from the barrel: cartridges in those days, before the invention of guncotton, were loaded with black powder which gave off a dense cloud of acrid, deep gray smoke. Through the upper edges of the cloud, however, Jim saw the leopard pass over his head, blood raining down on him, his clothes and the rock upon which he was seated.

He was not a little worried. His confidence in the gun was such that he expected to kill the leopard outright, not merely wound it. He knew, from the quantity of blood spilled on himself, that the leopard was badly wounded but he lacked the experience as yet to be able to tell from it whether or not the shot was fatal: in later life, he could judge from the colour, mobility, temperature and quantity of blood just where he had hit his target and with what result.

Terribly worried that the leopard would escape to die in a thicket or cranny on the hillside where he could not obtain it as his 'trophy' and, at the same time, aware that a wounded animal of this sort would be highly dangerous for the rest of its life – if it was to survive – Jim set off to track it in order to despatch it.

For a hundred yards, the forest was thin and flat before sloping down a rocky drop for fifty feet to another flat area. On the slope there was a thick cover of bushes and boulders and Jim, cautious as his quarry, started down this slope with his every sense pricked to the utmost.

Halfway down the hillside, he saw the leopard's tail and hind foot sticking out from behind a boulder: after a few minutes of observing this and wondering if the animal was dead, it moved its leg out of sight. To be sure of killing it with his next bullet, Jim knew he had to hit the creature in the head and so he crept forward with slow and measured caution.

One has to imagine this scene to appreciate the courage of the hunter, a small boy under five foot in height and not yet eleven years old, making his way deliberately towards a wounded leopard on very rough and uneven terrain.

Without making a sound, Jim reached a position from which he could see the leopard's head. It was facing away from him but, as he came to see it, the leopard sensed him looking at it and, in turning to catch sight of its antagonist, it was killed by a bullet that penetrated its ear.

Jubilant as only a young lad can be in such circumstances, Jim went to his first big game trophy and pulled it by the tail from the pool of blood in which it was lying. The blood, in congealing, would mat the fur and ruin it. That much brother Tom had told him. What Tom had not told him was that, the leopard being on the higher bank and facing Jim as he originally hit it, the chances were that the leopard would leap towards him on the shot and, being badly wounded, would fall short of the opposite bank and land on him.

Jim could have jumped and danced with joy but he did not: he stood, he said, and trembled with wonder at the animal that lay at his feet. It was a mature leopard in prime condition and, as such, was exquisitely beautiful. With it, Jim was launched into a career of tracking down and killing big cats – leopards and tigers in India and, in his middle age, lions and cheetah and other leopards in Tanganyika and Kenya.

He ran the three miles home to Arundel to break the news with considerable boyish pride: then he and Maggie returned with two servants to bring in the leopard which was skinned and kept by Jim for many years before it eventually grew so tatty as to be worthless.

Maggie's going with him to collect the leopard was indeed prophetic. For the whole of his life from this very first time, it was always Maggie who shared in his hunting victories and the worries that they engendered.

The bagging of the leopard did more than raise Jim's self-esteem. It gave him credibility in the eyes of his jungle guru, Kunwar Singh.

From a very young age, Jim was close to the local Indians. His contacts were not made simply through the intermediaries of servants but also through those whom he met in the forests – the woodcutters and timber workers, charcoal burners, farmers, poachers, *dak* runners, travellers and pilgrims. Being from a 'domiciled' family, often referred to by those Europeans for whom 'home' contact was maintained as 'country-bottled', Jim was regarded by the Indians more as a local himself than an expatriate. After all, though he was of the ruling nation, he was himself already a second generation Indian albeit of a different colour. He had a command of local languages and an understanding of the local mind not to mention a fair appreciation of the culture in which he lived and of which he was, in truth, an integral part. His family was one of the wealth-earners of the society in which they had, by Jim's grandfather, been transplanted. That he was already a knowledgeable *shikari*-in-the-making added to his position in the eyes of the local Indians who were themselves proud of his interest in them and their world.

Amongst his many local friends was Kunwar Singh, a Thakur by caste and the headman of the nearby village of Chandni Chauk. He shared with Jim a hero-worship of Tom Corbett for whom he acted from time to time as bearer on shooting expeditions: he also had business dealings with Tom in his role as a post office official. In addition, Kunwar Singh was a poacher.

Quite what this meant in those days is a little hazy. There was no prohibited shooting of animals as there is in modern, conservation-conscious times: licences were not required before the bagging of tigers and the plenitude of game made territorial hunting pointless. There were no estates as such from which the public were barred although most maharajas and princes had sections (blocks) of jungle, sometimes quite extensive, which they reserved exclusively for their own hunting purposes. It has to be assumed that Kunwar Singh poached either into a maharaja's land or into areas of forest that were the preserve of other villages or communities. That his poaching included shooting animals out of season is out of the question: like all true hunters – especially those native to their area – he respected the implicit laws of nature over and above the imposed laws of men.

It had been Kunwar Singh who had assisted Jim with the derelict Dease gun and upon whom he called for advice and ripping yarns of the jungle. Kunwar Singh was full of both, dispelling fears, rationalising caution, guiding and correcting, assisting and criticising with a kindly, polite but insistent determination. His tales were often educationally inspired, seeking to teach Jim what not to do in the forests; one story Jim himself retold over and over throughout his life as a lesson to others was based upon the advice that wherever one is in the forest, one is safe if there is a tree nearby to climb. Tigers, unlike all the other cats including the lion, supposedly cannot climb trees.

The story centred upon a day spent bird shooting when Kunwar Singh and Har Singh disturbed a tigress with cubs laid up nearby. Har Singh's stupidity brought the tigress's fury upon them for he had shot a roosting jungle fowl he knew to have been put up by the tigress, assuming that the report would not only provide supper but scare off the tigress. It did the opposite. With a furious roar, the tigress charged. Kunwar Singh, ever wary of the nearest trunk, sprinted for a runi tree and shinned up it, with his gun. Har Singh was not so lucky: not having learnt to climb as a boy, he was caught by the tigress and, rather than mauled, was pinned by her to the tree. Standing on her hind legs, she thrust her forepaws on either side of Har Singh's body and began to claw the bark in a rage. As the average body of a tigress, excluding the tail, is about the size of a big man, the experience must have been horrifying.

Har Singh's screams were mingled with the tigress's roars and the tigress was only driven off when Kunwar Singh fired his gun in the air. Har Singh fell in a faint as soon as she sprang from him.

One of the tigress's claws had ripped Har Singh's belly open from the navel round to the spine and his intestines had fallen out. The two men discussed in whispers – they were afraid the tigress might return – whether to shove the entrails back in or cut them off and beat a hasty retreat. They decided to shove them back in along with the humus and dead leaves and twigs that were by now adhering to them. Thus temporarily reconstructed, Kunwar Singh wrapped his puggaree (turban cloth) around his friend's midriff and they set off on the seven miles back home, Har Singh holding the puggaree to prevent it – and his innards – from coming loose. Darkness fell. They headed for the hut of a hospital at Kaladhungi where the young doctor gave Har Singh some 'very good medicine' and packed him off home to the two men's by-now grieving wives who assumed them to be dead at the hands of either dacoits or wild animals. Har Singh survived to live to old age.

The runi tree was known to Jim and Kunwar Singh as Har Singh's Tree. Every *nullah*, ravine, substantial tree, glade or clearing, rock outcrop or cave had a name known to the two of them and by these they knew the jungle intimately. The runi tree which the tigress had mauled, became known as a landmark for anyone who hunted in the forests around Garuppu. It was burned down in a winter forest fire just before the outbreak of the First World War.

News travelling at speed in rural, close-knit communities like Kaladhungi and the surrounding hamlets, it was not long before Kunwar Singh heard of the successfully shot leopard and, accepting now that Jim was a serious hunter, he arrived that same day to see the beast and offer Jim a hunting trip to commence the following day, before dawn.

One of Jim's greatest fears was that of forest fires. The jungle dries out in the dry seasons to tinder. To see a forest burning is an awe-inspiring and terrifying sight. The power and rapidity with which the flames spread and the seeming lack of logical direction to the advance of the fire-front give added horror. The ability of the fire, in a breeze, to jump ahead of itself is also most worrying.

At five in the morning, just before dawn and fortified by a cup of tea provided by sister Maggie, Jim arrived at the rendezvous on the Garuppu road to find Kunwar Singh sitting by a small fire. After an altercation about Jim's shorts – which were just then coming into fashion – and Kunwar Singh's comments that they were indecent and looked more like underwear, the boy and the man extinguished their camp fire and set off into the awakening morning and birdsong.

Just after sun-up, they reached Garuppu and took a path through the scrub cover. Beyond the scrub was a long area of nal grass, five hundred yards wide and three miles long. Nal grass is fourteen feet high when fully grown, sectioned and hollow like bamboo. It grows on damp ground and seldom dries out – but when it does it is brittle and very flammable, burning with a high temperature and loud crackling bangs as the hollow sections explode.

As they made their way along the watercourse, black clouds filled the sky and the sound of burning nal grass reached them. Rounding a turn they saw the fire ahead of them. A wall of mobile flame was whistling on the bank with the blaze curling in as it sucked upon the air. In the hot currents overhead circled a vast flock of starlings, drongos, minahs and other insectivorous birds, feeding on the insects forced on to the wing and up in the thermals of the fire: in the watercourse ahead of them, peacocks and jungle fowl with woodland partridges were feasting on the insects fleeing ahead of the flames. Beside them, a herd of cheetal were eating the red blossoms that were dropping from a samal tree being whisked by the fire-mad breeze. All were either oblivious of the fire or industriously taking advantage of it. It was then that it occurred to Jim that he was the only frightened creature present and his fear, with knowledge, left him for ever.

Jim's childhood passed by in a pattern of learning his books and learning the ways of the jungle. Either Tom, Kunwar Singh or the animals themselves gave him daily instruction. He perfected his mimicry of birds and monkeys. He studied and understood the behaviour of what he was to always term 'the jungle folk' – the animal inhabitants of the forests. He wandered alone not only in the Farm Yard and the forests around Garuppu but also in the hills about Naini Tal. He began to learn to fish as well – in the submontane rivers and the hidden lakes of Kumaon.

In school, he was neither academically brilliant nor under par. He was an above average pupil who read fairly widely and who had, as an obvious consequence of his jungle experiences, an inate command of common sense and logical thought.

When the time came for him to pass into secondary education, he left Oak Openings and its barbaric captain and entered the Diocesan Boys' School, subsequently retitled Sherwood College.

As he grew through his teenage years, he started to think seriously about what kind of a career he would like and he decided to plump for one of the two traditional Corbett family professions: not wanting to be a doctor, he set his sights on becoming an engineer.

There was, however, a major obstacle in his way: money. The family was not rich. Tom had married and was now obliged to support his own family. The others had variously married or left home, but there still remained Jim's mother, Mary Doyle, himself and Maggie and Archie, the youngest son. In addition, there were the two Nestor children, Ray and Vivian, both of them still under the age of ten. To become an engineer required further education and that was out of the question.

The house agency business still operated with a modicum of success and Mary Corbett still had her husband's meagre pension but she now also had adults to cater for, not just children. Maggie and Mary were unable to contribute to the finances of the house, although both helped with the business.

It was therefore necessary for Jim to lower his sights. He accepted with characteristic stoicism that engineering and he would never come together though he maintained a lifelong interest and curiosity in it. Furthermore, he knew within himself that he was now the man of the family and by the time he was seventeen he was fully conversant with the fact that it would be his responsibility to look after his mother and Mary Doyle in their old age, and his sister who showed no inclination to seek a spouse. Indeed, she was quite devoted to Jim and that took the place of her wanting a husband. Quite possibly, Archie would relieve him of some of this burden in time, but in the meanwhile, he was the head of the clan.

At the age of seventeen and a half, he left home. He had several options open to him as a domiciled white. He could have followed in his father's or brother Tom's footsteps and entered the Post Office (he had, aged fifteen, already once tried to obtain a job with the postal service but been told to return to his studies): he could have gone into a business in one of the centres of the land – Delhi, Bombay or Calcutta – as a ledger clerk or office worker of some description with the prospect of rising to a middle management position over a career span of forty years: he could have joined the Customs and Excise: he could have signed on with the army or, as a viable alternative, the police. Instead, he chose the only other main option. He chose to go to work on the railways.

In the second half of the nineteenth century, the railway system was the expanding backbone of India. It was the railway network that united or, as history might have it, perhaps disunited the country, crossing political, social and cultural barriers that had stood since the settlement of India in prehistoric times. It made possible great advances not only in travel but also in trade and it aided and abetted the spoliation of much of the land. It was the railways that brought about both the deforestation of vast tracts of northern India and the turning of swamps or otherwise infertile areas into agricultural farmland for it was the railways that carried away the trees as timber or as fuel and subsequently, took the produce to market.

The road network of India was still haphazard: tracks and roads varied their courses according to the season, the activity of dacoits (bandits) or the whim of local peoples. They were prone to wash-outs in the monsoon and reduction to waterless, semi-desert paths in the dry seasons. They were unsuitable for any form of travel other than the immediately local except when used by officials or Europeans with the resources to challenge whatever the land had to throw at them.

The railways were different. The track beds were stone-chip based, built on embankments. Rivers were adequately bridged, lines had proper causeways and stations were well manned and operated. Fuel was plentiful for the trains were, for the most part, wood-fired. The railway was permanent and it seemed, in the years prior to the internal combustion engine, that it would be everlasting. To enter the employment of the railway was to join an organisation that promised job security, stability and, for a domiciled European, a position of some authority in an important institution.

For Jim, the job security and steady if not over-generous salary meant that he could accept his responsibilities for his family more readily.

He was almost refused a job. He was called for interview but informed that he was too young. He countered this by remarking, 'You tell me I am too young to begin work, but if I came next year you would tell me I was too old.' His perspicacity prompted an offer of a job on probation.

It was to the Bengal & North-Western Railway (the BNWR) that Jim was contracted as a temporary fuel inspector posted to Bihar on a salary of one hundred rupees per month.

Bihar was a main city in the state of the same name. It was situated in the north-eastern corner of India between the countries of Nepal to the north and the modern-day Bangladesh to the east: only Assam and a few minor states were more easterly. For a boy not quite eighteen who had never travelled beyond Naini Tal, Kaladhungi and the jungles of his home area, it was a considerable way to journey, over 750 miles by country road and railway. It took him more than a week.

The landscape into which he found himself projected was alien to him. After initially signing on with the company, he was sent into the flat forests of the Ganges plain to organise the felling of timber that was cut into regulation size, thirty-six inch long billets as locomotive fuel before being transported by bullock cart to the nearest railway line for collection. To conduct this work, Jim had a sizeable labour force over which he had absolute control. He had to organise the tree cutting, the shaping and stacking and carting of the prepared fuel and pay his workers.

His allotted patch of forest was ten miles from the railway and he established his camp with a tent pitched on the left bank of the Ganges near Bakhtiyarpur, twenty miles east of Patna where the Gandak river joined the main flow of the Ganges itself.

For nearly two years, Jim's life was very hard indeed. He worked long hours in torrid heat, regardless of the humidity of the monsoon or the scorchingly hot dry season. He was plagued by mosquitoes which in turn were carriers for not only the scourge of malaria but also a wide variety of other tropical diseases. Since the site was near the banks of the river, snakes were a commonplace and dangerous. His workers frequently succumbed to disease, decamped for home or were injured. Elephants were used to move the timber at the felling site and the tracks in and out of the forest were either choked with thick dust or cloying mud, according to the time of year. For months at a time, Jim saw no other Europeans at all except as fleeting faces passing in the trains ten miles away or the auditor delivering the salary in canvas bags held inside a steel-bound chest. It was a miserable existence, though suited to a domiciled person: after all, he was little more than a cut above the Indian labourers over whom he held sway. His task was just as wretched as their own: although he claimed to have enjoyed every hour of it, one has to accept this as only partial truth. He was in his beloved forests but under circumstances he would have gladly changed.

It was at the forest felling sites, however, that Jim proved himself. His organisational skills were developed, he learnt to keep the books of his unit and he became admired and even loved by his Indian workers.

He had a considerable rapport with his labourers. Not only was he unusually knowledgeable for a European about the forest in which they were working, but he was also quick to learn the dialects of their language, he understood their culture and religion, he appreciated the caste system and its importance and he was scrupulously fair. It was his role to be not only glorified foreman but also arbitrator and chief justice, guide and mentor, strict and patronising leader, counsellor, doctor and teacher. It was a heavy responsibility to place upon one so young and it has to be assumed that the employers did not necessarily expect him to carry it off. Certainly, it was a dead-end job to which he had been sent and the description is not amiss: such a job killed a good many, either from disease or alcoholism induced by boredom and loneliness. To the employers, a domiciled man was almost as expendable as an Indian coolie.

Jim's success was not based wholly upon his relationship with his multitude of staff. He was a self-contained person, quiet to the point of introversion who was used, through his childhood years alone in the jungles of Kumaon, to relying upon his innermost soul. He was – even at such a young age – inwardly self-assured and self-reliant and it was this combination of qualities that helped him to survive. He did contract malaria on the Ganges, but his being 'country bottled' gave him a distinct advantage over his more illustrious expatriate peers. He had a built-in immunity to many of the Indian sicknesses and where he was not immune he was strengthened against the worst of the ravages.

He yearned, throughout his two years near Bakhtiyarpur, to hunt. He was in forest in which game teemed although it understandably kept well clear of the timber-cutting activity. Cheetal, wild pig, the Indian four-horned antelope, forest hares and a wide variety of birdlife inhabited the forest and Jim longed to stalk. However, his working day began at sun-up – he had to have broken his fast at dawn – and did not cease until late dusk or later if the planned production of billetwood hadn't reached the day's set target. The hottest hours of the day were left free but no one undertook any activity then. The labourers lay in the shade of their tarpaulins or bivouacs and the foreman lay in his tent. As for the animal life, it too kept to the shade and did nothing. Occasionally, he tried rod fishing but with little success: even the fish stayed deep and still.

Night hunting was the only option left and Jim was obliged to shoot then not so much for sport but for the pot: the only meat available was that which he brought down and in the moonless quarters of the month he was perforce a vegetarian. He ate the same food as his work force, very basic Indian fare, and what meat he could add to it was welcomed not only by him but also by his coolies. He had bought himself a light calibre rifle before leaving home and it was with this and a shotgun that he hunted, learning a lesson that was to stand him in good stead and save his life in years to come. He had not shot at night before and he soon found out that it was best to shoot by the waxing moon for it was essential for a good hit that the bright moonlight catch the foresight on the rifle barrel. He took to chalking his foresight to accentuate the available light. A waning moon was not sufficiently bright to show up the bead, chalked or not. He also did a good deal of fishing, though with a nightline rather than a rod, setting out his baited hooks at dusk and collecting the exhausted fish in the morning.

His forest camp life taught him his first lessons in ecology as well as night shooting.

Ecology, conservation, wildlife preservation, retention of environment and habitat: these were phrases unheard in the first two-thirds of Jim's life. India was a vast and overabundant hunting ground. People were plentiful but the population explosions of the twentieth century were unknown. The human mass was kept to naturally controlled sensible numbers by the deprivations of disease, starvation or poor diet and very high infant mortality. Animals killed by the gun or the lance or the local villager's trap were very soon replaced by others. The forests were widespread and rich and the animals took maximum advantage of the harvest of berries, nuts, leaves, flowers and bark: in their turn, the predators made the most of the untold millions of deer, antelope and other herbivorous mammals. Even tigers, hunted for sport in great numbers, were so plentiful that it was claimed that when one was shot in Kumaon another simply moved into its territory from the mountains of Nepal where, seemingly, there was a never-ending supply of fecund tigresses dropping cubs at an astounding rate.

It was Jim's job to see that between one and two acres of forest went under the axe, the machete and the saw every day. In fact, he was personally responsible for the cutting of five hundred thousand cubic feet of timber. In his work at Bakhtiyarpur, he was personally responsible for the clearance of over one thousand five hundred acres. As there were similar gangs of workers employed at regular intervals along all the railways of India, this meant that vast areas were being cut every week.

The tree felling brought about its casualties and not only in the labouring company. Creatures too frightened to move were hit by branches and toppling trees and killed or injured: young animals were abandoned by their parents or orphaned; all were driven from their homes never to return. This destruction had an impact on Jim. He did not see it as an evil, more a necessity of life, but it saddened him nevertheless. As an animal lover and student of nature, he took pity upon those creatures his work affected and he soon had about his tent a menagerie of injured or displaced animals found by him or his workers. Young birds were the most common: Jim kept them in man-made nests and tended them, where he could, through to eventual flight. Injured deer he splinted or crudely bandaged whilst he fed the orphans and guarded them in an enclosure by his tent, releasing them to the wild when they were old enough although some became too tame and remained in the vicinity. Surprisingly, for Jim had a not-inconsiderable aversion to them, he also kept a pet python named Rex.

The tameness of his orphans led, from time to time, to their downfall. A four-horned antelope fawn that he nursed through its suckling stage refused to leave him and, when he moved his camp to be nearer to the timber sites, the creature followed him and, being unafraid of humans, approached a man working in a field who saw in her a meal rather than a pet. He struck her with a stick, breaking her front legs. Jim discovered his pet later that day when he found her in his tent, in which she had sought refuge. The man, realising that she was a pet, had stayed to accept responsibility. Jim called for the nearest village bone-setter, an old man who untwisted the legs which had spun on themselves so that the broken bones protruded through the fur, added poultices of green paste and castor oil leaves and bound the legs to jute stalks with twine. The fee was one rupee and two annas and the antelope survived to skip and prance once more.

At the completion of his contract, Jim was faced with redundancy. Not only had his contractual period come to an end but so too had the billet-cutting. Coal was being rapidly phased in as the new locomotive fuel for financial reasons and the labour-intensive forestry work was curtailed. Jim was called to the regional office of the railway at Samasti-pur, across the Ganges and just south of Darbhanga, to receive the documents for the completion of his employment. Taking with him his account books, he presented these with their immaculate entries well-balanced and a rebate of two hundred rupees on his transportation costs.

Tipped off by another fuel inspector that it was not done to show a profit, so to speak, Jim surreptitiously deposited the money on the desk of his senior officer, Mr Ryles, and quietly left. He was soon ordered back to an audience with the Agent, a Mr Izat, the following day. He was made to explain how the money had come to be retained unpaid and Jim explained that it was, in fact, owed to one of the bullock cart operators but he had gone back to his home village and there was no way now of tracing him. Izat asked Jim why he had not simply kept the money and avoided the problems of his interview and reprimand. His answer was simply that he considered it wasn't his money to keep and to have pocketed it would have amounted to stealing. His honesty impressed Izat who immediately re-employed him at the regional offices in Samastipur. The money, to make the company accounts balance, was not re-entered but given to a railway charity.

Honesty was important to Jim: a religious upbringing at the hands of the two Marys (Corbett and Doyle) had impressed upon him and all his brothers and sisters the need for moral fibre and it showed in Jim. However, his forest clearance work had another side effect that stayed with him for life. He was very efficient and a very astute man when it came to matters of business and the handling of money.

For a year, Jim was employed variously around the offices in Samastipur as an assistant store keeper and deputy station master, learning the ways of the railway and furthering his command of local dialects and those who spoke them. He worked for a while as a guard on goods trains that travelled between Katihar to the east and Motihari to the north, on the line that went to the Nepalese border.

Occasionally he travelled as far as Gorakhpur where the railway head office was situated, accompanying the pay officer and his armed entourage. His knowledge of railway fuel, gained by felling and cutting it, was put to good use by his being sent on the footplates of the locomotives to assess fuel consumption on certain routes. In this way, he learnt something of the engineering side of the railways to which he still secretly aspired, hoping for an eventual specialist apprenticeship to the repair works or carriage building yards.

His year's general employment over, he was sent to Gorakhpur and offered a rise in salary amounting to fifty rupees a month to take over the contract for transhipping goods at Mokameh Ghat, forty miles southeast of Samastipur and twenty east of where he had been felling timber. His hopes of an engineering-biased job finally quashed, Jim accepted and was sent off to meet his new superior, Mr Storrar, the superintendent of ferries at Mokameh Ghat.

Mokameh Ghat is on the south bank of the Ganges across the river from Simaria Ghat on the north. At the height of the monsoon, the river at this point was five miles wide and fast flowing and there was no bridge either for rail or road traffic. A rail bridge would have been of no use in any case as the gauge of the railway on the north bank was a standard metre whilst that on the south bank was broader. There not being another crossing point for some hundreds of miles down river, Mokameh and Simaria Ghats were the focal point towards which all passenger and cargo traffic converged.

The result was unmitigated confusion, chaos and congestion. It was compounded by the fact that Jim's contract was to move the goods from the broad gauge railway to the river shore and across on the steamships:

once on the far bank, the Labour Company took over to load the cargo on to the metre gauge line. Originally, the Labour Company had done the whole task but they had, for some illogical reason, lost the south bank contract.

The course of action was that, on one bank, all goods were offloaded and passengers disembarked. These were then taken across the river by steamboat to the opposite shore where everything (and everyone) was reloaded onto the next size track system. The stations were inadequate, having been built for a smaller volume of traffic than they now saw: the marshalling yards were also inadequate and godowns or warehouses were in short supply.

Upon arrival at his new base in high summer, Jim was confronted with the pandemonium of transhipping a backlog of half a million tons of merchandise. The few resident European railway staff were surprised that the powers-that-be had sent a mere youth under the age of twenty-one to take on the task and dismissed him as not up to the job. It had broken others in the past and would no doubt break the newcomer. This may well have been the superintendent of staff's intention for the role was not one from which an employee could hope to advance a career in the railways. This, too, was a dead end job in more ways than one. Domiciled Europeans being expendable, this type of work was that upon which they were expended.

On seeing what he was faced with, Jim took heart rather than dismay. He ignored the resident staff and became friendly with the Mokameh Ghat station master, Ram Saran, a man twenty years Jim's senior but only recently promoted to the post. His assistant was a Mr Chatterji who was in his late fifties. It was very much a case of the boy overseeing men.

It was characteristic of Jim to form such an alliance for he felt much more at home in the company of Indians than he did with his own compatriots, be their status domiciled or otherwise. With the Indians, he knew where he stood and they accepted him more readily than they might other Europeans. He knew how to act with them, how to behave and his knowledge of Indians and their India impressed them. He was, bar the colour of his skin, one of them in so many ways. His friendship with the station master remained firm until the man's death thirty-five years later.

After several hours' conversation, Ram Saran said he believed the two of them – the Indian station master and the domiciled lad of twenty – could do it. Jim telegraphed his acceptance of the job to Gorakhpur, much to the cynical amusement of the other Europeans, and set about his workload with a vengeance.

As it turned out, Jim was in charge not only of a considerable labour force of coolies, hitherto formed into one vast organisation, whose role it was to manhandle goods, but he was also supervisor of a staff of over two hundred tally-clerks, ledger-clerks, line-tappers, points- and signalmen, shunters, guards and watchmen. He had to control not only the movement of goods but also that of trains in the sidings and he was additionally responsible for the handling of the fuel coal.

Since it was summer, the traffic at Mokameh Ghat was at a peak and the railway authorities had been faced with such congestion that they had been forced, much against their financial wills, to cease bookings through the junction. If Jim could succeed in sorting out even a part of the bedlam it would do his employers more than a passing favour.

He realised soon after his talk with Ram Saran that the main fault lay in the fact that the labour organisation was too big, too unwieldy for efficient management. Jim, to overcome this, decided to split the work force and delegate. He appointed twelve headmen from the work force and instructed eleven of them to recruit their own units of ten men each: the twelfth man was to recruit a band of sixty men and women to handle the movement of coal. This was a shrewd move as it did away in one sweep with the problems of who would work with whom according to caste: the men sorted themselves out into compatible groups. Instantly, Jim had a unified group under him. Soon, as others were required, so his headmen took on more labourers.

At first, the crews worked for sixteen hours a day, seven days a week, ignoring Sundays, religious festivals and fast days. Meal breaks were kept to a minimum and the work continued through the sweltering middle of the day. Within three months, the backlog was fully cleared and the transhipment regularised on a daily basis so that no goods remained in Mokameh Ghat for more than twenty-four hours. On the first pay day – the labour force and Corbett were paid quarterly – all hands had a half-day holiday and Jim slept for fourteen hours. In addition to the basic wage, it was possible to earn extra income on a piecework basis depending upon how much traffic was dealt with and the efficiency of Corbett's team brought him a continual salary 'on commission' which he shared with his workers, keeping twenty per cent for himself and dividing the rest equally. The pay for such labouring (and the organising of it) was about the lowest offered by the railway authorities who paid Jim according to the weight of goods handled. His own salary was far less than any other European would be offered and his men's wages were less than their own peers' incomes.

With the bulk handling bonus added, however, Jim's men earned much more than they had under the previous administration and more than the opposition earned in the Labour Company on the opposite bank of the Ganges. Everyone was content for Jim, being paid by weight himself, paid his workers by the wagon. Those who worked in the sheds were paid by their headmen, to whom Jim gave a set sum to be divided as felt appropriate whilst he paid the coal handlers directly himself. The workers were paid forty pice (ten annas) per wagon emptied and any odd pice left over after the payment of a work team was given to one of the workers to buy salt which would then be shared equally by all. It resulted in the workers being grateful for a job that paid three times as much as they could expect to earn in the fields and which was permanent rather than seasonal employment.

Jim stayed at his post at Mokameh Ghat, in charge of goods tranship-ment, for twenty-two years without a break other than for brief annual holidays. As for tiger hunting, he fitted that in here and there . . .

At Mokameh Ghat, Jim was housed in railway quarters, a rambling bungalow near to the river bank which he occupied for a few years with Storrar, until the latter was promoted out of the area and Jim took over the house on his own. He had three servants – a personal servant who saw to his laundry, housework and cooking, a water-carrier and a punkah wallah.

Once the initial hard months were over, Jim settled down to a regular life. He rose early in the morning, at dawn and had breakfast before setting out to work. The noon hours were spent in paper work or resting and the late afternoon or early evening had him back at work supervis-ing. He bathed every evening at eight, took a light supper and went to bed. He read what books he could and spent his leisure time fishing or shooting in the surrounding countryside.

It was in some respects an easy bachelor's life. He seldom saw other Europeans, very rarely a European woman. His mother, Mary Doyle and Maggie visited him and stayed on a number of occasions. So did the nine-year-old Ray Nestor who remembered the broad Ganges, the flat countryside and the steamboats: it was to him a 'horrid place, very hot and very nasty'. As a boy there he spent his time 'creeping around to a place where they had a billiard table – in the evenings, Jim played his guitar.' His life was governed by a comfortable routine and he saw no reasons to change it. He missed the jungles of Kaladhungi and Naini Tal, the friends he had in the local Indian population but he returned there every year for his holidays – usually in the winter months – and kept up more than a passing acquaintance with the animals, the jungle folk.

The Ganges offered him not only fishing, a sport of which he grew increasingly fond in his early years at Mokameh Ghat. The river was surrounded by birdlife and Jim collected birds' eggs, building up over the years an enviably fine collection. The mudbanks of the river, especially in the dry seasons, attracted multitudes of butterflies as well and he collected these, becoming an authority on them. He did not regret these pastimes. Birds' nests and butterflies were only too abundant.

He found, more and more, that he did not need the continual companionship of those of his own race. He was at home in India and with her. India was his country and he was in his own mind more of an Indian than he was an Irishman. He was, he knew, a sahib and not merely because he was white but because he was accepted, respected and loved by those over whom he held sway.

His relationship with his staff and work force did not rest solely upon the fact that his ability to manage brought them increased salaries. The Indian peasants, for all the ills of colonialism or imperialism, liked being governed. They enjoyed being patronised and looked after, guarded and employed and organised. They appreciated being controlled. At the turn of the century, this control began to turn more to exploitation but until then, it had been less a system of advantage-taking and more one of a sort of benevolent dictatorship. The British ran the place and took their 'cut' for doing so: the common Indians, by and large, benefited from it.

For his whole life, Jim was a representative of the earlier sort of Raj. He was a benevolent patron as much as a member of a ruling class. He accepted that he was in charge, in a small way, and saw it to be his responsibility to cherish and succour the natives. And yet there was that enigma always running in his blood. He wasn't an Indian and yet he was one – by birth, heritage and domicile.

His benevolence was soon to show in Mokameh Ghat. Once he was settled in, he and Ram Saran erected a simple square building near the railway station and established a school for the children of some of his labourers and low-paid clerks. Such a thing was virtually unheard-of. Education was much sought after by the Indians who rightly saw it as the only way in which they could conceivably better their lot. Schools for Indians were set up by the government, trading companies and by missionary societies but rarely by individuals and in this manner. The school started with twenty boys – girls were not educated at all – and a single teacher who dealt with the most rudimentary of the three R's. The pupils paid a minuscule fee to attend. Within four years, the school had grown to accommodate seven teachers and nearly three hundred boys: it was so large that the government then took over its running and expanded it further. Jim had been faced with one problem over the foundation of his school: the caste system decreed that pupils could not mix in the same classroom. This was overcome by Jim knocking out the rattan and mud-and-daub walls of the building and extending the roof so that the pupils now no longer sat in the same room but merely under the same roof.

Believing in the Victorian view of the importance of sport, almost as a virtue, Jim then joined up with Tom Kelly to institute a local tournament.

Tom Kelly, another domiciled Irishman, was for many years the station master at Simaria Ghat and came into constant contact with Jim over the movement of trans-river cargo. He was a large, strong man with a powerful presence and he intimidated his Indian staff but they respected him as they did his opposite number across the Ganges for Kelly shared Jim's concern for his men. The two of them established football and hockey teams and the two railway gauge networks staged league matches against each other, the simple Indian workers enjoying not only the actual playing but the spectacle of Kelly's bulk looming in goal with Jim's more wiry frame zipping about the field. (It was an uncommon enough sight to see Europeans playing in such a way with Indians, never mind making occasional fools of themselves into the bargain.) However, decorum had to be preserved and, if Jim or Tom Kelly slipped into the dust, play was suspended until they had stood up and removed the dirt from their clothing.

It was with Tom Kelly that Jim sometimes enjoyed an evening's shooting. The former was a keen hunter and in the winter months, when the rail traffic was lighter, the two men would go off in the evening on either a two-man, beam-operated trolley cart or a flatbed trolley pushed by four coolies, travelling nine or ten miles down the Ganges shore to a point just upstream from the town of Monghyr on the south bank. Here, the river divided into a series of islands and the two would stand and wait in the dry reeds or tall crops beside some water storage reservoirs, known as the tanks, and bring down migrating barheaded and greylag geese as they rose from the river to come inland for a night's feeding on the farm wheat or lentil fields or the water weed growing in the tanks. These shooting expeditions took Jim away from the humdrum routine of his daily work and lifted him back, just for a few hours, to his childhood. In his sixties, he still remembered those evenings:

'After crossing the railway line, which was halfway between our positions and the Ganges, the geese would start losing height, and they passed over our heads within easy range. Shooting by moonlight needs a little practice, for birds flighting overhead appear to be farther off than they actually are and one is apt to fire too far ahead of them. When this happened, the birds, seeing the flash of the gun and hearing the report, sprang straight up in the air and before they flattened out again were out of range of the second barrel. Those winter evenings when the full moon was rising over the palm-trees that fringed the river, and the cold brittle air throbbed and reverberated with the honking of geese and the swish of their wings as they passed overhead in flights of from ten to a hundred, are among the happiest of my recollections of the years I spent at Mokameh Ghat.'

Other recreational pleasures were provided by the railway company which built a small mess for the European staff at Mokameh Ghat and equipped it with a tennis court and presented the billiard table which Ray Nestor recalled. The former was little used for the men were often exhausted at the end of their working day, but the billiard table became a great centre of evening activity and it was here that Jim learnt first to play billiards and, when it became more fashionable and common later, snooker which was a game he continued to play for the rest of his life whenever the opportunity arose. Kelly, being proficient in both billiards and tennis, taught them to Jim who, until late middle age, continued to play the latter well.

Not all his life was so pleasurable or free of worries. Within months of his appointment to Mokameh Ghat, an administrative error caused a long delay in the delivery of the cash box from which the workers were paid. For three months, no payments were made despite Jim's continual telegraphing for long overdue funds. One day just before the monsoon broke, he was forced to spend three intolerable hours with Tom Kelly rerailing a locomotive at Simaria Ghat with the aid of hand jacking equipment. They strove to get the locomotive on the tracks in a burning, sun-dancing wind but it only came off again. At the third attempt, as the sun was lowering, they succeeded in moving the locomotive and packing the tracks with oven-hot sand. His eyes sore from the dust and wind, Jim was exhausted and just sitting down to his evening meal when a deputation of his headmen arrived on the veranda of his quarters where he was eating. Before approaching the sahib, they noticed what he was being served and asked of his servant why the master was eating only a chapati and some dal. The servant replied that, as there was no money left, that was all that was available. The headmen withdrew, one, a Moslem, returning after the plate was removed and Jim was leaning back in his chair smoking. Jim remembered the words of their spokesman for many years:

'We came to tell you that our stomachs have long been empty and that after tomorrow it would be no longer possible for us to work. But we have seen tonight that your case is as bad as ours and we will carry on as long as we have strength to stand. I will, with your permission, go now, Sahib, and, for the sake of Allah, I beg you will do something to help us.'

What the Mohammedan did not realise was that Jim had already used his one hundred and fifty rupees savings to pay the men whilst Jim knew that the men had pawned everything they could to keep going. He went immediately to the telegraph office and threatened a strike if the money wasn't immediately forthcoming. It arrived within forty-eight hours.

With the departure of Storrar, Jim received overall charge of the cross-river steamers as well as the cargo shipping. This gave him a huge added responsibility as well as a much increased staff. He was, by the time this extra work was placed upon him, well acquainted with what it involved, but it was nevertheless a strain. The increase in salary was not commensurate with the increase in responsibility but every little bit helped as he was sending a large proportion of his income back to his mother in Naini Tal. However, accepting management of the steamers did give him some advantage: firstly he was now seen as a slightly higher ranking official than he had previously been and this gave him more pride of position in the eyes of European travellers. It was not that Jim was proud. He was far too modest throughout his life to be one who sought such elevation, but it must have given him some inward joy to know that he was at least climbing in his career, albeit only in a small way. Secondly, being in charge of the steamers, he was obliged to cross from one bank to the other on business and this gave him a morning and an afternoon break in his working day. From early manhood, Jim had been a cigarette smoker, usually preferring native Indian to Virginia tobacco but his work in the cargo sheds prevented him from smoking. Many of the cargoes he and his men transhipped were dangerous, especially in the dry months – flour dust was explosive as was the coal dust that hung with equal unpleasantness in the air and cloth and many other items of merchandise were inflammable. It is to Jim's credit that there is on record not one instance of fire or any such calamity striking Mokameh Ghat during his years there although some workers, despite his strict safety rules, died from time to time from coal-gas poisoning.

The passage by boat across the river was a chance therefore for Jim to have a relaxing smoke and carry out what he called his other hobby – the study of human beings – to which he applied himself with much the same avidity as he did the study of animals. Indeed, at Mokameh Ghat, humans took the place of animals in the continual exercising of Jim's wits and powers of observation: the steamer and railway junction being such an important one, a great and varied multitude of people crossed there at all times of the year. It was in the company of a young European, out from England to join the railway, that Jim gave one of his many exhibitions of acute human observation and was caught out.

In the first decade of the twentieth century, the railway authorities recruited increasingly for staff in Britain, bringing out to India young men to learn the job under the instruction of the old hands and Jim, aged about thirty, was now considered an old hand in no uncertain terms. He was utterly familiar with the work of which he was in charge and as knowledgeable – if not more so – on India and the Indians. He was a regular teacher for expatriates who were still pink-kneed and starry-eyed.

It was a task Jim relished. He greatly enjoyed showing the ropes to the young men partly because it indicated to him (and his superiors) that he was doing his job well and partly because he was always keen to pass on his knowledge of animals or humans. He liked the company of young people, especially children, and recognised in them the vast repository of the future.

Crosthwaite had spent a fortnight at Mokameh Ghat with Jim, assisting and getting in the way, learning and questioning. At the end of his stay, Jim went with the youngster across the river to Simaria Ghat where he was to put him on the train for Gorakhpur. Each river crossing of the steamship took not only cargo but also seven hundred passengers and Jim and Crosthwaite stood on the upper passenger deck, looking down on the crowded lower deck upon which thronged the bulk of the Indian travellers.

When Crosthwaite expressed a curiosity in them, Jim began to indicate to his junior what was the station in life of every person on the deck below. Jim showed him three Brahmins carrying copper amphorae sealed with clay, explaining that they were taking holy Ganges water (from the holier right bank) to their employer eighty miles inland from the left bank, a maharaja to whom Jim knew the men were servants. Next he pointed out a Mohammedan whose job was as a *dhoonia*, a teaser of old cotton knots in mattresses to make them into comfortable floss once more: he had on the deck beside him his unique work-tool. There were two Tibetan Buddhist priests feeling the heat to which they were unused. There were four Nepalese pilgrims from the holy city of Benares also taking with them glass vessels of holy water which they would sell in their home villages. Finally, he reached a farmer, the father of one of his work force, travelling to till his fields on the left bank. It was, Jim explained, all a matter of seeing what the eye saw – of looking, not just watching – and, from reasoned study, understanding and correctly interpreting the signs.

To test Jim as much as from wonderment, Crosthwaite asked him about a man squatting on a bench on their own deck. Jim stated that he was a Mohammedan leather merchant on route from Gaya to Muzaffarpur. At this, the man lowered his legs to the deck and started laughing, much to Jim's discomfiture and this was quickly followed by his acute embarrassment. The man spoke in excellent English, saying that he had heard all of Jim's synopses of the passengers below and agreed with them for the most part. He also admitted that he was a Mohammedan and that he was indeed travelling from Gaya to Muzaffarpur though how his observer had arrived at this conclusion was beyond him as he had yet to be asked by the inspector for his ticket. Jim was, however, humorously informed that he was mistaken about one thing: the man did not deal in leather but tobacco. Jim had noticed the man's stained hands and assumed that this was caused by tanning fluids.

Indian royalty, maharajas and princes, servants and peasants, holy men and criminals, those of very high and very low caste, soldiers and their officers, Indian Civil Service and Forest Service officials, traders and businessmen, missionaries and drifters all passed through Mokameh Ghat and Jim grew to know the regular travellers and was known to them. He knew the Prime Minister of Nepal quite well, was on familiar speaking terms with him and was treated by him with courtesy and honour. It was through the Prime Minister's secretary that Jim was given one of the many of his insights into the mysticism of the east.

One night, as Jim was filing his quarterly report on goods movement, the Nepalese secretary was ushered into his office. The man, whom Jim had previously seen only a few weeks before dressed in court robes and finery, was dirty and unshaven, dog-tired and hungry. Jim gave him a meal and then found out what circumstances had led to his present state.

On a recent trip to Calcutta, the Prime Minister had purchased for his concubines a suitcase of gemstones from Hamilton & Co., paying for them in silver. The suitcase was then placed in the care of the secretary but on the return of the party to Katmandu, it was found to be missing. The secretary having been in charge of it was given a week's leave to find it: failure to return with the gems would mean certain execution for he was considered guilty of a heinous crime not only against common morality but against his powerful ruler as well – and that spelt death.

The man's chances of finding the suitcase were slim: anyone else discovering it would doubtless make off with the contents and live happily ever afterwards. He was distraught with fear, not only because of his impending doom but also because he had let his employer down. To try and know where to start searching, he had visited a famous hermit known for his clairvoyant powers. After a night's meditation on the part of the hermit – and no doubt a sleepless night's sweating on the part of the secretary – the hermit informed him that the suitcase was still intact and unopened in a room which he described in some detail. It was, he divined, not far from a great river, in a room with only one door that faced east: furthermore, it was in a corner and hidden by other bags and parcels.

Jim accepted this as gospel: he was conversant with the accurate foretellings of such mystics and had heard the priest at the temple in

Naini Tal prophesy minor events that came to pass as expected. After all, it was said that the gods would wreak vengeance on the Europeans by drowning one annually in the *tal* at Naini Tal. That prophecy was indubitably being carried out and Jim knew it.

The problem was to find the room. It might have been in Simaria Ghat, Mokameh Ghat or back at the town of Mokameh where there was a large rail junction and storage facilities for goods waiting to be moved by Jim's men to the river crossing. And in each place there were many godowns, sheds and storage areas. With the secretary, he left his house and they toured Mokameh Ghat by lantern. No room fitted the description. Then Jim stated that one might: it was the parcels office at Mokameh Junction. Ram Saran and the secretary went off to it. The parcels clerk denied all knowledge of a suitcase in his store but Ram Saran insisted on a search: the suitcase was intact, seals unbroken, in a far corner. An enquiry showed it to have been found by a low caste carriage cleaner who, discovering it under a seat in the Calcutta-Mokameh train, and not knowing what to do with it, had put it in the unattended parcels office.

Other excitements enlivened Jim's life at Mokameh Ghat. On one occasion, he was trapped in the darkness of his bathroom with an angry cobra. The lamp had been knocked out by Jim's frantic and ill-conceived attempt to remove his toes from within a few inches of the snake which was hissing, spitting and had flared its hood to its fullest extent. That one of the workers had died from cobra bites only a few days previously did not help to improve Jim's frame of mind. He was trapped, with a trapped cobra, in a dark bathroom. After half an hour, his bearer came to call him to dinner and heard the sahib's voice through the door explaining what was going on inside. After much palaver and abortive attempts to get a lantern through the window, Jim succeeded in dropping the heavy woven rush bathmat on to the snake and leaping for the door. The snake attacked the floorboards and was cudgelled to death.

A dangerous snakebite in those days was uncurable. There were no developed anti-snakebite serums and one's only hope of survival was to be in the vicinity of a holy man or some such who knew of a folk remedy, although these were often useless. Jim felt that as many people died from the psychological fear brought on by being bitten as by the actual poisons: most Indians believed all snakes were poisonous, whether or not they were constrictors or venomous only to small mammals and birds. A snakebite was invariably fatal and that was that. To recover from one was indeed a miracle or gift from the gods.

What was a far greater cause for fear was disease. In the summer months, cholera ravaged the indigenous and European population alike. As with the snake venom, there was no antidote available. Typhoid was common and malaria killed hundreds of thousands a year until well into the middle of the twentieth century. Tetanus was another risk all ran in a country where animals were so widely used: though Jim seldom came across cases of tetanus, those he saw horrified him as much as rabies victims did and, in Naini Tal, he was warned as a child to keep clear of the polo ground which was known to be heavily infected with tetanus. Whenever an outbreak of a disease – especially cholera – occurred, Jim was on hand at all times to help the local Indians. He had to preserve his work force for the sake of the railways, but his motivation was humanist rather than capitalist. His medical knowledge was sketchy and as reliant upon folk medicine as was the holy man's but he did his best, rubbing powdered root ginger on the hands and feet of the sick to raise their temperatures and purging them with herbal teas. In 1905, he saved the life of a cholera-stricken passenger on the steamer: he not only kept the man for a month and nursed him back to health after the local doctor proved his incompetence and was obliged to leave the area, but also bought him a ticket to Gaya and lent him five hundred rupees without security to establish himself in his grain business which had fallen upon lean times. It was a sum of money Jim could ill afford but eleven months later, the man returned with the loan complete and a gift of twenty-five per cent interest which latter sum Jim refused as being out of the court of friendship. For the next eleven years, the rest of his time at Mokameh Ghat, Jim received an annual gift of plump, ripe mangoes from the grain merchant's garden.

On another occasion, Jim noticed one of his coal labourers absenting himself annually for two or three months upon receiving a postcard from his home. Whenever the man and his wife, who also humped coal, arrived back at the coal yards they were noticeably thinner, haggard-looking and tired out to the point that they could barely do a day's work: indeed, coal-lifting seemed a lighter load for them after their absence. Jim asked a few questions and was told that the man and his wife were bound to a moneylender who had been usuriously draining the man's family for three generations, to the tune of twenty-five per cent interest per annum. The moneylender was getting his interest settlement in kind by forcing the man and his wife to slave for him in his fields every harvest-tide. Jim, partly by bluff and partly with the aid of a lawyer, succeeded in getting the moneylender to drop not only his claim but all documentation to it. The freed debtor agreed to be bound to Jim for saving him, but Jim characteristically declined this and was, instead, given the greatest show of gratitude an Indian can offer by having his feet embraced and kissed.

For over fifteen of his years at Mokameh Ghat, Jim was aided by his coal-labourers' headman, Chamari, a man of the lowest caste possible – he was an Untouchable. Jim had initially taken him and his wife on out of pity but finding the man had not the stamina for heavy cargo shifting, never mind coal-shovelling, had made him a tally-clerk for he could read and write a little Hindi. He later rose to become pay clerk. A strong friendship grew between the two men, the European being unrestricted by the caste system. Both were generous to a fault, hard-working and sympathetic. Chamari assisted Jim with his medical work, always willing to tend the sick and dying: he died in Jim's arms from cholera. His funeral was attended by a huge crowd of mixed castes and religions, such was the respect in which he was held.

Festivals, holy days and Sundays were generally ignored even after the pressures of the first months at Mokameh Ghat. Jim and his workers kept a seven-day week which was interrupted only by Christmas when the very high esteem in which Jim was held by the Indians was shown at its most poignant. On that day, he remained in his bungalow until 10 a.m. when he was called for by Ram Saran and ceremonially taken to his office where he sat at his table, decorated with a bowl of flowers, under a bunting made of signal flags, whilst the station master made a speech followed by Jim replying to it. After this came a handing out of sweets to all the children and then a solemn and grateful sharing out of eighty per cent of the profits made by the team during the year. All the labourers wore their best clean clothes and Jim was garlanded with a chain of jasmine flowers. As each worker collected his share of the profit, he placed his hands together and bowed low to Jim. Until 1939 there were Indians still at Mokameh Ghat who remembered the kindness, generosity and humanity of the sahib who shared his profits with his labourers and coolies.

No doubt, Jim's life would have continued through to retirement at Mokameh Ghat. He enjoyed the work there, shifting in an average year over one million tons of cargo. He earned a safe and steady salary, was able to make a profit on bonus payments and maintained his family back home in Kumaon. He visited them annually on holiday, spending his time with them hunting or fishing. It is also true that, on occasion, he was side-tracked into other activities of *shikar* . . .

Mokameh Ghat made Jim. It taught him organisation, leadership, an even greater love of the Indian people. It gave him security of a sort and self-esteem. He arrived there as a boy and left as a man verging upon middle age. Only one thing could really drag him away from Mokameh Ghat and that was patriotism. He was fiercely patriotic about Britain. And, in 1914, the First World War began.

6

Captain Corbett

When the Boer War broke out, Jim wrote to the railway company to ask for permission to enlist. He was refused it. The railway authorities, having only comparatively recently appointed him to a full-time post and quick to realise that he was exceptionally efficient in it were loath to let him go. Mokameh Ghat was a key junction and to have it operating so well was a considerable asset to the network as a whole.

Jim was disappointed at the failure of his application. The war against the Boers seemed one to which he could ideally apply himself for it was an Imperialist war in which the honour not only of Queen and Country was at stake but also the pride and stability of the British Empire as a whole. He was filled with patriotic jingoism and wanted to fight, to prove himself in yet another field. He anticipated with some delight the prospect of being able to serve under the officer who had readjusted his sights for him in the shooting display at Naini Tal a decade or so before. Yet he was not to press his request to the railway head office in Gorakhpur: he knew that he at least had a job and a safe one, and that was an undeniable asset. He could have resigned but to do that would be to destroy his reputation and, when the war was over, he would be unemployed and considered unemployable – a man who broke his bond. All that would remain would be the Indian Army and, as a domiciled man, he could not expect to rise fast through the ranks, if at all. An ultimate commission was out of the question. Besides, he had already considered the army as a career prospect and had passed it over as untenable.

There were other mitigating factors that influenced his decision to remain at Mokameh Ghat. One was a terrible blow to the family that had caused Jim to return to Naini Tal at very short notice. His younger brother Archy had died tragically aged only twenty. After the funeral, Jim realised that he was now the remaining son and the youngest child whose prime responsibility it now was to provide for and look after his mother, half-sister and sister. He had had thoughts that perhaps Archy would take over the load from his shoulders when he came of age but that hope was now extinct. Jim was now the Corbett family protector and that was that.

Jim's sister and mother were not so upset that his eagerness to take the Queen's shilling met with a solid rebuff. From Mary Corbett's point of view, she wanted Jim to remain tied to the matrimonial home. With no husband, a tiny pension and a small business which she knew she would not be able to run for ever, it was imperative that Jim remained available in case of need and she set about securing that end with the same diligence that she applied to all matters of importance in her life, be they house renting, religion or the keeping of the family home.

So Jim continued to work at Mokameh Ghat, take his annual leave and entertain his mother and sisters on the banks of the Ganges every so often. He saw few Europeans, except for travellers, itinerant railway staff or the local residents who were mostly men. He continued to take an almost fatherly interest in his workers and in the Indians around his homes in Kumaon. This interest led him to become involved in a fascinating and sad story.

In the July of 1914, some labourers building a road near Ratighat, within fifteen miles of Naini Tal, had seen an animal working through cover by their site. Taking up their tools, they surrounded the cover into which the animal had vanished and drove it out. What they found was a naked human being that then fled on all fours. They followed and captured it, put it in a wicker basket and sent it to Naini Tal.

The press reported the finding of a wolf-child and this aroused Jim's curiosity down in Mokameh Ghat. Legends of such creatures were rife in the hills, but none had ever been found. He telegraphed to G. W. Lawrie, who was a professional photographer who had a studio in Naini Tal, and asked him to photograph the child which was now in the Crosthwaite Hospital near the bazaar. Lawrie could not take any photographs because the child refused to come out of a pile of straw under which it lived in the corner of its room.

When next in Naini Tal on leave, Jim received a letter from Sir Bampfylde Fuller in London (whom Jim knew through his railway work and who knew of Jim's hill knowledge) asking him to look into the matter of the wolf-child.

He found out that the child was a girl in her mid-teens who was healthy and strong but covered with dirt and a thick coat of hair. She spoke no language and was dubbed *Goongi* ('dumb') as a result, though she had a vocabulary of bestial sounds. Her nails were long claws and she tore up any clothes or coverings given to her. Refusing human food, she ate only raw meat, vegetables and fruit and growled or cooed, with displeasure or enjoyment respectively. She did not use her hands to hold her food but ate as a dog might, though she carried her food into her straw on the backs of her hands. She was very agile, cunning, not house-trained and climbed up pillars to escape those coming towards her. From her colouring and physical features, she was assumed to be a girl from the hill tribes. She was quite obviously intelligent and, in her own terms, quite sane. She also bit the nurses badly. A fortnight after admission to the hospital, she was transferred to a lunatic asylum in Bareilly on the Indian plains. It was high summer and the wolf-child not surprisingly died of heat-stroke within days.

Jim was intrigued and although he never saw the child, he gave her case much study believing, finally, that she was not a wolf-child – which relationship he very much doubted could be allowed by the laws of nature to occur – but a bear-child. He concluded that her behaviour was more ursine: to add to the possibility was the fact that it was a commonly accepted legend that bears were reputed to molest women at certain seasons of the year. A rumour soon sprang up that a Forest Officer friend of Jim's had shot a bear accompanied by 'its human-like cub' and indeed a bear had recently been shot in the area but it had been a lone animal.

After his researches, Jim felt sad on two counts. He was sorry and disappointed that the child had died before further tests could be carried out, especially his own of taking the child to Lucknow Zoo and seeing to which animals there she related. Yet he was also saddened by the fact that the child had died, thus robbing not only men of further study and understanding of the jungles but also depriving nature of another innocent animal.

At Mokameh Ghat, Jim's life was masculine. He toiled physically for long, hard hours and his recreation – when time afforded him some –

was manly. He hunted, shot, collected birds' eggs and butterflies for his collections, played billiards and outdoor sport and maintained a rigid, bachelor existence.

He was not necessarily monastic. It is assumed that he was celibate for all these years, for women of any race hardly ever entered into his life unless they appeared as part of his labour force, but that is not necessarily so. It was certainly not uncommon for Europeans to consort with local Indian girls and Jim must have seen this accepted, if under-cover, sort of dalliance going on all around him. Whether or not he regarded it as acceptable practice himself and on occasion indulged in such relationships is not known, but it is possible. Certainly, later in his life, Jim was known to have had such liaisons. Some of his closest friends at the time, whether in Naini Tal or Mokameh Ghat, did surreptitiously (or, in a few instances, fairly openly) build up considerable affairs with Indian girls of quite good background. Those of the lower strata of Indian society were kept well clear of except by the British troops: venereal disease was rampant and the cure – for what it was worth – was prolonged, inconvenient, embarrassing and exceedingly painful.

There has over the years been qualified speculation that Jim was a homosexual: he did not marry and he lived in a male-orientated world, to return from it to his mother and spinster sister. There is, however, absolutely no foundation to the assumption. Jim's problem was not suppressed homosexuality but unfortunate circumstance. He simply rarely saw women of his own race or class or had the time or the opportunity to court them. Any sexual relationships he may have had were necessarily fleeting and any amorous ones were broken almost before they had begun.

Jim was domiciled and from this social position stemmed much prejudice in the first half of his life. Young women out from England looked down upon the likes of the Corbetts not only because of pure snobbery but also practicality. To marry a domiciled man was to commit oneself to the same state of permanent expatriation and few young women viewed a lifetime in India without many misgivings. It was one thing to do just a tour of duty there but quite another to be resident.

On top of the enforced residency came the position in society. The young women Jim would have met 'out from Home' were of a certain standing and they were loath to lower it. The general idea was to marry well. A domiciled, country-bred, railway official of Irish stock, living in a

God-forsaken railway junction on the Ganges plain, surrounded by thousands of natives, mosquitoes and forest, with a poor salary, long working hours and no club in which to relax was not considered to be much of a matrimonial catch.

Also to Jim's disadvantage was his own demeanour. He was, throughout his life, quiet and almost shy in the company of other Europeans, preferring to be away from crowds and in the presence of only one or two others. He was truly very modest and this too prevented him from fitting in with mixed company. His self-effacing and withdrawn manner made him hard to converse with in a large gathering and, when with young women, he seemed almost ganglingly clumsy. He was tall and thin, wiry rather than muscular and his slightly gaunt appearance made him somehow formidable to young women. It was all rather sad for inside this quiet man there dwelt another who was full of fun, humour and a fund of knowledge, stories, jokes and conversation. What was more, there was in Jim a man longing to be loved and eager to share his life with a communicant soul like his own. It was just that he prevented this second person from emerging, feeling embarrassed at letting his barriers down and worried, at the same time, that by doing so would somehow be to desert or let down his mother and sisters. His mother, for her part, knew of this conflict within her son and did her level best, in subtle ways, to encourage and maintain his state of uncertainty.

The same motivation that caused Mary Corbett to inwardly rejoice that her son was not being sent to fight in South Africa operated in her attitudes towards all her sons' hopes for wedlock. She was intensely jealous of her boys and strove to make any relationships that they sought to develop cool off: she had placed countless obstacles before brother John's romances with the result that he did not finally succeed in marrying until he was thirty-four years old. With Archy dead, her resolve to protect Jim from young women toughened considerably. The odds were more than loaded against him.

In 1902, whilst on holiday from Mokameh Ghat, Jim met and fell in love with a young girl who was staying with her parents in Naini Tal, out from England for a matter of months. Information on their courtship is hazy, indeed. Mary Corbett did her damnedest to make the romance fail though quite how is lost. John was straining at the leash – or the apron strings – at the time and, perhaps knowing that he was a lost cause, the mother concentrated her efforts on her now youngest surviving son. She was closely aided in her designs by Maggie who was just as jealous of any member of the opposite sex who paid her brother the least attention.

It may be that Mary Corbett was eager to see them all into better marriages: Thomas, the firstborn, had done very well for the son of a domiciled former army apothecary and local postmaster: he was married to Lord Allenbury's daughter. Christopher, the next son, had married a Nestor from Kaladhungi, the sister of Richard Nestor, the husband of Harriet, the second Corbett child. Richard Nestor left much to be desired both as a father and a husband and Mary Corbett obviously wanted no repetition of that sort of alliance despite the fact that Christopher was happily married, but to a domiciled wife.

Somehow, though, this socially conscious concern seems out of character for Mary Corbett. She was really just a very, almost pathologically jealous mother who wanted to be quite sure, beyond all doubt, that she had a son with undivided loyalties to stand by her in her old age.

Her fears were groundless, of course. Jim was far too kind and sympathetic a man, not to mention devoted, to have abandoned his mother in her last years. He would have seen to her every comfort – as indeed he did – and protected her with a depth of filial love few mothers can command or rightly expect from an adult son. She, for her part, took away every possibility of the happiness of a woman's love from Jim. By the time she died, he was well past the marrying age.

Jim's first serious expedition into the jungles of romance was, therefore, an utter failure. He caught nothing and the girl disappeared from his life to marry an officer in the army. Jim made very few attempts after this to woo anyone. He returned, no doubt crestfallen and not a little apprehensive now that he had seen the writing on the wall, to Mokameh Ghat and his bachelor routines.

In 1914, the Great War broke out. Jim was thirty-eight years old when hostilities commenced yet he nevertheless immediately travelled by train to Calcutta and offered his services to the army. This was no war against a rabble of insurgent Boers: this was a struggle that would rock the foundations of Europe and the Empire and Jim realised that this was a much more terrifying threat to his world than the South African situation had been two decades previously.

Inevitably, he was rejected on account of his age and once more retreated to Mokameh Ghat. Once again, the railway authorities were much relieved. However, as the war in Europe ground on and developed into a battle of attrition rather than military action, and as the deaths mounted, the mother country had to start drawing upon her reserves of manpower and that meant seeking volunteers or conscripts in the Empire. India was the largest of the Empire's dominions in the terms of a population that was as yet untapped. Word was sent to Delhi for the formation not only of fighting units for the Western Front but also for sappers, labour corps and general cannon-fodder.

Being deemed too old to fight, Jim was not considered too old to command and, in 1917, he was given a wartime commission as a captain.

This move not only upset but also annoyed his superiors in the railway. He received a none too polite letter from the head office at Gorakhpur to which he replied that he saw that he must carry out his duty to his country whilst at the same time acknowledging that he owed more than a passing debt of duty to the railway. He assured them that the transhipment contract would not lapse or fall into its former chaos. It was with complete confidence that Jim could make this assurance as he had already spoken with Ram Saran about the station master taking over the role of transhipment contractor. It is a credit not only to Ram Saran but also to Jim's fine ability as an organiser that, for the years of his absence on military service, there was not one hiccup in the service.

He left Mokameh Ghat amidst much sadness, with promises from all his workers that they would daily pray for his safety and return to them. The love for him which these simple folk displayed touched Jim greatly and, with a heavy heart, he headed for home, now Captain E. J. Corbett, though he signed his army forms 'J.E.' as he usually did in everyday life. His orders were to raise a labour corps to take to France.

The esteem in which he was held in Kumaon did not make his job very difficult. From the jungles he reputedly raised five thousand volunteers and recruited a personal unit of five hundred young Kumaoni men from the total, optimistically and rashly promising to the head of the family of each that he would bring every single individual home safely when the war was ended.

In the late summer of 1917, Captain Corbett and his unit embarked upon a troopship at Bombay, headed first for England and then Flanders.

It was with very mixed feelings that Jim set sail. He knew he was going to war and that he might never return: similarly, he was responsible not just for his own life but also for the lives of his men. This was no labour force shifting timber or coal, farm produce, baggage and general goods from railway box-cars into sheds and on to steamers. These men would have to dig trenches, lay communication wires, fill sandbags and cut duckboards: they would be under fire from whining bullets not whining mosquitoes. New, 'European' diseases were a major risk for the hillfolk, especially influenza: seasickness and even homesickness could kill them as readily as bullets or bacteria. The countryside in which they would be living would be totally alien to them: indeed, he realised that it would be just as alien to him.

He was leaving not only India and his life there, but his elderly mother, his half-sister Mary Doyle (now verging upon the elderly herself) and his dearly beloved sister, Maggie. That they were financially provided for he was certain: his life had taken a few twists for the better since the turn of the century in addition to his having continued to build a modest profit from the Mokameh Ghat contract but he was nevertheless worried about his family. He was, after all, their only hope.

On the positive side, he was excited. Forty-two years old, he was going off to war, to active service as had so many of his forebears. The Indian Mutiny hero, Tom, was in Jim's blood: his father had been a soldier, and his grandfather, and now it was his turn. What was more, he was going 'Home'.

This was a very strange feeling for Jim. India was his home. He was domiciled. And yet, like most of his breed, he was fiercely patriotic and 'British' and related to Great Britain even though he had only ever seen it in faded photographs or steel engravings in editions of the *Illustrated London News*. He was intensely curious to see the Tower of London and the Houses of Parliament from which stemmed the flow of history and the power of the Empire.

Where his troopship docked is uncertain though it was probably Southampton. Where he and his men were barracked prior to departure for the front is also unknown but Jim did not have the opportunity, before 'going down the line', of visiting London. He had problems enough with which to contend.

His men, known as the 70th Kumaon Company, were sad, dispirited, depressed and lost. The winter weather was damp and chilling and the Front Line was unmitigatingly terrible. Their work was hard, dangerous and awkward not only because of the risks of warfare but also because of the complexities of the differing cultures the men carried with them. Religious beliefs had to be stretched or waived, attitudes altered. By crossing the ocean, the men had lost their caste and would have to regain it on their return – if they returned.

Some of the Indian troops sent to the war, facing the pleasures of the recreational facilities behind the lines, went berserk with hungry glee. White women were available as well as the regular army ration of rum. Wine was to be had quite easily and every vice of the European was on hand. Religious observancy with respect to alcohol was ignored by some native troops and they suffered badly, both physically and through military discipline, for their lapses. Additionally, the tommies took the Indian troops for a ride as often as they could: crown-and-anchor and Find-the-lady games took their pay and they were generally ribbed, hassled, scorned, mocked, abused and taken advantage of by turn.

Jim saw to it that his men did not become corrupted. It was bad enough that they were taking part in the horror of 'modern' warfare and, besides, when he promised to look after them, he meant more than just caring for their physical well-being. By example, he taught them restraint and the respect he carried was enough to make his rule effective.

Not once did he quit the side of his men. He did not take a leave in Blighty because they could not. If they were up against it, whatever it was, so was he.

Jim seldom spoke of what he called 'The Kaiser's War' and, for him, its aftermath. It was a period of his life he would rather forget: no doubt, he arrived at the Front Line full of patriotic fervour only to find – as had so many tens of thousands before him – that the glory of war was no longer a truism. Modern warfare was a filthy, degrading ante-room to hell.

His unit was variously posted to a number of scenes of action along the Western Front. That he and his men saw active service is certain but Jim seldom wrote home of this and whatever letters he did write were first censored by Jim himself and later by the army mails officer: none survive. When he did send a letter home, he was careful not to record too much of the bloodiness of war for he did not want to concern or worry his mother and those at home in Naini Tal. His natural cheerfulness seems to have won the day in any case. His Kumaoni men looked up to him not as an officer but as a *sadhu*, a guru who would guard as much as lead them: his reputation as a fearless hunter as well as a gentleman and lover of Kumaoni hillfolk – not to mention India in general – was well known and inspired his men. The reasons for his being so highly thought-of and trusted by his men and their families in India was based upon events of more than a decade before: his men placed in him a well-founded and simple faith. They knew what he had done, in their eyes the impossible, and therefore he would go on in a like manner.

His labourer-troops faced many vicissitudes apart from the bullets and the bombs, the disease and the drizzling cold and the rats and trench foot. Their food was scanty and poor and often inappropriate – tinned beef stew, a staple for army rations, was out for them on religious grounds. Pork wasn't readily accepted by many. His men came from different religious backgrounds, different cultural foundations and, most of all, were of mixed caste. Whatever the conditions in the trenches, the caste system could not be totally ignored.

Jim had to not only face and share his men's problems but also had to alleviate them wherever he was able. His immense skill at organisation, improvisation and ingenuity was invaluable to him and, fortunately, there exists a unique and fascinating document that shows Captain Corbett at war and gives a tiny insight into his life in Flanders.

Lord Ampthill, in overall charge of foreign labour corps troops fighting in France towards the end of the war, visited the trenches and front line in the first week of January, 1918 and met Corbett. Three extracts from his tour report are worthy of mention not only for what they say of Jim but also of the conditions of the war: the third extract refers to a man who was to become a close friend and associate of Jim's in the post-war years.

The weather had been severe in the extreme for a fortnight: biting winds, sleet and snow had greatly affected the troops and Ampthill had felt it necessary to look at the circumstances of the men. He called on a number of units:

'*No. 70 KUMAON COMPANY*

This Company has headquarters at LA CHAPELLETTE and detachment at TINCOURT and HANCOURT. I visited the two former. Captain J. E. CORBETT, who impressed me as a competent and resourceful man, gave me a cheerful account of his Company. He said that the men are standing the cold very well and that there has been practically no sickness. The method of heating the Adrian Huts at the LA CHAPELLETTE Camp is the best of the many varieties that I have seen and I believe that the credit of devising this particular pattern is due to the Group Commander, Lieut-Colonel H. A. PERROTT. It is on the trench system, which is now most in favour, but its efficacy consists in the small details which have been improved as the result of much experiment. I was astonished to see a substantial brick building which I have not noticed on previous occasions, and on my enquiring how it came to escape the ravages of war Captain CORBETT told me that he had built it himself with salved materials and no labour except that of his own men. This building contains a Bathroom and a Drying Room both of which are to be heated by an Incinerator. It has good solid walls of red brick and the mortar was made with nothing more than chalk and rice water.

The Detachment at TINCOURT has two exceptionally good Officers, namely, 2nd. Lieuts. O. O'DONNELL and H. LEE, both of them men with a great deal of experience of travel, sport and the management of labour . . . The camp of this Detachment is not at all a good one and the men have been greatly inconvenienced by the repeated theft of their ablution benches, and other things capable of being turned into fuel, and of canvas from the huts by the men of neighbouring Units. They themselves are suffering a good deal from shortage of fuel but they remain cheerful and there is no abnormal sickness. Frozen feet are the chief cause of trouble especially when the Employer urges the Officers to 'Push them along'.

'No. 26 LUSHAI COMPANY

This Company which used to be among the best has suffered cruelly from constant moves and the consequent hardships such as that of having to sleep on the cold ground.'

[Within 27 days in November and December, the unit had moved to Aisecourt; to Norlu to build roads; to Mont St Quentin with the German attack on Cambrai; to Haute Allaines for ammunition dump construction; back to Mont St Quentin for road and dump work; back to Aisecourt and finally to Rosiel.]

'The Adrian Huts at ROSIEL are insufficiently heated and application for some of the numerous stoves lying on the neighbouring dump has not received attention. The men have no gloves with which to handle metal and are often crying with the pain of frozen hands. They are being overworked and it is the constant night work which does for them. There were 96 morning sick on the 1st. January, the day of my visit.

All the British Officers from England have gone sick and only the two Officers who brought the Company out from India, Captain NEEDHAM and 2nd. Lieut. BADDELEY remain. I found the former in bed with fever but he has been carrying on pluckily in spite of this illness . . .

'No. 73 *KUMAON COMPANY*

This Company were not given half a chance of showing what they would do at ROSIEL and were suddenly moved to AISECOURT on the 17th. December. I was unable to discover any plausible reason for this transfer but I saw some correspondence which led me to form a very high opinion of Major R. T. BELLAIRS and an opinion which was not very high of the D.A.D.L., Captain ROBERTSON.

I found Major BELLAIRS recovering from an attack of Mumps and 2nd. Lieut. REGNARD very sick and sorry for himself. 2nd. Lieut. MURPHY had gone to Hospital having collapsed, in almost tragic circumstances, in consequence of the sudden move in which under the orders of the D.A.D.L. he was sent in charge of a detachment to a separate place; and that in spite of the fact that he had only just joined the Company and is a very elderly gentleman. Colonel PERROTT when visiting the detachment on the morning after the move found 2nd. Lieut. MURPHY shivering over a stove and eating rice with his fingers out of an Indian vessel. One of the Indian Officers had had to sit up with him all night and rub his limbs to keep him alive. Colonel PERROTT of course removed him at once in the Medical Officer's motor ambulance and sent him to hospital. This episode suggests two considerations, viz: (1) that D.A.D.L.'s should not be allowed to usurp the duties of Company Commanders, and (2) that the War Office might be informed that the officers whom they appoint to the Indian Labour corps have to lead an outdoor life and ought to be sufficiently young and robust to endure a certain amount of exposure. The health of the men of this Company is fairly good but there were no less than fifty sick on the day of the move.

They have been kept waiting for some time for clothing to replace deficiencies. Their present camp is a good one. They would have been better able to endure the harder work and discomforts of ROSIEL than the LUSHAIS as they are quite accustomed to snowy winters. The detachment of this Company at HAUTES ALLAINES is in a miserable Camp.'

Ampthill's comments brought about by the illness of the elderly Murphy were echoed by others in his staff in the months to come: as for

Jim, although he was into middle age, the rigours of his jungle life had sufficiently toughened him for trench warfare. His ability to make the most of a situation, heightened by his work at Mokameh Ghat and to be of such use to him in the forests of Kumaon, shows in his building the bath-house which was not merely to keep his men reasonably comfortable but also to overcome a caste problem. Those from different groups used the facility according to a rota and all kept clean and comparatively dry at least every third day.

Major Bellairs, in the sister company to Jim's own, was an officer who thought in Jim's manner. He was keen on the welfare of his labourers and he and Jim struck a friendship that saw them through the horrors of the Flanders mud. As at Mokameh Ghat with Kelly, Jim organised such pastimes as he could for his men, raising their spirits and keeping them going. When the war ended in 1918, he and his men gathered up their belongings, war souvenirs and 'trophies', as if they had been out hunting, and returned to India via Britain. Of the five hundred Jim took away with him from his beloved Kumaon hills, only one did not live to return. He had reputedly died not of disease and war, but of seasickness.

Jim returned to England promoted to the rank of Major. He felt no small pride at the promotion: he had not only served his King but had done so in such a way as to merit a tangible acknowledgement of the fact. He also knew or hoped that the rank would hold him in good stead once he was back in India.

Having not accepted leave from the trenches because it would have meant that his men would have been without him, Jim was now eager to see London on his way back to Naini Tal. With his men safely ensconced in a Home Counties barracks, he took a very different train from the ones to which he was used and headed for the capital. Once there, using his military travel pass, he booked into a hotel in Great Russell Street, opposite the portico to the British Museum: the building subsequently became a YWCA hostel.

When he had left Mokameh Ghat for the war, he had been much ribbed by his fellow Europeans, especially those who were not domiciled, who asked him how he would feel in the old country, 'back home' in Britain. He would be lost, they maintained. Until he embarked for the war, he had been no further south than Calcutta and no further west than Mussoorie except for one trip to Dalhousie on the India/Kashmir border.

He found London instantly fascinating. The history of the place, the excitements of the discovery of things that hitherto had only been tales; he was not only gripped by Buckingham Palace and the Tower of London for simply being surrounded by tall, stone buildings was a unique experience for him. Few buildings in Naini Tal reached three storeys and Mokameh Ghat consisted of bungalows save for the marshalling yard goods sheds.

He spent his first afternoon sightseeing and returned to the hotel for dinner. He rushed through the meal, intent on getting out once more into the streets, to absorb and observe and understand as much as he could. He was, whenever something new came to him, inordinately curious and would examine and pore over whatever it was with the almost naïve thrill of a schoolboy being presented with a new and wonderful toy. Even his hands would shake with the wonder of the new: it is no surprise that he gulped his meal and left the hotel.

Not only did he leave the hotel, but he left the immediate environs of Bloomsbury. Used to walking for fifteen miles without a pause through the Siwalik hills, traipsing the streets of London was easy indeed. He strode along, looking about him with more eagerness than any ordinary tourist would and, after a few hours, found that not only was he lost, but that the streets had emptied of people. Never at ease in crowds, he had tended to ignore the throngs on the evening pavements and walked in his own inner world. Seeking now to return, he approached the only person he could spy – a policeman on his night beat.

Quite what the policeman thought would be worth recording: standing before him was an army major, recently the hero returned from the trenches, asking the way to the hotel. The policeman reiterated that there were many hotels in South Kensington – which did the major want? He did not know its name. The major also did not know the name of the street in which it stood. After all, in Naini Tal, there were but a few hotels and although the streets had names, everyone knew where they were without needing the exact location. The flummoxed constable admitted that he was unable to assist the major and abandoned Jim to his own devices.

Needless to say, he found a solution to his dilemma by applying the only craft he knew for such a situation – that of the jungle.

Forgetting that he was surrounded by buildings, he assumed he was back in the forests around Kaladhungi. He turned about and retraced his steps as far as he could see. Then he stopped. Scanning about him, he looked for a mark that had caught his eye or registered in his subconscious – a street sign, shop name, painted door, broken window, tram stop, pile of horse dung by the gutter and so on. Yard by yard or street by street, he reached Piccadilly Circus which confused him. It was, to all intents and purposes, a jungle glade into which fed a large number of game trails: that a winged statue stood in the centre was immaterial. He took the only bushcraft course open to him. He ranged: one hundred yards up Regent Street and nothing recognised so a hundred yards down Haymarket and again a blank. He walked to Leicester Square: nothing. Up Shaftesbury Avneue, he saw a clue and off he went. What might have been the hairs of tiger caught on a thorn bush in the Farm Yard was here the ragged edge of a theatre poster. He was again confused at Cambridge Circus but recognised an alley between two buildings and had sensed when passing it previously how the wind had blown down it on to his right cheek. Keeping the alleyway to his left, he proceeded. Eventually, he reached the hotel in the hour just before dawn.

How much truth lies in this tale is perhaps dubious: he must surely have known from the start that his hotel was opposite the world-famous portico of the British Museum and he might have given this information to the policeman. Or possibly he really did not know, having only just arrived, and he did get genuinely lost. Yet the fact remains that he probably did work his way across central London in such a manner, if only to prove that he could – and he certainly had the jungle lore to manage such a feat. He was never a man to avoid testing himself when the opportunity arose.

His jaunt in London over, he returned to his men and, as a unit, they embarked at Tilbury for the voyage home to India. The excitement was over, for the time being. Or so Jim thought. He was not demobilised in Britain but was to remain in command of his men until they were repatriated to their families and dismissed active service. The ship on which they sailed journeyed by way of the Mediterranean and the Suez Canal: at Port Said, the northern entrance to the canal, Jim left the ship and travelled on to Cairo where he visited the pyramids on a camel and purchased two pewter vases as a souvenir gift for his sister, Maggie. He rejoined the ship at Port Suez on the Red Sea.

The troopship docked in Bombay and Jim travelled to Naini Tal where his unit was disbanded and he took his leave.

The railway authorities were eager to have him back at Mokameh

Ghat. Ram Saran had done sterling work in Jim's absence and the efficiency of the transhipment operation was unhampered in any way but the headquarters office wanted Jim back in their operations. Partly they wanted him to continue with his contract across the Ganges and partly they wanted him to continue in a job he had held for some years, as a sort of labour adviser and general transhipment inspector: in 1916, he was listed as the transhipment inspector for the railway based at Gorakhpur even though he spent most of his time in Mokameh Ghat.

Jim hummed and hahed about his rejoining the railway. He was, for a number of reasons, in two minds about returning to the banks of the Ganges. He was now in his forties and Mokameh Ghat was neither a healthy nor an exciting place; he had seen the goods contract operate quite effectively without his presence (though he still held the contract and therefore continued to take the small share of the profits he divided with the work force). He did not need the money and he wanted pastures new in which to test himself.

In truth, Jim was in the same quandary as many a man who had served in and survived intact the Great War. Until the outbreak of the war, he had known only his home territory, exotic though that may have been: like every plough-hand or cowman, factory worker or ledger clerk back in England, he had had a taste not only of horror but also of excitement, thrill and foreign travel. His horizons had been opened and although Jim was not, by a long way, sorry to return to India, he was nevertheless bitten by the bug of greater adventure. Peace hung heavily upon him.

It is a comment upon his stamina and lifelong curiosity that he still sought new pastures. His jungle adventures before his mobilisation would have been sufficient to have satisfied even the most rabid taste for excitement in most ordinary men. But then Jim Corbett was extraordinary.

Sensing that he might want to remain nearer to his family – Mary Corbett was now a very elderly though far from frail woman – the railway authorities toyed with the idea of offering Jim a position with the Rohilkund and Kumaon Railway Company which operated into his home area and which the Bengal & North Western Railway owned as a subsidiary.

In a letter he sent to Maggie and his mother from Lucknow on 8 Feburary 1919, Jim wrote that

'Miller told me that Walker (a senior railway official) had written to England after he saw me in Naini recommending me for promotion and that on receipt of the home board's reply, he had applied to the Military Authorities at Simla to return my services to the railway. The home board have given me Rs. 500 to start with . . .'

He continued by going into the ins and outs of the situation before finishing,

'What do you all think of the whole matter? I must do something for I don't feel ancient enough yet to sit down and wait for old age. The only question is whether I could do anything better for us all than take this billet at Gorakhpur. I would have liked to go to British East Africa and British Columbia, but the question is whether we could have stood the transplanting at our time of life. After my free and easy life I will not take very kindly to an office stool but I could stand it if I thought it was for the best.'

He might have considered the offered 'billet at Gorakhpur' but any decision was removed from his – or the railway's – domain by the army high command which did not demobilise him. They had seen his qualities as an officer in command of native troops and he was called back after the expiry of his leave to lead a labour corps to the fighting against Afghanistan. This was a surprise to Jim and his family. Facing tigers in the forest was one thing, but fighting the wily Pathan was quite another. With a heavy heart though a distinct sense of the new excitements promised, Jim set off for the North-West Frontier, once again following in the military steps of his forebears. This second stint of military life was far removed from his experiences in Flanders.

In the middle of February, 1919, the Amir Habibullah Khan was assassinated whilst out hunting in Laghman, north of Jalalabad. After a short period of political wrangling, rivalry and machination in the Afghanistan court, the deceased Amir's third son, Amanullah, took control having first wisely assured himself that the army was behind him. There was to follow a period of anti-British feeling in the court, which had been somewhat suppressed by Habibullah Khan, leading to the beginning of a holy war against the British in India.

The North-West Frontier had long been a battle zone between the British and the Afghans: each disputed ownership of the barren mountains and the British were also apprehensive in case the Afghans showed Russian sympathies. One Imperialist power in the area was enough: ironically, the Afghans were the first foreign government to recognise the new Bolshevik state of Soviet Russia and so the British, it seems, had good reason to be concerned.

In the spring of 1919, the Afghans started to establish pockets of unrest deep inside India. They summoned Indian tribal leaders to Kabul, sent secret emissaries into India with caches of arms and ammunition and stirred up anti-British politics, aided and abetted by a strange underground group calling themselves 'The Provisional Government of India'.

Their timing was well-chosen. The army was war-weary from European and Middle Eastern service and in the throes of demobilisation. The best Indian troops were still in Mesopotamia and the Indian Army and British Army in India consisted mostly of territorials who were fully capable of local garrison or domestic tasks but hardly battle trained for the bleak hillsides of the Afghan border country.

Rioting broke out in Peshawar and the railway from that city through the Punjab to, ultimately, Bombay was attacked. The policy of 'indianising' the railways had not been completed at the time and there were still large numbers of Europeans, domiciled or otherwise, and Anglo-Indians to keep the trains running. The uprising in the Punjab was put down without too much effort and the political unrest prevented from developing but the Amir, in the meantime, had moved heavy troop concentrations to the Afghan/Indian border. On 3 May 1919, a contingent of the famous Khyber Rifles was turned back by Afghans from escorting a caravan. From then on matters moved swiftly with Afghan troops advancing well into Indian territory. Within a week, the Third Afghan War was well under way.

In another letter home from Lucknow, addressed to Maggie and posted four days before the one concerning his railway job, Jim wrote:

'There is some talk of our being demobilised in May, in fact Walker writes and tells me he has seen it in orders.'

His brother John was ill – as were the rest of his family – and Jim made plans to visit him, nostalgically recalling his own childhood and giving his views on marriage and its accompanying drawbacks; whether or not these comments were specifically made for the benefit of the eyes of

Mary Corbett and Maggie can only be conjecture, but it appears as if Jim was reconciling himself yet again to the fact that he would not be allowed to marry as long as his mother was alive. His letter continued:

'If I can get out of the army by May or earlier, Kathleen (John's wife) will then be away in Naini or somewhere else, and I will then go and spend a quiet ten days with John. I love kids, but seven would get on my nerves. When mother had all her big family of Doyles, Deases and Corbetts round her, I am quite sure she made a better job of looking after them on an income of next to nothing, than some people do on a pay that in those days was unheard of. That Dad never got more than R's 150, on that small sum Mother clothed and fed us and kept us fit and well and I am sure that there was no happier family than ours in all India. I can't remember that you ever had more than one frock, one hat and one bit of ribbon (sometimes it was the fringe of an old durry) nor can I remember that small details of that kind ever interfered with your health or happiness. Glad I am that I have not got a modern wife and family of seven to provide for. In the old days, a wife and each child as it came was written down on the credit side of a man's ledger. In these days they all, wife included, go down on the debit side. If any man contemplating matrimony was to ask my advice, I would tell him if he wanted to be happy, to marry the poorest girl he could lay his hands on. Poorest people are the happiest in all the world.'

His plans to rejoin his favourite brother, the other slice of bread in the 'Jam Sandwich' from long ago, were frustrated. Instead, Jim was sent in late April or early May to Peshawar where he joined a relief force heading towards the frontier town of Thal, via Kohat. Thal had been under siege by the Afghan general Sardar Mohammad Nadir Khan but he knew, as did his trapped enemies, that it was only a matter of time before reinforcements arrived. In the last week of May, there arrived in Kohat two battalions of the 69th Punjabis, quickly followed in the next few days by two brigades of the 16th Division from Lahore with the 45th Brigade of the Field Artillery and a battery from Peshawar. They set off by rail, truck and on foot on their fifty-odd mile advance to Thal: by five in the morning of 1 June the force was within striking distance of Thal and engaged the enemy. The battle that followed was fierce and raged all day in stupendous heat and dust. Daytime temperatures in June in the

North-West Frontier could reach well into the one-hundred-and-twenty degrees Fahrenheit range: the ground could get so hot that rocks could be used by the troops as cooking stoves. By four in the afternoon, the Afghan forces and a mercenary army of Khostwal and Waziri tribesmen under the command of a Zadran chief called Babrak were beaten: the artillery had routed Babrak's men and destroyed the Afghan guns. Dawn the next day showed the Afghans vanished into the mountains.

Quite what Jim's role was is uncertain. Most probably, he was in charge of the supply line for the advance but he did see some of the action and at close quarters.

From Thal, Jim was sent south to Waziristan where the South Waziristan Militia had been virtually annihilated and the local native troops were in disarray. A number of massacres of convoys and columns forced the British to retaliate in no uncertain terms, for the deaths of large numbers of militarily innocent recruits and their officers had to be revenged. The campaign to bring this about in the district of Zhob took until the end of July and involved skirmishes into the mountains to punish those local tribes that could be rounded up.

Localised fighting continued in Waziristan off and on for years afterwards, as indeed it had done before, but the real core of the Third Afghan War was over and Jim was at last allowed to return to his homeland late in the year and relinquish his military position. Having seen fighting, he was eligible for a war bonus which, with characteristic Corbett generosity, he donated towards the building of a canteen for the troops.

That done, he did not return to the railway. He did have his family's welfare in mind but he also had a secure financial foundation and saw a different course for his life. New vistas and opportunities were opening for him and he longed to face them.

7

A Man of Substance

By 1902, Mr Frederick Edward George Mathews – or Matthews for he was known by both spellings and signed his name both ways – was well established in Naini Tal. He was much respected by the local European population and regarded as a pleasant gentleman with an exceedingly shrewd business head on his shoulders. Exactly when he first arrived in Naini Tal is unknown but by the turn of the century he was well established with a business that indicated that he had quite the foresightedness of Mary Corbett. Indeed, it is possible that he either took over part of Mary Corbett's house agency or built his own up with her occasionally acting as a subcontracted agent under the umbrella of his firm. Whichever was the case, he was listed in the directory for Naini Tal as 'F. E. G. Mathews, house agent and hardware dealer'.

To state that he was a hardware dealer is rather a misnomer. He owned the town hardware store which sold everything bar foodstuffs and was akin to the sort of store one sees in the classic Western movies – tin tacks to typewriters, hammocks to horseshoes, bullets to bolts of hessian. In a 'frontier town' such as Naini Tal, it was a smart investment, for the hill tribesmen, pilgrims, local farmers, Europeans and travellers all came through the town for one reason or another and all would need such provision. To append estate agency on to such a store was sheer business brilliance for those who owned or needed to rent a house would also need paint and repair it – the climate in Naini Tal was such that all the houses often required structural attention for what the sun did not peel the termites consumed. Mathews artfully provided an all-round service.

The store was run, at the turn of the century, by an assistant named H. E. Crawford while Mathews himself lived in a large house called Newberry (or Newbery) Lodge. He was married but childless and the couple occupied only a part of the house, renting the remainder to single Europeans or Anglo-Indians working in the town or passing through on contracts of a few months' duration. He additionally owned or handled on commission a very large number of properties in and around Naini Tal which he let both seasonally and on longer tenures.

In time, he became a central figure in Naini Tal for he was one of the richer local inhabitants, on paper if not in ready cash, who had invested wisely in the town and made good as a consequence. Yet comparatively little is known of him now. He was on the town council for sixteen years and was a champion of the rights of the local Indians and yet he appears to have been a somewhat withdrawn and elusive man, not exactly a recluse but someone who kept himself to himself unless matters financial were concerned. That he went to the Naini Tal Club is indisputable – many were invited there in the turn of the century years, even Jim who was not a member – but he was nevertheless a private man and inwardly saddened by the lack of an heir.

How he came to get to know and like Jim can only be surmised. Possibly he had known him as a child or they may have met later through Mary Corbett's house dealings or on other social occasions: Jim's reputation in Naini Tal as a hunter and lover of the hills was widespread and Mathews might have come upon him through that channel, both of them sharing a loving if, in Mathews' case, a slightly patronising concern for the welfare of the hill peoples. Whatever was the cause of their meeting, they formed for each other a bond of friendship, the older man for the younger. Both were quiet and both were, in their own ways, India hands who were committed to Kumaon.

Whatever the cause of their relationship, Mathews brought Jim into his hardware company as a sleeping partner. This too was a wise move for Mathews was in considerable ill health after the turn of the century and had been, for several years, neglecting his business somewhat. An injection of capital, no matter how slight, was useful in boosting the coffers and bolstering confidence: Mathews was only too well aware that estate agency depended on trust and confidence.

When Mathews died on 21 September 1906, his widow

Mary inherited the company. On 15 December, she sold it to Jim for sixty thousand rupees. More accurately, she transferred a mortgage for that amount, due to the Allahabad Bank, from herself to Jim.

It was a considerable sum and one seemingly beyond Jim's reach to repay on his salary from the railway but Jim had, before Mathews' death, made that investment in the company. Any small price he might have paid to Mary Mathews, therefore, was partly covered by his own share and dividend extant in the firm: possibly, she took Jim's small share as part payment, retaining this as a form of pension for herself. As well as gaining the shop with ten thousand rupees' worth of stock, Jim was also given most of Mathews' Naini Tal properties – Dudley Grove, Mary Ville below Deopatha hill and above Sukha Tal, Woodstock nearby (with its operating lime kiln), Newberry Lodge – and he added these to his own recently purchased Mullacloe which was a quarter of mile west of Mary Corbett's Gurney House. In all, the properties totalled over thirteen or fourteen acres. Quite possibly, he released the mortgage by selling a few of these properties or maintained the mortgage with some of them as collateral security. Certainly, he could not raise enough ready cash of his own to pay off the bank.

His taking over the store and estate proprietorship was definitely not an act of inevitability. It is possible that Mary Mathews was keen to be rid of the company in any case. That she was, in some way, following one of her husband's wishes that Jim should eventually have the firm after his death is perhaps fortuitous. In the sale deeds, there lies a clause to the effect that the sale was made 'according to the wish of the late Mr Frederick Edward George Matthews': it is likely that Mathews had wished that, on his wife's death, the business be passed on to Jim. She simply decided not to wait; in fact, she would not have had long to wait for she herself died in Lucknow in 1911, leaving her few belongings to the Catholic mission in Jeolikote. She died with but sixty rupees to her name.

However it came about though, in 1907 'F. E. G. Mathews: house agent and hardware dealers' had added after its name on the signboard outside, in smaller letters, 'J. Corbett, proprietor: A. D. Wood, manager'.

It appears that Jim took over more than Mathews' business, too. On 1 July 1907 he was nominated to take his benefactor's place on the town's municipal board as a representative of the 'class of proprietors'. He accepted, but resigned in 1909 having been unable to attend any but a few meetings.

At the time, of course, Jim was working in Mokameh Ghat and so had to have a manager in the business. Wood ran the hardware side of the concern and Mary Corbett advised on the house agenting which sister Maggie began to learn. She was an adept mathematician and was quick to pick up the principles of book-keeping and finance: she looked after Jim's business affairs for many years. Until Maggie was ready to take on the job, Mary Doyle ran it for a while.

Mary Corbett was predictably a force behind the firm, too. She encouraged Jim in his expansion into more properties and she herself bought Grassmere, east of the church of St John-in-the-Wilderness, in 1911; two years before, Jim had bought three more houses from expatriates returning 'home' – Aberfoyle, next door to Mullacloe, Mount Pleasant just above them and Hutton Hall. All were on the 'safe' non-landslide side of the town on which Mary Corbett had wisely built thirty years before. These three properties alone earned a gross rental income per annum of fifteen thousand rupees.

It is likely that Jim's initial investment in the Mathews business was made with his share of the bonus paid to him under his contract with the railways. This was an added income, over and above his or his family's immediate needs, for he lived simply, and he was clever enough to ensure that his money worked for him. It was a most fortunate investment with dividends beyond his wildest dreams and the beginnings of his career as a businessman of no small success.

Quite why Jim stayed on at Mokameh Ghat after obtaining a steady income in his own home town is hard to understand. Many theories suggest themselves – he liked the comparative freedom from European contacts in the life of Mokameh Ghat where he was the undisputed sahib free of the domiciled tag; he preferred being with the local Indians whom he did not want to let down; he preferred this exile on the Ganges after being disappointed in love in Naini Tal where his mother scotched his chances of romances; he was bound by contract; he preferred the security of the railway job to the possible risk of the business failing; he liked doing a job he was confident he was doing well . . . It is indeed hard to guess why a man born and bred to the Kumaon hills and forests could accept being away from them for so long after the opportunity arose for him to return.

F. E. G. Mathews & Co. continued to prosper after Jim took it over.

Indeed, it expanded considerably. Mr Wood managed the shop until 1914 when he disappeared from the scene: he was most likely called up or volunteered for service in the war. From 1916 until 1918, the management of the shop and the estate agency lay firmly in the control of Maggie who was named as the manager and held power of attorney for Jim during his absence in Europe and the North-West Frontier.

When, on his return from the fighting against the Afghans, Jim resigned finally from the railways, he passed the whole of the tranship-ment contract over to Ram Saran who had operated it so well during the later war years. Jim concentrated on building up F. E. G. Mathews & Co. and in getting to know, once again, the jungles, flora, fauna and people of Kumaon.

The company needed expansion. Naini Tal was growing in size and population and, for the company to continue to prosper, it would have to keep pace. In 1921, Jim expanded the house agency to include not only the properties he owned, but also the supervision of others' houses. He extended the premises of the hardware store and, as a natural pro-gression from such a business and going one better than Mathews had done, established a sideline as a local contractor. He now owned or looked after the houses which he repaired or rebuilt with nails from his own shop. When called upon, the company also acted as an auctioneer-ing firm. This latter especially shows how much he was respected as a trustworthy character. J. E. Corbett as he signed himself, the local businessman, now had his finger on the pulse of local trade and his honesty brought him other plaudits of trust and position. He was voted on to the town council and, by 1924, was vice-chairman of it: he remained a member until 1928.

With Mokameh Ghat no longer calling upon his time, and the business secure and flourishing, Jim could turn his attention towards other matters. His main 'other matter' was a combination of hunting and jungle lore and in that pastime he had a staunch ally and chum.

Percy Wyndham was appointed District Commissioner in Decem-ber, 1914. Educated at Giggleswick Grammar School and Queen's College, Oxford, he was appointed by examination to the Indian Civil Service (ICS) in 1886 and arrived in India for his first appointment on 13 December 1889. He was posted to the North-West Province as assistant commissioner at Oudh. Within five years, he was to be made deputy superintendent of the family domains of the Maharaja of Benares. From this post he rose to be a deputy commissioner, tax commissioner and then deputy commissioner (1st Grade). He followed the typical path of success in the ICS for an expatriate. A bachelor, he was an eccentric of the first order, spoke a number of Indian dialects fluently and was an expert shot.

Few records exist of the likes of Wyndham: unless they were involved in a major event of history, or a substantial scandal, or promoted way beyond their expectations to become 'famous', they are largely un-documented, which is one of the sad losses to colonial and social historians. Often, they were odd and extraordinary men who faced a lifetime as diverse and exciting as any explorer's or missionary's but which, because it was of little historical import, has been left unresearched. Fortunately, there exists a brief indication of what Wyndham was like as a DC, a district commissioner, the viewpoint coming from an Indian civil servant.

In his memoirs of life as a schools inspector, *naib tahsildar* and eventually senior civil servant in the United Provinces, now Uttar Pradesh and of which Kumaon is but a small area, Govind Ram Kala gives a detailed account of his working under the commissionership of Percy Wyndham, whom he describes as a most colourful person.

'... dour and foulmouthed, a man who spoke the dialects like a native. He devoted all the leisure he had to tigers, maintaining a retinue of his own Mirzapur trackers.'

The first time that they met indicates Wyndham's uncompromisingly forthright attitude towards his inferiors, be they European or Indian. He was rough and ready in some ways with his men, incredibly devious and skilfully manipulative with others: he stood for no nonsense and he had the perfect soul for a colonial administrator. On their first meeting, Wyndham had inspected Kala's tent – he was touring schools at the time – and asked ingeniously pertinent and mannerly impertinent questions about the contents: why do you carry cooking utensils? Can't you get them from the villages? Why do you carry flour? Why not buy it? What is your salary? How much you pay for cart hire? He asked of the village headman, in front of him, after his character; he grilled him on his servants and way of life. Several months later, Wyndham appointed Kala *naib tahsildar* at Ranikhet, in the mountains.

The relationship they had over the ensuing decade ran hot and cold as did all Wyndham's associations with his staff. In his affairs with Indians, he was arrogant and cruel one minute, patronising and kind and considerate the next. When Kala applied to join Jim's Flanders-bound Labour Corps, Wyndham gave him a sound character reference, though poor health prevented him joining up. Despite them often arguing, Kala believing that Wyndham had upset his chances for promotion, he states categorically that he feels Wyndham was 'one of the greatest members of the Indian Civil Service'.

The enigma that was Wyndham confused Kala and many other Indians, in and out of government employ. He could be moody and capricious, awe-inspiring and frightening. His temper was short and as loud as his voice. Yet he was scrupulously honest, was utterly beyond bribing and unstintingly fair and just. He was a clever manipulator of the Indian population and an excellent exponent of the divide-and-rule theory by which the British kept much of their control over the subcontinent. He was generous, too. Kala cites the case of two *naib tahsildars* caught for corruption for which most DCs would have sacked them but Wyndham reduced them to a clerical rank so that they might not starve. He was never one to deprive a man of his living. He knew all his considerable staff by name and knew all their business, too. He was brave in the face of adversity and as courageous facing a tiger. In short, he was hard to grasp, difficult to understand and downright contrary when it suited him. He ran his office by terrorising his staff – bawling, 'Damn, silly hell!' when things did not go his way. He was short, moustachioed, bright-eyed, of medium build yet sturdy and noted by both the Europeans and Indians who came upon him for his distinctly unsartorial dress. He was most at home in shirt, riding breeches and boots, at camp in the jungle.

How he and Jim came to be bosom friends is unknown. That they shared a common interest in tigers and hunting seems to have been what brought them together, though Jim's work, with his hunting down of his first man-eater, could have come to Wyndham's ears before they necessarily met. On the other hand, as they both lived in Naini Tal, and Jim was known as a local businessman and councillor as well as for his jungle lore, even though he was absent for most of the year at Mokameh Ghat, Wyndham would have found it hard to avoid him.

They were as unlikely a pair of friends as ever could have joined together, a true proof of the maxim that unlike poles attract. Wyndham was the District Commissioner and Jim was a domiciled railway inspector and top grade box-wallah; Wyndham was brash, occasionally coarse and bluntly spoken whilst Jim was quiet and found the uncouth abhorrent; Wyndham was powerfully in command of the natives and Jim was, as Kala put it, quite 'unlike the general run of the hoity-toity white man' which Wyndham necessarily represented; Jim was kindly, generous, considerate and approachable and Wyndham put on the appearance of being very much otherwise, even if underneath it all he was not. And in this lies the common ground between the two men for they were staunchly in love with Kumaon and the Kumaoni people. The love simply manifested itself in different ways.

Of course, they were also both *shikaris* of the top order. Both were expert marksmen, fearless and determined. Wyndham knew tigers better than anyone else and he spent all his spare time hunting the big cats.

In the heyday of *shikar*, the accepted way to shoot tigers was to beat for them in a manner not unlike the beating of English fields for pheasant or partridge, but on a much grander and more thrilling scale. To go into the setting up and conducting of a beat in detail would be tedious for it required much organisation and skill but to know the basics is essential for an understanding of what Jim's life involved, off and on, for many years.

Briefly, the average beat was operated over an area of about a square mile, the terrain not so awkward as to produce obstacles to movement. The vegetation could be varied and provided little concern so long as the cover was not so thick as to reduce visibility. The 'guns', those doing the shooting, would be established in a rough line at the base in a 'V'- or 'Y'-shaped formation. This base was up to two or three hundred yards across, depending on the number of 'guns'. These would be safely esconced either on *machans* (platforms especially built) in substantial trees or on the backs of elephants where they would ride either in howdahs or on pads. The former, the howdah, was a wood and rattan basket rather like a roofless sedan chair that was strapped to the elephant's back. It was cumbersome, heavy and inconvenient in thick forest but its advantage was that the hunter could stand upright in it to fire. The pad was a mattress-like affair placed on the elephant on which the passengers sat and clung to the securing ropes. Often the pad supported a wooden device rather like a large, upturned rectangular coffee table called a *khatola*. On this one sat, holding on when needs be to the projecting 'legs' of the table-like structure. One could not stand up without the considerable danger of falling off, which would certainly result in injury as an elephant's back can be up to twelve feet from the ground. The pad and *khatola* were not too heavy for the elephant and were easily carried through thick, high undergrowth.

The guns safely placed, a second line of elephants would, on a signal, start from the open top of the 'Y' and commence to move slowly forward simultaneously, the mahouts (owner-jockeys, so to speak) shouting and whistling with a few other beaters on the pads behind clapping, banging sticks together or generally making a din. Down the sides of the 'Y' would be positioned stationary elephants (or Indians in trees) who would, as the advancing line drew level with them, also start up a shindig. Any tigers in the area would be flushed into running ahead of the noisy line but kept in the 'Y' by those on the sides. Gradually, the beating and side elephants would close in until the tigers were restricted to running the gauntlet through the area of the guns. The shooting came fast and furious at the end of the beat. That area covered, the whole company would move off to another pre-designated square mile where the whole process would be repeated. Up to half a dozen tigers a day could be shot in this fashion by no more than five average ability guns.

In the years before the First World War, it was to this kind of *bandobast* (jamboree) that Jim often went as a guest of Wyndham who, as District Commissioner, not only shot tigers in this way to maintain face, to show his position, but also arranged such shoots for friends. Attending such a *shikar* (hunt), Jim seldom missed the opportunity to bag a tiger. For someone of his exceptional skill with a rifle, it was like shooting rats in a barrel. Furthermore, such a day's (or even week's!) hunting was a social event. The well-to-do Europeans and their few Indian counterparts used such gatherings much as Edwardians used tea parties or African colonials used sundowner drinks parties in the fashionable 1920s. Quite often, Wyndham would ask Jim's advice in arranging the beats and, as the years passed, he increasingly called upon Jim, when he was available 'on leave' from Mokameh Ghat or visiting Kumaon on railway business (as he did occasionally), to oversee them himself, to act much as a modern day landowner utilises his gamekeeper to find and train and position and command the beaters.

Jim accepted these invitations, either as hunter or co-master of ceremonies, gladly. They afforded him the opportunity to meet people in an environment with which he was familiar – far more so than the club in Naini Tal – and gave him the chance to indulge himself in his favourite hobby, hunting. He did not see this kind of hunting as a massacre of wildlife or an act of degrading nature. It was simply a part of living in India. And those he met were useful contacts, especially in the business he was running after he acquired the F. E. G. Mathews firm.

Yet his own brand of hunting was more to his liking and to Wyndham's. This was far removed from the social calendar and the safety of *machan*, howdah or pad. In this form of *shikar*, Wyndham and he would wait in camp – a few tents with provisions for their servants and basic needs – and send out trackers to find the whereabouts of local tigers. (Wyndham's own trackers were reputedly the best team in the entire subcontinent.) The Indian trackers would spend several days studying the ground and would report back their every find of spoor. Jim and his friend would then decide which tiger they would go for and would set out early in the dawn to track it on foot, close in on it and shoot it.

Tracking a tiger on foot – indeed, simply walking in jungle in which one knows there is a tiger – is one of the most terrifying experiences an ordinary mortal can expect to undergo. Despite the fact that a tiger is a huge animal, sometimes bigger than a lion, it can hide itself better than a hare: one can pass within ten feet of a tiger and not know it. Its camouflage is perfect. Only if it growls, or the wind is in the walker's favour and he gets to smell the distinctive scent of the tiger, can he assess its whereabouts. That can, in the case of an angry, threatened or defensive tiger, be just a little too late. A tiger's pounce is astoundingly rapid: it is very rare for a man to escape from or survive the determined attack of a tiger.

Jim and Wyndham would pinpoint their quarry and approach it from an angle of 90 degrees to each other. The first man to see it would shoot. Sometimes, to ensure that it stayed put in roughly the same area as they had located it, they would have one or two men sitting in trees ahead of them, banging sticks to keep the tiger *in situ*. This, in turn, alerted it to whatever was going on around it.

To wound any animal is not only unsportsmanlike but downright cruel. It is the universal code of hunting to track down and finish off any wounded beast, be it even so insignificant as a winged duck. The clean kill is the aim of all true hunters. To kill outright requires that the hunter gets close to the prey. In the case of Corbett and Wyndham, close could mean a range inside twenty feet. To wound and be unable to track and despatch a tiger (or leopard) was tantamount to murder, not the murder of the animal but the subsequent death of every person that creature killed and ate. For infirm tigers and, to a lesser extent leopards, became man-eaters. Sadly, not all hunters are true to their sport's morality and those amateurs or inconsiderate 'hunters' were to prove to be the bane and central cause of danger throughout Jim's adult life.

Together or alone, Jim and Wyndham claim never to have left a wounded animal. If, by some chance, they hit but did not kill a tiger, they were unceasing in their efforts to catch up with and kill it even if the follow-up took days, as it occasionally did. Both were true hunters. And they seldom missed.

It was not only trophies of deer and carnivores that they hunted. Before the First World War, Wyndham had been charged with founding what was called the Special Dacoity Police Force of three hundred hand-picked men under the command of a brilliant and courageous young police officer, Freddy Young. Their primary task was the capture of a famous dacoit called Sultana.

From time to time, the bandit lived with his gang in the forests between Kaladhungi and Ramnagar and every so often Jim would come upon abandoned camp sites when hunting: once, when out walking with Maggie in search of a leopard, they met a fleeing herdsman who reported that Sultana's men were after him and coming along behind him. He had a badly gashed leg to prove it. When a tenant farmer at Lamachour, seven miles from Kaladhungi, was shot dead by Sultana's men, Jim's anger was aroused and he offered his services to Young. He took part in an attack on one of the dacoits' camps which they discovered empty but were soon caught in a crossfire from bandits hiding nearby. One dacoit and a policeman were killed.

Some time later, when the band of dacoits was shrunk to about forty members, it was decided to launch a concerted attack. Jim was invited to join in by Percy Wyndham. It was to be a memorable, if brief, campaign. During the course of their approach to the camp, they were mistakenly marooned on an island, nearly drowned in a fast flowing river which Wyndham had proved to be fordable by stripping his clothes off and crossing with his arms around a young Indian policeman, and the other three Europeans with Jim (Freddy Young, Wyndham and Young's cousin) were nearly blinded by pollen from some tall grasses to which Jim was not allergic. Then, to round off the excitement, they met a rogue elephant. That night, they camped under a banyan tree and Sultana had them at his mercy but did not counter-attack.

They did not capture Sultana: Freddy Young did so the next day, when Jim and Wyndham had left. He was later executed and Jim regretted this for Sultana had the reputation of being a kind of Robin Hood who never robbed the poor.

The friendship between Jim and Wyndham extended beyond the jungle. By the time Jim went off to war, leaving Wyndham as DC in Naini Tal, he was rich enough to go into business with his friend. Together they had hunted tigers and, in 1922 (or possibly as early as 1919, just before Jim went off to fight the Afghans), they shared a different form of speculation. Coffee.

Percy Wyndham was getting near to retirement age and did not intend to spend his last years in India: quite why he decided not to remain in the country he so evidently enjoyed and felt for is only to be guessed at but it is likely that, as a shrewd politician, he saw the writing on the wall, that in the long run the British would be driven out of or choose to leave India. Africa, however, he saw as another matter.

Whereas India was long settled by the end of the nineteenth century, Africa was not. It was still only just opening up and it offered the sort of prospects India had had two centuries before. What was more the country, in particular East Africa, was still more or less virgin with untold tracts of land unmapped and unsettled. It appealed to Wyndham's sense of adventure, both financial and physical. What was more, it was abundant in game just waiting to be stalked, shot and mounted.

To line his nest egg for the future, Wyndham purchased a farm called the Kikafu estate in the then country of Tanganyika. Before the Great War, Tanganyika had been German East Africa but after the war it became a British protectorate and any German-owned properties were confiscated and later redistributed by sale to predominantly English and Afrikaaner settlers.

Kikafu was in a spectacular part of East Africa. Situated twelve miles west of Moshi, to the north of the Moshi to Arusha road, it had as a backdrop to the north the stunning panorama of the snow-capped cone of Mount Kilimanjaro, the extinct volcano that is the highest mountain in Africa and the only African peak, though virtually on the equator, to bear a mantle of snow all the year round. To the west was the smaller but still majestic peak of Mount Meru. Only one hundred and fifty miles away was the Ngorongoro Crater, not long on the map and to this day, despite the predations of men, one of the wonders of the natural world with such abundant wildlife that it takes the breath away. (At the time

Wyndham purchased Kikafu, the wildebeest annual migration population through the area was estimated conservatively at two million animals).

It was a small estate by East African standards. One thousand four hundred and fifty acres in extent and lying at an altitude of three thousand five hundred feet, most of it was covered with heavy thorn bush and scrub timber. It was unsuitable for cattle raising, save for the local breeds that were economically unviable, due to the tsetse fly infestations that carried incurable stock diseases and the seasonal water shortages: but it was suitable for coffee and Wyndham's first task was to clear about ten per cent of the bush and plant it with coffee.

Before this, however, he needed some financial assistance and Jim, who had thought of emigrating to East Africa after his demobilisation in 1919 and was by now making very comfortable profits from his house agenting and the hardware store, agreed to invest in the land with his friend. How Jim came to purchase his share is a little complicated but worthy of the telling for it shows not only his canny handling of money but also his great generosity and kindness to others, in this instance not an Indian but a fellow European.

In the trenches of Flanders, or even possibly on the way to the war, Jim had come across Robert Bellairs who was, in the mud of northern France, another volunteer officer in a sister company of labourers from the Kumaon. They billeted together when the opportunity arose and became firm friends in adversity, having heard of each other back in India: Bellairs was also a *shikari* and had hunted several man-eaters. The adversity was to last longer than the war years.

In 1919, probably during his leave from Flanders and before he was called to serve against the Afghans, Jim and Bellairs went on a hunting and fishing trip to the lower slopes of Trisul, the twenty-three and a half thousand foot mountain visible from the peaks behind Naini Tal, sixty miles or so away. By now, Bellairs had been demobbed and was appointed Settlement Officer at Kausani, near Almora. It was his job to apportion grants of government-owned land to Indian ex-servicemen. He also joined a forest officer, J. E. Carrington Turner, in the hunting and killing of a man-eating tigress at Gwaldam, north of Kausani.

In camp one evening, Bellairs bared his soul to Jim. He had a lingering problem – his father, James George Stevenson. He was a successful tea planter who had changed his name from Bellairs by deed poll and was determined to disinherit his son. Robert Bellairs, without the hope of inheritance, had little to which to look forward. Stevenson, seeking to retire with his money secure, sold his first plantation but, on offering the second for sale in early 1920, was confronted by Jim who bought it for himself, giving rise to the subsequent inaccurate rumour that he owned tea estates in Assam.

The Stevenson plantations were at Berinag and Chaukori in the hills beyond Almora. Having purchased the Berinag property, Jim then incorporated it into his holdings alongside the assets of F. E. G. Mathews & Co. and visited Bellairs at Kausani offering it to him firstly as a gift and then for a fixed rent of four thousand rupees a year, well below its market price.

For his part, Bellairs felt he could not accept this generosity so Jim temporarily put a manager called Kadar Datt in the estate and placed it on the market. He found no difficulty in selling it a matter of months later to Kadar Datt. Writing to Maggie in the May of 1920, Jim told her of his estate matters and reported on his visit to Bellairs and his feelings for his wartime comrade:

'I did not tell you of my visit to Kausani. Bellairs sent his horse to Sameshwar[?] for me and walked three miles down the road to meet me. We got to his place at about 5 p.m. and I left the next day at 11.30. Bellairs appeared to be quite happy and is taking a very great interest in the 10,000 acres he is lord and master of. Kausani house has been built regardless of expense and has a lovely setting, the view is supposed to be the best in Kumaon, but I saw nothing of it owing to the heavy smoke from forest fires. I sent my things direct to Bagashwar and only took a toothbrush with me. I was glad I had done this for Bellairs had a bed and everything ready for me, in fact he feasted and treated me as though I was a long lost brother. Poor old chap, I feel very sorry for him – nothing but a dog to welcome him home in the evenings. If he had a nice wife who would stay with him and take an interest in his work he could settle down and be happy at Kausani for the rest of his life. As it is, all he can look forward to is dying like the man before him, forgotten by the world and buried any how and any where by strangers. A fate that awaits all the last of the Mohicans.'

Regardless of his thoughts on marriage of the year before, perhaps Jim still yearned secretly for the happiness he wanted for Bellairs.

With the money realised from the sale, he invested in Wyndham's Tanganyika estate.

Being still the District Commissioner for Naini Tal, Wyndham had no time to visit his farm in East Africa and he left the management and running of it to Jim who in turn, and thus saving Bellairs from bankruptcy, installed his wartime companion in it as overseer. He managed the farm for a quarter of a century, leaving it only in 1947 when Kikafu, long since sold by Jim and Wyndham, changed ownership and Bellairs entered into partnership with some neighbouring cattle farmers: Bellairs moved to Rhodesia in about 1950 where he subsequently died.

Kikafu was a rough and ready place. When Percy Wyndham bought it, it had no farmhouse upon it and one had to be constructed for the manager to live in. The first house was a mud and wattle hut with a thatch roof built in the traditional native style. After Wyndham retired from Kumaon in December, 1924 and went to live at the farm, a proper and substantial house was built of cedar shipped from the Lebanon. Even then, Wyndham did not live all the while at Kikafu for he also owned a tea plantation at Kericho, in Kenya, and he often went there: he was also one for returning at regular intervals to Britain where he had property he had inherited. Nevertheless, Kikafu was very important to all three men. For Wyndham, it was a base of sorts: for Bellairs it was a haven of employment: for Jim, shrewd as ever, it was an investment. In no time at all, Jim purchased another tract of land to the west of Mount Meru, thirty miles away. Quite possibly, Jim saw himself, years hence, following in Percy Wyndham's footsteps. To some extent, he did just that.

From 1922 until the mid-1930s, Jim travelled most years to Kenya for a few months. His trips combined several purposes. He wanted to guard his investment and see it was being maintained. He wanted to see Wyndham and, if Wyndham was involved, hunting would be, too. It was easy for Jim to travel, for Maggie could mind the home business affairs whilst he was itinerant, but he hated the act of travelling. In 1928, on his way to visit friends in Britain, his second trip 'home', he wrote to Maggie:

'The older one gets the less inclined one feels to travel about. If it had not been for my promise to P.W. (Percy Wyndham) and Ibbotson, I would gladly have chucked this trip. I can't stand trains a little bit and simply hate steamers, however I have got to go through with it now and instead of groaning should, I expect, think myself very fortunate to get the chance of some fishing (would much rather catch mahsir (sic) in Naini lake) . . .'

Interestingly, Jim has never referred to his African hunting trips. In the hunting books he was to write in his later years and which made him internationally famous, African game hunting is not mentioned. Nowhere does he write of the lion or the cheetah. For him, they were secondary to his major love and admiration, the Indian tiger.

Kikafu, F. E. G. Mathews & Co. and assorted other temporary property purchases were not all that Jim bought. These were activities from which he, as a businessman, sought to make a profit. Some time around 1915 – the date is a little hazy because the matter is wrapped up in local legend now – Jim made another purchase from which he could not have a hope of turning a profit. He bought the now near derelict village of Choti Haldwani, close to Arundel, the Farm Yard and the places of his childhood.

Quite why he thought to purchase the village is a puzzle. It may well be that he suffered from Mathews' awareness of not having an heir and wanted to leave something substantial behind him when he died. There again, he may have sentimentally wanted to hold on to his family past: he was now an established local figure and to be a 'landowner' as well as a mere property developer and agent would give him added credibility and position which could only be enhanced by his having well defined roots. Domiciled Europeans were regularly reminded of their lost inheritance. Or, quite simply, he wanted to do something for the poor peasants of the *terai* near Kaladhungi. Knowing Jim's character, it is safe to assume that all three factors were present in his decision.

When he took possession of the village, the majority of the houses were in ruins and had been unoccupied for some years. Originally, those working in and catering to the small industries of the Kaladhungi area had lived in them, but with the decline of trade and the shifting of the centre of such activities to Haldwani, the population had drifted away. A few still lived on, subsistence farming in the few fields they could cultivate. Most of the land was weed-strewn or had reverted to a semi-scrub forest. The watercourses that had previously been banked had washed through and rocks had been deposited on some of the fields. A small portion of the village area was waterlogged in the monsoons, as if the swampy *terai* was seeking to reassert itself. For this state of agricultural decrepitude, Jim paid one thousand five hundred rupees.

At first, he cleared the fields of cover and stones, using as a labour force the few inhabitants of the village whom he organised with all the efficiency of his Mokameh Ghat squadrons. This was backbreaking work in which Jim shared from time to time but really he only set it in motion after giving the small number of villagers a strict pep talk and a dream of what the future could hold for them. For much of the time it was going on, he was back on the Ganges, moving cargo.

For the beginning of the sowing season in 1916, Jim purchased some seed and this was set in the few fields that were suitable for immediate cultivation. The harvest later that year was not encouraging and an agricultural revenue report dated 4 December 1916 stated bluntly:

'Cultivation increasing slightly, probably owing to the new pig-fencing put up by Mr. Corbett last year at his own expense. It is a pity that he is always in arrears with his payments; he does pay eventually but in the meantime trouble is caused to everyone concerned.'

Evidently, despite the success he was making in business in Naini Tal, Jim was somewhat overstretched by the purchase of the village which was his own, personal venture. It was not something he could write off against his other business affairs. This supports the idea that he bought the village for philanthropic or sentimental reasons rather than to turn it into a new source of income. He often said in later years that he had had to skimp and save to set Choti Haldwani in motion.

Jim had never been a farmer and buying the village in order to make it into a model settlement was a near mistake for him. He did not realise just what was involved. He had thought it was just a matter of setting the land to rights, planting it wisely and harvesting correctly. There was much more to it than that and it is surprising that he, a country dweller, had not realised it before he signed the deeds and paid the rupees over. He certainly should have appreciated the fact that the forces of nature would be the first to start to move in once the humans moved out.

As the revenue report indicates, the biggest problem was the local tribe of wild pigs. Looking much like their European counterparts, the wild Indian pigs are greyish brown, bristle-covered creatures with tusks under their longish snouts and a temper that would suit many an empress dowager. They are, like all their cousins, rooters. They not only clear what grows above ground, but they also turn over and eat the roots and can devastate a field in hours. They are also destructive in the way that wild elephants can be – they trample that which they don't consume. An early priority at Choti Haldwani was to keep the pigs out and wire fencing was the quickest effective method: it was also the most expensive. Jim had tried bamboo hurdles before buying the wire (no doubt from his own store) but the pigs simply pushed them over or bit their way through them.

One of Percy Wyndham's famous maxims was that if one was faced with a famine, it was pointless handing out food to the starving: better to stand on a hilltop with a bag of rupees. Soon, people with food would appear to sell to the bag holder. Whilst not a safe assumption today, it might have been eighty years ago and Jim's farming village was much like Wyndham's bag of rupees. Once it was seen to be there, people arrived from out of the forests and plains to take up the offers of tenancy.

Gradually, the population increased, so the work force grew, so the possibilities of the place began to be realised. Over the years that Jim was away at the Front Line and up until 1925, the village continued to expand and prosper. Jim arranged for more derelict houses to be repaired and for others to be built of stone. They were mostly traditional Indian rural houses with a stone-flagged (later concreted) courtyard in front with a veranda, and a number of rooms with a separate kitchen hut out the back and proper – if crude – sanitation. They were rainproof and considerably better than most common Indians could ever expect to occupy.

With the increase in population, Jim constructed a cement watercourse system to deliver water to all the homesteads. As the field systems extended and the scrub forest was cleared and burned off, so the problem arose of having to keep the pigs out of a bigger area than the wire protected. To wire in the whole village area would cost a small fortune and make the farming unviable. Jim and the Indians, knowing the way of pigs, had a solution for which Jim paid and with which he helped, toiling alongside his tenants in all but the hottest hours of the day. It took a long time to complete, almost a decade . . .

Pigs, for all their artfulness, cannot climb a vertical object because they cannot lift their back legs up. All it takes to keep a pig in his pen is a wall he cannot push over that is higher than his chest when he's standing on his hind legs.

So Jim and his Choti Haldwanians built a stone wall nearly six feet high entirely surrounding the village and all its fields. Gates, stiles and entrances were put in it to allow passage into the forests for firewood or fodder collecting or for the herding of cows or goats. The wall stands to this very day, though it has lost its top and is now between four and half to five feet high. The wild pigs have all but disappeared from the countryside around. Covered with creepers or lantana bushes, alert with lizards, it is an amazing *nine* kilometres long.

Over the thirty or so years that Jim owned Choti Haldwani, he encouraged the villagers to grow new crops. Corn and barley were not uncommon when Jim took on the village but he introduced new, disease-resistant strains. He encouraged market gardening for profit and to improve the villagers' diet: soft fruit bushes were taken from cuttings of the rampant plants left in the former gardens of Arundel, new banana trees were imported from Tanganyika, grape vines and fruit trees purchased. His most successful imported introduction was a new, large kernelled maize he obtained on one of his trips to East Africa and which he brought back in a number of flat cigarette tins bound with twine. The cobs these produced were over a foot long and the descendants of those first plants are still cultivated in the village which remains to this day a thriving almost model community in which Jim's name is revered and loved more than thirty years after his death and forty after his departure from India.

Not all the plants Jim introduced were successful. His bananas did not last long: they were small and hard and not at all palatable. He enthusiastically served them up for dinner once to European friends on the veranda of his own house in Choti Haldwani: they were swallowed only for the sake of decorum. For a short time, he experimented with grapefruit but they would not develop sufficiently. The vines died. Attempts to grow coffee failed abysmally.

It was in the village that Jim constructed his own winter home for himself; as his parents had quit Naini Tal in the cold months for Arundel, so he moved to this new house. It still stands, although today it is a museum to his memory, one of the very few such monuments to a European anywhere in India.

Built as a single storey bungalow, it is a big house, set in a large garden, with an orchard to one side and tropical fruit trees standing elsewhere: by the kitchen – a small, separate building at the rear of the property – there is still growing the papaya tree Jim planted.

The house at Kaladhungi is well appointed. Built solidly in stone, it has a deep veranda, several main rooms and bedrooms and an inside privy. Next to it is a separate, single roomed building said to be Jim's bedroom, though he very rarely slept in it. It was more often used as an estate office. Maggie slept in the house and Jim lived in it, but at nights he preferred to withdraw to his tent which was pitched in the garden to the west of the house in a spot through which now runs a garden path: unknowingly, but ironically, the museum staff have erected a bronze bust of Jim on a pedestal almost exactly where his tent used to be placed.

The gardens were trim and neat. Maggie and the mali looked after them and tended the rose trees and flowerbeds with care and skill. Today, the house is painted in the same brilliant yellow colour one sees on holy buildings throughout India although in Jim's day, it was either bare stone or whitewashed. Although garish to western eyes, the colour is somehow appropriate for Corbett is regarded as a *sadhu*, a sort of holy man who could perform miracles where mortals had failed.

Some years after Jim's death, Maggie dictated to a friend, Ruby Beyts, some notes that might be of value to a future biographer and in these she said of Choti Haldwani:

'Often as I walked along its paths as the sun went down with the evening light on the ripening corn and the blue hills in the background, I would think there could not be a more beautiful village in the world.'

And so it remains. The fields around Jim's house still wave with corn and barley and the women of the village still make their ways to the fields in the early morning light to reap with hand scythes. In the evening, the light glances across the fields and a peace descends on the farmland that is utterly heaven-like.

To the locals – *his* locals – Jim was known as 'Carbet' or 'Carpet Sahib', his surname so twisted by the Indian accent, and he was seen as the patriarch of Choti Haldwani. The Indians loved and feared, respected and admired him. Of simple peasant stock, they saw in him not only a benefactor and surrogate tribal leader of sorts, but they prided themselves on being of his village. As the years passed by and Jim's reputation swelled throughout India and, finally, the world, their pride increased *pro rata*. To be one of Carpet Sahib's men was considered an honour.

Jim, Maggie and Mary Doyle, for as long as she lived with the other two, looked after the welfare of the villagers. Those in trouble were assisted out of it and those in debt helped. Those who required or sought advice were given it. Those who did not fit in were told off, those who sinned against their fellows castigated and those who skived their village duties were severely reprimanded. Children who needed schooling were schooled. Yet it was in the matter of medical help that the Corbetts were best known.

Maggie picked up from Mary Doyle a good deal of the latter's simple diagnostic tricks, adding these to her own medical knowledge gleaned from their mother and the household library. Jim also knew a thing or two of doctoring from his family background, his military career and his awareness of jungle lore and folkcraft. A chest was kept in the house stocked with the common medicines of the day – quinine tablets, potassium permanganate, gentian violet, calomine lotion, splints and bandages. A surgery of sorts was held in fine weather under the mango trees in the garden. In poor weather, it moved to the veranda of the house. Malaria was the most common illness they saw, but every other variety came to them in time, most of them the results either of tropical diseases or of malnutrition.

Jim Corbett, the baron of Choti Haldwani as some of his European and Indian *bêtes noires* called him, ruled with a fair but iron hand. He was regularly asked to act as mediator in local arguments which tended to be both common and heated as the local population in the nearby small town of Kaladhungi were made up of half Hindu and half Moslem families, continually bickering amongst themselves. He defended his village against the pigs with the wall and, when parakeets threatened the crops, he would walk the fields and shoot them down. At night, he would guard the potato fields against porcupines or lend a villager a gun for the same purpose. Defending the peace as well as the produce was also his concern. He once reputedly thrashed a man whose cats kept people awake at night and was not averse to boxing ears if he thought fit. This sounds cruel and outrageous nowadays, but in those times this type of behaviour was accepted – it was not unheard-of for a British farmer to so lambast his workers and certainly it was not unknown for the local policeman in an English village to thump a petty criminal to teach him his lesson without bothering the courts. Such an encounter often did the trick and cured the miscreant.

However, Jim did regard Kaladhungi and the surrounding area as his own. He became very annoyed if Europeans encroached into the area to hunt without asking his permission. In the years before 1930, their actions annoyed him as they were – as he saw it – poaching his domain. After 1930, his reasons for wanting them out were somewhat different and altogether more laudable and less selfishly motivated.

The stories of Jim's bailiffing of 'his' jungle are many. He strictly applied the seasonal and sporting rules brother Tom had taught him in childhood even to the extent of belabouring with his tongue and his fists a party of hunters who wounded and failed to follow up and despatch a tiger. He claimed the animals in the area were 'his' and he objected to them being hunted and shot without his permission. This caused him to be labelled as an upstart who patronised the lower class Indians but ignored the upper class and Europeans.

The antagonism felt towards Jim was deep rooted in some of the expatriate people of his own nationality. He was the archetypal piggy-in-the-middle in their eyes, a man whom others found it hard to assess or categorise. He was domiciled, only one step up the social ladder from Anglo-Indian (or half-caste) and yet he was well-known and mixed with the mighty to such an extent that, by the time he was in his mid-fifties, he was on first name terms with successive governors of Kumaon and, ultimately, with the Viceroy himself with whom he not only had a close personal friendship but was also a confidant in certain matters. He was considered by some to be not much more than a box-wallah, a senior office clerk, and yet he was the proprietor of his own company which did thriving business and he was landed in so much as he owned his own village as well as chunks of equally profitable real estate in Africa. He lived in the sticks and was not a man of fashion or society: indeed, he and his sister shunned large social gatherings.

In short, in the eyes of many of his fellow Europeans, he was one of their number who had let the side down by 'going native', as the term put it: hardly surprising, his detractors considered, seeing he was 'country bottled'. That is to say, he was white but had cast off his heritage in order to associate with and side with the native. He ate native food, followed native customs and religions, spoke a number of dialects fluently, understood the 'Indian mind' and was generally at home in his supposedly alien environment. To cap it all, he knew his way around the forests better than many a native tracker.

As for the well-to-do Indians, he was as much an enigma for them as he was for his fellow Britishers. For them, he was a white man who identified with the lower classes (not to mention castes) and took on their causes not just against the rulers of the Raj but also against the upper echelons of Indian society. He took upon himself the role of supporter of the underdog and it was hardly surprising: he was one himself who had, by dint of good fortune and bravery and hard work, risen upward but not forgotten his roots. In time, he defended not just the underdog Indians but also the 'underdog' that was the very Kumaon region itself.

This affinity with the downtrodden, be it a man or an animal or a tract of forest, was but a part of a man who was inwardly very private and very complex. He loved India and the Indians with a passion that was never dampened and, because he allowed this to show more through his modest and quiet manner (as opposed to the brash bawling and bum-kicking of Wyndham, for example) it gave him, in the eyes of some others, the reputation of being a do-gooder in the most derogatory sense of the word. Certainly, many high-born Indians regarded him as such. To them he was a European who had 'gone native' and that was as distasteful to them as it was to their white counterparts.

Another thing about Jim that galled the strait-laced was the fact that he not only preached but acted accordingly. And he was seldom wrong. If he set his heart on something, he achieved it. Often, what he achieved brought him notoriety, fame and honour well beyond his station.

To be fair to Jim's detractors, he could be stubborn, downright troublesome and persistent to the point of intense annoyance in order to get what he believed to be right. He did not like to be proved wrong on the albeit few occasions that he was. What he didn't want to hear, he ignored. He listened to criticism but did not necessarily act upon it. He was also most certainly a man who had little time for bureaucracy, red tape and officialdom which he saw as human evils. He was outwardly, even sometimes belligerently, contemptuous of authority when it was, in his eyes, wrong. He would not tolerate adverse argument.

Several anecdotes illustrate these sides to Jim's character only too well.

Apart from great Christmas festivities at the house at Kaladhungi, over which Jim and Maggie lorded like a local country squire and his lady, in which all the children of Choti Haldwani were given toys and sweets, and games formed a good part of the afternoon, there was also from time to time a children's day in the forests of the Farm Yard. On these days, a group of the older children from the village, all of them boys, would be taken by Jim into the forests where he would teach them to beat for birds, to track and know their surroundings. He would shoot the driven game and then distribute it amongst the lads for them to take home.

One day in the mid-1920s, a forest officer, a European member of the Indian Forest Service, was staying in the rest house near Kaladhungi and, one evening, the officer shot a leopard, an animal still reasonably common in the area. When Jim heard of this, he sent a runner from his home to the rest house to complain that the hunter had shot one of 'his leopards': the officer, in high dudgeon, returned the reply that he did not realise it was a Corbett leopard as it did not wear a collar.

It all came down to the fact that he was envied, despite his faults. He was a man of infinite courage for whom tens of thousands of hillfolk showed a love offered to no other European and to few Indians of position. He was a success in his own business dealings and, being a shrewd and hard business nut to crack, was begrudgingly admired. He was at times mild and understanding, kind and generous and filled with humanity, truly modest and withdrawn, honourable and upright: he was also opinionated, stubborn, determined, harsh when it suited him, patronising, tactless and undiplomatic, and a stirrer. In other words, he had in him all the traits that made the British feared, loathed, respected and admired and sound colonial administrators and imperialists. The paradox was that he also loved India as much an ordinary man would a woman and, in this way, he defended India (or his part of it) with a fierce possessive jealousy and pride that on occasion jumped over the bounds of discretion, propriety or reason. India was his surrogate wife. He would have duelled for her honour if he had had to . . . And in time, he did.

8

The First Man-eaters

Jim's first man-eater was an immigrant. She was a tigress who had reputedly killed over two hundred people in Nepal before the local hill tribes organised themselves into a massive beating operation and drove her west over the border into India. There she established herself, in the winter of 1902/3, in the region of the Lohaghat river valley about forty miles due east of Naini Tal and began to prey upon the local population. As the toll in India began to mount and word reached the authorities in Almora and Naini Tal, an expert sportsman was sent to despatch the tigress. He failed.

Over a period of four years, the tigress was hunted by small parties of *shikaris*, units of Gurkha troops from their base in Almora, sportsmen, government and army officers, all to no avail. She slipped through the net every time. Few saw her long enough to get in even a hopeful shot. By 1907, the tigress had claimed more than two hundred additional victims and the list was mounting weekly, for she was killing on average once every three days.

When he was on leave that year from Mokameh Ghat, Jim was approached by the deputy commissioner in Naini Tal who shared his growing concern over the tigress's operations. As Jim's knowledge of tigers was great, he was asked if he would have a go for her. Sharing the commissioner's anxiety, he agreed but set down two conditions under which he would hunt and which he always demanded when, in the future, he dealt with other man-eaters.

The first condition was that he was not to be rewarded if he was successful. There was a bounty placed on the pelt of all such killers in the hope that it would encourage their hunting before that of other tigers. Jim waived this, not wanting to be considered a mercenary bounty hunter.

His second demand was that, for as long as he was hunting the man-eater, all other attempts to kill it would be withdrawn. This was a wise decision of self-protection. Apart from the risk of being shot by another *shikari*, he was keen that he should be on almost personal terms with his prey. This was not just a show of his pride in his abilities as a hunter and his keen sense of sportsmanship but also essential if he was to be successful in tracking and shooting the creature. Man-eaters are utterly unlike other tigers.

Any animal must be cleverer than its diet. If the fox cannot outwit the rabbit, he starves and the tiger must be more artful, more powerful, more skilful in catching a sambhar or a cheetal than the latter is in escaping. The balanced laws of nature operate in this way. However, once an animal starts to see men and women as his prey, then he must become that much cleverer than the humans.

This is not difficult. The average human cannot run faster than a tiger over a short distance. He has not the highly attuned senses of a wild animal. He has not the camouflage or the instinctive sixth sense of the wild creature. Many humans, even those who live in forest areas, are out of their familiar environment in the jungle. They are as much at a disadvantage in the trees as the tiger would be in a city street full of traffic. And the man-eater has more than an edge on them because, as they are his prey, he knows them, has studied them, has absorbed their ways into his mind and he can predict how they will react, behave and operate. Just as the ordinary tiger knows the cheetal . . . For this reason, the man-eater is doubly dangerous for he isn't just waiting for his meal to appear. He goes out and gets it by applying his knowledge of men.

Most tigers, on seeing a man, will flee. Unless cornered or protecting their young, when they will stand their ground and fight to defend their rights or preserve themselves, tigers are wise cowards. They know what men can do to them. Jim maintained that tigers know when a man is a threat to them and he had had tigers walk past him, within a matter of a few feet, because he had 'told' them that he was not a danger to them. He informed those who asked that the best thing to do when confronting a tiger on a narrow path on a head-on course, was to step slightly aside, stand still and slowly raise one hand up level with the breast, holding the fingers in a certain manner, rather like the pattern one sees on the idols of the Indian gods in temples. Whether or not the finer points of the shape of the hand were of importance is doubtful. Jim most probably picked up this refinement from a village priest or hillsman, for it is a detail that is passed down today to those who venture into the forest.

Jim was, therefore, conscious that when he went after the tigress, he would not be hunting a wild tiger but an animal with which he was on almost equal terms in that it had the intelligence of men and he had the intelligence of tigers. It was a rare, if somewhat risky, opportunity to conduct the ultimate hunting experience. Although Jim had his love for the hill people in his heart at the time, it is certain that he also had the simultaneous thrill of what he was embarking upon – the one-to-one relationship with his quarry – in his mind. His penchant for danger was another factor in his provisional acceptance of the task.

Within a week, his demands were agreed and he received word of the latest human kill at the village of Pali, twenty miles east-south-east of Almora and thirty miles from Naini Tal. With his bearer and six men to carry his gear, he set off and walked seventeen miles in the first day.

Throughout his life, Jim walked great distances in Kumaon. Seventeen miles, carrying only his rifle, may not seem very much but it was an astounding feat. Not only did he walk throughout the day, regardless of the Indian sun, but he walked over terrain that would quite literally defeat a common goat.

Kumaon is made of ridges and ranges of hills, most between one and three-and-half thousand feet high. These were predictably crisscrossed with tracks made by wild animals, humans and mule trains. They wound to and fro, hairpinning and twisting back on themselves so that to travel five miles as the arrow flies entailed a journey by path of up to five times that distance. At the bottom of each valley is usually a fast-flowing, submontane torrent. Its width and depth depends upon the season and it could be crossed by fording, rope bridge or, in some instances, by inflated cowskin or goatskin bladders or rafts.

Jim forsook the paths. If he was in a hurry he walked *in a straight line* up and down the hillsides. In the sun, already at an altitude of perhaps three thousand feet where the air was thinner even when in a valley, across loose scree slopes, through forest and cover and always aware of the animals around him, this was a remarkable achievement even for one bred in the hills. Jim's stamina was quite extraordinary.

On the third day out from Naini Tal, he arrived in Pali where the population of fifty was in a state of complete terror. He arrived at mid-morning to find the village locked up tight. It was not until he had brewed up a pot of tea on a fire he had made in the village courtyard that the inhabitants began reluctantly and cautiously to appear.

It is very difficult for a reader far removed from Kumaon to appreciate what it is like to be living in the domain of a man-eater. Such a tiger is, by comparison with his peers, fearless. He will not baulk at drawing close to a village, he will not be driven off as easily as another tiger and he will persist with his quarry until he gets it. Whereas a wild tiger, if unsuccessful, will drop his chase of one deer and rethink his strategy, the man-eater will as like as not carry on. Escape from an efficient man-eater was, therefore, highly unusual. The only effective course of action was to climb a tree, for tigers, unlike all the other cats, are unable to climb trees. In such circumstances, the man-eater then prowls around the base of the tree until either tired or fed up or driven off by a very superior force of rescuers.

To inhabit a man-eater's territory was to live in constant, twenty-four hour fear for one's life. To go out and herd the village cows, go to the river to draw water or wash clothes, to collect firewood, to gather fodder, to cross the village compound to visit a friend, to step out of doors at dusk, to visit the nearest temple or bazaar, to answer a 'call of nature' was to invite an instant and horrible death. Going to market, to another village to trade, to a distant field to sow or harvest was out of the question. Village to village intercourse was conducted by hollering at the top of one's voice across a valley or up a hillside.

Each small hill community was therefore all but cut off from its normal life. Farming could not be conducted so food grew short. Water was collected only at some considerable risk and was used only for drinking so hygiene standards dropped, exacerbated by the need to excrete as close as possible to the door of one's hovel. The natives' shortage of firearms increased the man-eater's chances of survival. The shoddy construction of buildings helped: man-eating leopards were not averse to actually entering villages (which tigers were most loath to do) and those Jim hunted took victims by demolishing doors or pushing through hut walls, not bothering with the door at all.

The amount of human excreta that was spread about the normally clean, well-swept courtyard of Pali told Jim its own tale: the villagers had barely been outside their houses for five days. The tigress was, they reported, still in the area because her growls had been heard on the track to the village for the past three nights and, that morning, she had been seen in a nearby field.

When out hunting, Jim often slept in the open air without even a tent for cover and, on seeing that the village headman had offered him and his men only a one-roomed hut to sleep in – and not wanting to lose face or insult the headman, Jim chose to sleep out that night. His men safely ensconced in the room, he set himself on the ground by the side of the road leading to the village, his back to a tree. The tigress was in the habit of using the road so he hoped to get a shot in by the bright moonlight before the tigress saw him. After a short time, he realised that this was not a sensible ploy: the deep-cast shadows set his imagination to work much as they had that first time he and brother Tom had gone hunting bears together. He was too frightened to stay under the tree: on the other hand, he was just as afraid to return to the village and admit his weakness. He stayed and, in the early hours, fell asleep to be so discovered by his men at dawn. Fortunately, the tigress had not appeared.

The last victim had been a woman surprised when cutting oak leaves for cattle fodder. As she had climbed out of her selected tree, the tigress had approached unseen, stood on its hind legs and dragged the woman from the bottom branches. Pulling her by the foot to a dried up watercourse beneath the tree, it then let her go in order to grab her by the throat, killing her. As soon as the tigress had taken the woman off to cover, her companions – a number of women and girls gathering fodder in nearby trees – fled for the village. The men returned to the scene but were driven off by the roars of the tigress which had been encouraged by one villager firing his ineffective blunderbuss in the air.

Jim spent the morning scouting the village area and afterwards stood guard over the villagers as the whole population gathered in their harvest. That night, Jim slept in a second room provided for him, with the doorway jammed with thorn bushes as a protection. The following day, Jim went out to shoot a goral (a mountain goat) but had the lucky chance to shoot three in quick succession, much to the delight and wonder of the villagers who, taking heart from this display of apparent near miracles, offered to take Jim to the scene of the woman's death. Little remained other than some blood-soaked clothing and thin shreds of skin adhering to the oak tree which the woman had gripped in vain. Jim gathered up a few splinters of bone so that at least a part of the victim could be cremated thus satisfying the urgent religious need of the dead woman and her family.

That evening, he visited the scene of an earlier killing. Here, the victim – again a woman, as tiger victims often were, for the women traditionally go into the jungle to collect fuel or fodder – was taken in a field and the tigress chased by the prey's sister. After going a hundred yards and being followed by an heroic, screaming, scythe-brandishing human, the tigress had dropped her now-dead victim and rounded on her pursuer who then took flight and made for the village, the whole terrible and courageous business having been watched by some of the villagers, struck still with fear and horror. It was then found that the woman had, after regaining her breath, lost her voice with the shock of her ordeal. Jim visited her in her two-roomed hovel where she was laundering her clothes. She had been dumb for a year by then.

It appeared that the tigress had moved her hunting ground from Pali and Jim did not see her to get in a shot. He set off into the surrounding forests, the plans he had made back in Naini Tal being discarded as he went. His greatest problem was that there was no one to whom he could turn for advice.

The tigress – subsequently known as the Champawat man-eater, for that was the substantial village nearest to where it was finally killed – was not, as Jim claimed, the first-ever Kumaoni man-eater. Others had been recorded in the last decade of the nineteenth century and for some years before, for as long as public records had been assembled or British authority well established in the area. Indeed, wherever tigers and humans have lived side by side, man-eating has been a possibility and, on occasion, a reality. Now, however, Jim had to deal with one and he knew of no precedent. It was very much a case of learn-as-you-go. His knowledge of wild tigers was of only limited use.

Joined on the road by groups of men, for no one travelled singly or in pairs, Jim and his party reached Champawat to be regaled with a hideous story from some men who had, two months previously, watched the tigress make off with a woman whom it was holding by the small of her back. The woman was fully conscious and bellowing for help. The tigress had carried her off, her screams for mercy gradually disappearing into silence. She had been collecting kindling.

Jim lodged in the *dak* bungalow not at but near to Champawat. Throughout India, there were (and still are) a vast network of bunga-lows, each with a resident caretaker, which were used by visiting civil servants, forest officers, policemen and the like when they were travelling on tours of their administrative areas. Others could stay in these if they were vacant. The *tahsildar* had suggested the *dak* bungalow as it was in the area in which the tigress had started to hunt again and had killed often in the past. Jim went there, studying the pug marks of tigers around nearby water springs (without seeing the man-eater's signature with which he was now familiar having seen it in Pali), being sidetracked *en route* by some men who told him the tigress had killed a cow: on reaching the shed in which the carcass lay, he discovered it had been killed by a leopard. He returned in the late afternoon to the bungalow where the *tahsildar* met him. They talked of the tigress and, just as it was getting dark, the *tahsildar* said that he had to be off home. Jim had expected him to remain the night at the bungalow. The man refused to stay and set off accompanied by his servant and a smoking oil lamp. It was four miles back to Champawat.

Jim went inside, pondering on the considerable bravery of the *tahsildar*. During that night, he found out why the man had declined to stay, rather facing the chance of meeting the man-eater than the bungalow.

Quite what happened was something about which Jim was forever reticent. That he had a night-long brush with the supernatural is without doubt for, although he claimed to regard superstition as a form of mental aberration that passed by much as measles does, he was nevertheless a man fully endowed with a staunch belief in it and its powers. Many of the old Indian houses in the foothills are haunted by spirits both friendly and antagonistic. Most seem to be varieties of poltergeist which are capable of moving objects, including men.

On one occasion, Jim and a friend were forcibly ejected from a building by a spirit: a fragment of an undated letter written by a third friend reports this:

'Jim and a friend arrived at a very isolated Dak bungalow late one evening & prepared to stay the night. However, after getting a scratch meal, neither of their bearers would remain at the bungalow and went off for the night.

'Jim and his friend occupied separate rooms, and Jim had a hurricane lamp on a table beside his bed. He was extremely weary after a long day hunting a man-eater, but about 1AM he woke up suddenly to "feel" as he put it an indescribable evil presence in the room. His light was then extinguished & whatever it was forced him to the door and out onto the hillside. He found his friend already there having suffered a similar experience, and he assured me that nothing in the world would ever induce him to stay at that bungalow again!'

It may well be that he spent his night in the *dak* bungalow near Champawat struggling not to be thrown out and thereby placed at risk from the tigress. Whatever had come to pass that night, he would seldom be drawn even to mention it.

One has to accept that Jim was psychic. Throughout his life he had experiences of the supernatural and, no matter how dismissive he was at the time, he was more than conscious of it and its power. He was also superstitious, sometimes irrationally so.

If he was to have a successful hunt, especially if he was after a man-eater, he believed quite sincerely that he would not make a kill until he had first shot a snake. He sometimes went out of his way to kill one. Lucky talismans, which were common amongst the Kumaon hillfolk were also something in which he believed and although there is no record that he ever wore or carried one he was more than careful, when killing a tiger, to distribute the lucky bones to Indian friends and he usually gave the skinned carcass away so that the fat might be eaten or saved for protection.

Although he came from a devoutly Christian background, Jim was not at all averse to the Hindu religion and made a point of attending major religious festivals, especially in Naini Tal where he would make a grand offering annually. He even very occasionally prayed in temples and, on the bank of a stream by the old path from Naini Tal to Kaladhungi, he erected a small wayside shrine to Devi Mata, the mother goddess.

Of his supernatural experiences, Jim was usually reticent, his attitude being that one should accept the supernatural and leave well alone. However, a few are worth noting and it is important to realise that Jim, a man whose life was based upon reality and fact, gave credence to the occult.

The most famous of his supernatural encounters took place in 1929 at the sacred hill of Purnagiri above a gorge on the Sarda River where he and his men were honoured to be shown – by the gods, one assumes –

the strange lights that move across the precipitous face of the hill: they were accorded this viewing by the goddess Bhagbatti, the goddess of increase, because they were on a mission to help the hill people, to rid them of the Talla Des man-eater. The event so impressed him that he included a chapter about it in the first book he wrote and repeated it in his penultimate one.

He also crossed paths with the supernatural in other *dak* bungalows such as the one at Ramgarh (as have other people) and one of the Naini Tal houses his mother looked after as agent, Braemar, was also haunted.

The most weird and terrifying of Jim's contacts with the occult came about in September, 1938. It was whilst he was hunting the Thak man-eater.

He was in a *machan* twenty yards from a dead buffalo to which he hoped the man-eater would return. In the moonlight, a sambhar hind and calf came to within fifty yards of the *machan* and a kakar started barking on the hillside just above the village of Thak which, because of fear of the man-eater, had been temporarily deserted. Quite suddenly, from the village, there was a piercing scream which Jim described as 'Ar-Ar-Arr' fading away on a long note. So surprised was Jim that he stood up in the *machan* with the immediate intention of going down to the village where he was afraid one of his men was being taken by the man-eater. Yet he recalled counting them all safely off back down the path to Chuka where they were staying. Jim's own words tell the remainder of the story:

'The scream had been the despairing cry of a human being in mortal agony, and reason questioned how such a sound could come from a deserted village. It was not a thing of my imagination, for the kakar had heard it and had abruptly stopped barking, and the sambhar had dashed away closely followed by her young one. Two days previously, when I had escorted the men to the village (to collect food), I had remarked that they appeared to be very confiding to leave their property behind doors that were not even shut or latched, and the Headman had answered that even if their village remained untenanted for years their property would be quite safe, for they were priests of Purnagiri and no one would dream of robbing them; he added that as long as the tigress lived she was a better guard of their property – if guard were needed – than any hundred men could be . . .'

The scream did not occur again, the tigress called once some while later and Jim was relieved by his men from his *machan* at dawn. Yet that is not the end of the tale:

'I questioned him (the headman) about the kill at Thak on the 12th of the month when he so narrowly escaped falling a victim to the man-eater.

'Once again the Headman told me in great detail how he had gone to his fields to dig ginger, taking his grandchild with him . . . and how a few minutes later the tigress had killed a man while he was cutting leaves . . . I now asked him if he had actually seen the tigress killing the man. His answer was, No; and he added that the tree was not visible from where he had been standing. I then asked him how he knew that the man had been killed, and he said, because he had heard him. In reply to further questions he said that the man had not called for help but had cried out; and when asked if he had cried out once he said, 'No, three times', and then at my request he gave an imitation of the man's cry. It was the same . . .'

If that was the eeriest of Jim's experiences, perhaps the strangest tale happened when, on his 1919 trip to Trisul with Robert Bellairs, they had lost one of their *shikaris* who was convinced that he had swallowed the demon of Trisul whilst singing round their campfire. Shouting and beating tin cans did not exorcise the demon whose presence the unfortunate man took for granted. A European doctor found nothing physically wrong with him: an eminent Indian doctor was called in who soon assessed the cause of the illness – the man was possessed and the doctor quickly moved away from the patient declaring that there was nothing he could do. The *shikari*, Bala Singh, whom Jim had known for some years and upon whom he relied as a good expedition guide, returned to his home village and simply died.

The following morning, Jim ranged through the orchard and tea plantation around the bungalow and, just before noon, stripped and bathed himself in a spring that irrigated the gardens. The *tahsildar* returned at midday and, as they sat talking, a man ran up from the village to report that a girl had just been killed.

On reaching the village, Jim met an agitated crowd and took one man aside to learn what had happened.

About two hundred yards from the village stood a gentle upward slope lightly covered with young oak trees. A dozen or so women were in the trees collecting kindling when the tigress appeared and caught hold of a seventeen-year-old girl. No one knew of the attack until they heard the girl choking and fighting for breath, the tigress characteristically having gripped her by the throat. The rest of the wood-gatherers had fled without looking round. One woman pointed out to him the oak tree on the ridge of the slope where the girl had been snatched.

Instructing the villagers to keep very quiet, Jim set off up the slope. There was very little undergrowth and the ground beneath the trees was quite open and he marvelled how the tigress had so easily been able to creep up on the party of women undetected.

Near the oak tree Jim came upon a thick pool of deep red, arterial blood which told him the girl had been quickly killed. Nearby lay a broken necklace of azure beads. The tigress had made off with its kill up a path and round the side of hill above the slope up which Jim had come.

The drag, the spoor of the tigress and her meal, was easily followed. The pug marks were non-existent in the dead leaves that covered the ground but on one side of the tigress's progress there were big dabs of blood where the girl's head touched the ground as the tigress walked: next to these were scuffs in the leaves where her feet were rubbing the ground. The tigress was carrying her victim balanced by the waist, in the usual manner for the portage of light prey: heavy prey is straddled and dragged between the front legs. Half a mile further on, Jim found the girl's *sari* and, a short distance past it, her sarong-like skirt. Further still, he found strands of the girl's long hair caught on a thorn thicket. From the thicket, the tiger had passed through a wide bed of nettles.

As he was wondering how he might work his way round this – for Jim was wearing only long socks and shorts over rubber soled shoes – he heard the sound of a footfall behind him. Spinning round he saw a man with a rifle approaching him. The *tahsildar* had sent him to help. Jim had neither the heart nor the inclination to send the man back: it would have lost him much face in the eyes of his fellows and would have greatly hurt his feelings. On the other hand, Jim wanted to hunt alone for the sake of safety. Ordering the man to remove his heavy and therefore noisy boots, and demanding that he stay close behind, they set off through the nettles which stung them both badly.

The tigress, once out of the nettles, had turned down a very steep slope covered with bracken and thin hill bamboo. Three hundred feet down, she had gone into a narrow and steep watercourse where she had

had difficulty keeping her footing on the soft earth and loose rocks. Together, the two men went down the watercourse for nearly half a mile.

All the while, the Indian – who was in mortal fear – kept tugging Jim's sleeve to whisper that he had heard or seen or sensed the tigress behind, above, to the left or the right or before them. This not only unnerved Jim but took his mind from the task at hand of protecting himself and the Indian and bringing the tigress down. Halfway down the watercourse was a huge pinnacle of rock projecting from the hillside: Jim instructed the man to climb it and sit on it until relieved. With considerable speed, he did just that and Jim continued down the watercourse. One hundred yards down, at the junction with a ravine, there was a small pool on the sides of which were bloodstains. Beside it was a strange white object.

Jim had disturbed the tigress at her feast. The pug marks in the mud were still filling with bloody water as he approached the pool. On the side of the pool itself was the white object, the lower part of a human leg, blood seeping from it into the water.

Struck by the horror and pity of the leg, Jim's guard dropped. It was one of the very rare occasions when it did. Then, quite suddenly and with the instinctive sixth sense jungle dwellers have, he knew the tigress was about to spring. He raised his gun with his fingers on the triggers – he was carrying a double-barrelled shotgun which was more useful than a rifle at the close range at which Jim expected to be shooting – and saw just a trickle of soil fall down the tall bank in front of him to land in the water.

Unable to negotiate the bank itself by ordinary climbing, Jim ran back and sprinted for it, jumping to grasp a bush growing out of the earth. With the aid of this, he hauled himself up. (Quite how, when he was also carrying a heavy gun, he doesn't say: certainly, he would not have put the gun down before his scrabble up the bank. It is one of those instances in his recollections when one has to accept a smidgin of licence.)

The tigress's track was revealed by the bent stalks of the plants through which she had travelled, carrying what was left of her kill. She had run off with it, hidden it temporarily under an overhang of rock, backtracked to look at her pursuer, returned to the kill to collect it and made off through a large area, some four acres in extent, of fallen rocks and boulders overgrown with creepers and bushes. For Jim to enter that would be to invite death. Yet he did.

Cautiously, so as not to be surprised but also so as not to fall or slip, he made his way through the boulders. Quite a number of times he came upon a place where the tigress had stopped to eat, only to be moved on by the approaching hunter. This perpetual interruption made the man-eater somewhat annoyed. She commenced growling and spitting but she was also intelligent enough to know not to attack and to remain out of sight in the undergrowth. Jim, for his part, wanted her to attack for that would give him the opportunity he wanted for a shot. Eventually, she abandoned her kill.

This tracking had taken four hours and by now it was late afternoon. The valleys were filling with shadows and Jim felt the need to regain the safety of the village whilst it was still light. He went back the way he had come, pausing at the pool to lift the leg up and bury it as protection against scavengers: it would be needed later for cremation. Collecting the rock-bound Indian, who had assumed that the tigress's growlings from the boulders meant that Jim was dead and who was wondering what might be his own fate, he returned to the village. For jungle safety, he made the man walk in front of him. It was now that Jim vowed he would never hunt man-eaters again with anyone else – though he was later to break this rule in the case of a close friend William 'Ibby' Ibbotson. The man tripped going up the watercourse and dropped his converted .450 rifle. Jim noticed it had no safety catch. Going down the watercourse, after the tigress, the muzzle must have often pointed at the back of his head.

The tigress, Jim knew, would return to the kill during the night and eat it and then, having eaten, would rest in the safe cover of the boulder-strewn area. It was unlikely that Jim could find her, never mind stalk her, over that kind of ground and he knew that he would only get a shot at the man-eater by driving her before a beat. The *tahsildar* agreed to try and raise the large number of men who would be required.

By noon the following day, two hundred and ninety-eight men had gathered at the village. The *tahsildar* had achieved this miracle by agreeing to ignore unlicensed guns and to provide ammunition for those with weapons. Jim outlined the lie of the land and the beat spread out to commence once Jim gave the signal. With the *tahsildar*, he set off to position himself but the beaters, waiting on the ridge above, either assumed they had missed the signal or mistook a movement from the *tahsildar* as being it: whichever was the case, they began their beating before Jim was in position.

Running down the dangerously steep hillside, Jim was forced to sit on the ground in a patch of two-foot high grass near the entrance to a gorge down which he anticipated the tigress would flee. Before him was the hill that was being driven at the foot of which was a small stream. Meanwhile, the *tahsildar* had positioned himself by a pine tree from which the signal was supposed to have been given.

Firing guns, beating drums, bawls and shouts, rolling rocks, clapping hands and smacking sticks echoed from the hillside.

As if from nowhere, the tigress appeared running down the grassy slope to Jim's right front, three hundred yards off. The *tahsildar*, two hundred yards above Jim's right shoulder, armed with a shotgun, let off both barrels. The tigress turned about and disappeared into thick cover. With little hope of success, Jim fired as she vanished.

The three shots gave the beaters the impression that it was all over. They fired off a few more fusillades and then were silent. Jim expected the tigress now to head upwards towards the beaters and sat waiting to hear the screams as she closed on the men. Instead, she suddenly broke cover in front of Jim and headed for the gorge, leaping the stream. Aiming his .500 rifle at her, he fired.

She stopped stock still thirty yards away.

He had aimed straight at her but realised the gun was sighted at sea level: the shot was taken at five thousand feet so it must have gone high and missed. She turned towards Jim and gave him a fine shoulder shot. He fired again. The tigress shuddered but did not fall. She laid her ears flat and snarled.

Jim waited for the charge with considerable apprehension. He had brought only three cartridges with him as he had wanted to travel light and had not expected in his wildest optimism that he would have had the opportunity for more than three shots.

Fortunately, the tigress did not charge. She made off across the stream, climbed some rocks to a narrow ledge and headed off along it until she came to a bush which she commenced to denude of foliage. Several times in his life, Jim was to see man-eaters he had wounded take their anger and pain out on a tree or bush.

Jim ran up to the *tahsildar*, snatched his gun from his hands and set off after the tigress. As he reached the stream the tigress quit the bush and headed for Jim. He threw the gun to his shoulder and saw, in that split second before firing, that the barrels did not meet the breech. The gun was old and although it would not explode in his hands, there could be a blowback that might blind him. With no choice now, he aimed at the tigress's oncoming mouth and fired. The ball – the gun fired a projectile rather like a ball-bearing rather than a pointed bullet – missed the tigress's head completely and hit her paw. Yet it was enough. She was nearly dead in any case. Stumbling, she fell with her head leaning over the rim of the rock ledge.

The beaters converged on the scene, screaming with rage at the dead tigress which had for so long terrorised them, but they soon calmed down and begged Jim not to skin the tigress there and then but to allow them to carry it through the neighbouring villages. He did and they marched off in triumph whilst he and the *tahsildar* headed for Champawat passing on the way the relatives of the last victim. During the beat, the girl's head had been found and it was now being given the last Hindu cremation rites.

Later that evening, the tigress was skinned and, the next day, the flesh was cut into fragments and distributed as talismans. Inside the tigress's stomach were found the girl's fingers which Jim was sent in a bottle of spirits: he buried them on the shore of the lake at Naini Tal, close by the temple.

Two sequels to the story of Jim's first man-eater are worth recounting. On his way back to Naini Tal, he took a detour to visit Pali where he showed the dumb woman the skin of the tigress. She, on seeing it, rushed to the other nearby houses shouting for everyone to come and view the pelt.

Several months later, at an official gathering in Naini Tal, the *tahsildar* of Champawat was presented with a new shotgun by the Lieutenant Governor of the United Provinces, Sir John Hewett. The man who had followed Jim down the watercourse was presented with a hunting knife.

As for Jim, who had refused any reward save the pride and joy of knowing that he had rid part of his beloved Kumaon of a terrifying menace, he was presented with a rifle that was to be used by him over and over again in his hunts for man-eaters as well as other tigers. It was from then on his favourite weapon, a British-made .275 (7mm) Rigby with a Mauser action, right-hand bolt and leaf-sights with settings for 100, 200 and 300 yards, though he was often to use it at ranges of ten and twenty feet. It was numbered 2516 and had been bought at the gunsmiths, Manton of Calcutta, to whom it had been supplied from London in April, 1905. Its weight was 7lb. 8 oz. with a 25-inch barrel and a 14⅜ inch stock of French walnut. The magazine was a five-shot firing a rimmed cartridge with a 173 grain bullet. It was a good choice for a woodsman for it was a gun that could be dismantled and cleaned without the use of tools. It cost twelve guineas.

On the left side of the butt, where Jim's cheek would rest when he fired the gun – he was right-eyed – was mounted a silver plate incorrectly inscribed:

'Presented to Mr. J.G. Corbett by Sir J.P. Hewett KCSI, Lieutenant Governor of the United Provinces in recognition of his having killed a man-eating tigress at Champawat in 1907.'

The Champawat man-eater was calculated to have killed 436 people. Jim did not agree with those who maintained that one could always accept these figures as accurate: a man wanted to be rid of his wife or an enemy – a tiger got them. The truth was liable to a margin of error, but even if this was as high as fifty per cent, it still left a tale of horror and enormous human disruption.

As a result of the Champawat hunt, Jim's fame was consolidated. Known before as an above average *shikari*, he was now elevated to the position of being the only man to bring down the devil. The local hill tribes believed, not without cause, that man-eaters harboured the devil himself in their skins.

The job done and the accolades sounded, Jim returned to his work as a newly established Naini Tal businessman and railway official. However, his skills, now sharpened by the Champawat hunt, were to be called upon again.

Whilst hunting the Champawat tigress, Jim had heard tales of a man-eating leopard operating in an area north and north west of Champawat. The leopard had gathered quite an infamous reputation: it was reputed to have claimed over four hundred lives and to be causing such concern that the question of eradicating it was raised in Parliament back in London. On reaching Naini Tal, Jim was requested by the provincial government to go after the leopard, but he refused to go immediately because business matters were pressing upon him. After a few weeks, Jim records, he was preparing to set off to deal with the leopard when he was summoned to the District Commissioner's Office in Naini Tal.

C. H. Berthoud, the Deputy Commissioner, asked him to forgo his hunting the leopard to try for another man-eater that was establishing itself in the region around the village of Mukteswar, between Naini Tal and Almora.

There is some confusion about the dates of the shooting of the Champawat tigress and the killing of the Mukteswar man-eater and the leopard. Official Indian sources state that the leopard was shot in September 1910 and the Mukteswar tigress in the early spring of that year. Jim, however, writes that he shot the Mukteswar tigress some weeks after the Champawat success. Then he went after the leopard and killed it.

The truth is that Jim got his dates wrong. He did shoot the Champawat man-eater in 1907 and he was asked if he would immediately go after the other two creatures. In fact, he did not or – if he did go after the Mukteswar man-eater in 1907 – he was unsuccessful and did not care to remember the failure. It was not until the early spring of 1910 that he finally went after the other two beasts: in the intervening years, they claimed many more victims. Jim tended to overlook this fact in later years and it seems that his love of his hill folk did not always take precedence over his pressing business affairs.

The Mukteswar man-eater was another tigress in the prime of her life. She took to man-eating only with her third victim: the first she killed because the fodder-gathering woman came too close, the second because the woodcutter came to chop at the fallen tree beneath which she was hiding. On the fourth day, she deliberately killed and ate her victim. Within a matter of a few weeks, the tigress had killed two dozen people and was becoming such a menace that her hunting was disrupting vital work at the veterinary research centre at Mukteswar. It was the director of the centre who had requested the government get hold of Jim.

Shortly after arriving in the Mukteswar area, the tigress killed a white bullock the whereabouts of which was shown to Jim by a brave little girl called Putli whom he had met walking alone along the road leading another bullock and whom he had guarded until she had delivered her bullock to her uncle and returned home.

Jim realised that the only way in which he would get a shot in at the man-eater would be to sit up over the kill at night. This was not a plan that would have given him the least worry with an ordinary tiger. With a man-eater, it was a different matter altogether.

There were no suitable trees near the kill in which to construct a *machan*, so Jim had to elect to sit on a stunted tree, its trunk covered with a wild rose bush. With the aid of a local friend, Badri, and two of his men, they erected a small *machan* and Jim hoisted himself into it at 4 p.m., had his .500 double barrelled gun handed up to him and settled down for the night. Badri was told to come for him, with companions, once the sun was well up the next morning.

At five o'clock, a muntjac deer started barking in a ravine two hundred yards below. It had seen the tigress which had moved nearby and lain down in sight of the kill but not in sight of Jim. After a long while, the muntjac left. Dusk fell. Then a twig snapped. The man-eater was moving nearer and towards Jim. It reached his stunted tree and lay down on the dry leaves ten feet under him. Clouds came over the sky, the night blackened to pitch and Jim could not see even the white bullock.

The man-eater moved to the kill and spent a few moments blowing off the lazy hornets that had been gorging on the bullock carcass. Then it began to feed.

From the sounds and knowing how the bullock was lying, Jim reasoned that the tigress was lying broadside on to him, on the right-hand end of the kill. Very slowly, he raised the gun, rested his elbows on his knees and listened, turning his head to range the gun sights by sound. Finally deciding he was on line, he fired.

In the dark, the tigress sprang up a bank behind the kill and Jim could hear it moving over dry leaves. He listened intently. Nothing. The tigress was either dead or unharmed. He lowered the rifle. The tigress saw this and growled. It now knew where he was. And it was twenty feet away. What was more, Jim's weight had bent the tree and rose bush so that he was now but eight feet off the ground, his legs lower still. It was 10 p.m. and first light was at 6 a.m., eight long hours of waiting away.

Now that the tigress was in the picture, Jim had no need to remain hidden so he lit a cigarette. He did this partly to calm himself and partly to keep himself awake. So long as he kept his balance and did not doze off, he thought he would be fairly safe.

At the scratching of the match, the tigress had moved off but it soon returned. At eleven o'clock, and three cigarettes later, it began to rain heavily. The tigress – as tigers do – headed for cover as soon as the big drops started to fall. It rained torrentially until four in the morning. The sky then cleared and a wind sprang up. Jim was frozen to the marrow. At sunrise, Badri arrived with a man carrying a pot of tea. The night's chill and the cramp had taken all the strength from Jim's legs and he was unable to walk until his calves had been massaged.

Badri's servant was despatched to the guest house in Mukteswar to light a fire. Jim inspected the bullock. His bullet had missed the tigress's head by six inches: the elevation was right but the aim just too far left.

Returning to the guest house twenty minutes later, Jim and Badri found the tigress's pug marks imprinted in the rain-softened earth over those of the servant. Luckily, the tigress had not had time to catch up with the swiftly walking man. She was lame and he was not.

After his experience with the Champawat man-eater, Jim decided to beat for this one, too. The drive was organised by Govind Singh, Badri's head gardener in the vegetable plots the latter operated as a market gardening concern a thousand feet below the Mukteswar Post Office. It drew a blank and at the end of it, Govind Singh and Jim stood facing each other to discuss another beat.

Of a sudden, the Indian looked over Jim's shoulder and stopped talking. Spinning round, Jim saw the tigress coming towards them, four hundred yards off. Between them was a stream, some open ground and thick bushes. Behind the two men were the thirty beaters, sitting in a group, chatting and smoking. As soon as the tigress entered the bushes, Jim instructed everyone to sit still and make no sound.

Making off at a run along the contour of the hillside, Jim came to another wild rose clump. He struggled through a tunnel in this, losing his hat and tearing his scalp open. The tigress was heading for a cow, dead a week, that was in a nearby hollow and which Jim had found before the beat.

The hollow, forty yards long and thirty wide, was entered by a path just above and to Jim's left. On its far side was a small cliff down to the stream. As Jim, who approached with caution, came to the rim, he heard a bone being crunched. He stood out of sight of the tigress, planning. There was a movement behind him. Jim looked round. There was Govind Singh coming up with Jim's hat: no European ever went out without his hat on.

Signalling utter silence, Jim pushed Govind Singh very gently into a shallow depression in the hillside. He squatted there shivering with fear. He could now hear the tigress feeding.

As he returned to the rim of the hollow, Jim heard the tigress stop eating, then he saw her going off. She was out of the hollow and heading for a group of saplings. With little hope of success, Jim threw up the gun and fired. He missed the tigress and hit a tree by her head. She spun about and came back towards him, fast, keeping to the path. He waited until she was *six feet* from him then fired. The bullet hit her in the back of the neck and the impact deflected her to one side. She missed Jim's shoulder and fell over a fifty foot drop to land in the stream below.

That evening, skinning the man-eater, Jim found the reason for her changing her diet to men. At some time in the not-too-distant past, the tigress had met a porcupine with results similar to, but far more drastic than, those which had taught Magog the dog his lesson all those years before. The tigress was blind in one eye and she had fifty porcupine quills, between one and nine inches long, embedded in her right foot and pad. Several had either broken off on hitting the bone or had bent back on themselves. Many had given rise to suppurating sores. The Mukteswar tigress had been forced to eat men through injury.

Many of the man-eaters Jim hunted had been forced to kill humans through infirmity or age.

The Panar leopard, the third of the trio of man-eaters, was credited with having taken four hundred lives. It was hunting in an area of over two hundred square miles to the north and north-east of Champawat and Jim set off after the creature in the April of 1910. He established his base at the *dak* bungalow in the village of Dol and was soon to come into contact with the leopard.

His first introduction to the beast came on the evening of his first day when he found its pug marks on a path which told Jim he was dealing with a large, male leopard. At the end of the path was a small hill farm and here he came face to face with the leopard's handiwork.

During the previous night, the young farmer and his wife had been sleeping in their one-roomed house with the door open – it had been a hot spring night. The leopard had sprung on to the veranda before the house, grabbed the farmer's wife by the throat and started to drag her, head first, out the door. She screamed and grabbed her husband. He took a firm and quick hold on his wife and, giving a sharp jerk with all his might, pulled his wife free and through the door, which he slammed and barred. For the rest of the night, the man and his direly injured wife cowered in a corner of their room whilst the leopard did his damnedest to claw the door down. In the hot room, the woman's wounds rapidly turned septic and by dawn she was unconscious from loss of blood and fear. All day, the husband had stayed with his wife, too afraid to risk going to the nearest farmstead for help. Jim was greeted by the farmer throwing himself at his feet.

The wife, aged about eighteen, was in a terrible state. Her throat was pierced by teeth holes and one of her breasts was badly clawed. All her wounds were filled with pus and covered with flies. Jim knew there was little he could do.

He decided to stay the night with the couple and, as darkness fell, he sat down in a firewood store under the balcony, his back to the wall, to see if the leopard would return. The farmer bolted himself inside the room above. A jackal started to call and Jim knew the leopard was in the area but throughout the moonlit night he saw no evidence of it. The following morning he left with his eyes tired from his all night vigil and saddened after hearing the night-long wheezings of the dying girl.

Unsuccessful in this attempt, Jim left the area, though not without spending some while attempting to shoot – for sport – a tiger reputed to be protected by the gods and therefore immortal. He failed to kill this animal as well, though he got a number of shots in at it.

One has to ask several questions here which throw some doubts upon Jim's character, suggesting that it was not as unblemished as his future legendary reputation was to make it appear.

He had possibly waited three years to go after the Mukteswar and Panar man-eaters, when he could have made attempts for them over that time. He was in the area of the man-eater on the night the girl was snatched back by her husband and yet, the next day, he seemingly did not seek to follow up the trail, lay a bait for the leopard (such as tying out a goat and sitting over it in a *machan*) or otherwise go after it although he knew it must still be in the vicinity. Finally, he obviously had enough time on leaving the area to indulge in a bit of would-be sport hunting after the temple-guarded tiger of Dabidhura: why did he not use this time to try again for the leopard?

These do not seem to be the decisions of a man wholly dedicated to his task of ridding the world of such horrifying creatures as man-eaters. Obviously his anguish at hearing the farmer's young wife die did not affect him too deeply.

From April to September, 1910, Jim was back at Mokameh Ghat. In early September, he returned to Naini Tal, saw to his business affairs (which Maggie and Mary Doyle had managed in his absence) and set off once more for the land of the Panar leopard.

En route, Jim had an experience as nasty as meeting the leopard. He stopped one night in a village where he found an empty room with no door. His men swept out the straw and rags that were in the room – there was no furniture – and Jim settled down for the night on a groundsheet spread on the floor. At sun up, he woke to find the room's occupant sitting on the floor by his groundsheet. He was about fifty years old and in the terminal stages of leprosy, regarded then as the most dreaded disease known. No one in the village had thought to tell Jim of the leper's existence as lepers were not segregated, their disease being regarded as a visitation from the gods rather than an illness. Jim's first action on leaving the village was to order his men to wash his bedding out and spread it in the hot sunlight whilst he stripped naked in the first stream they came to and thoroughly scrubbed himself and his clothing with carbolic soap.

Sanouli, an isolated village to which Jim was heading, had been the scene of the most recent human kill and it was evidently a spot favoured by the leopard for he had killed four human beings from the same small settlement, each time carrying them to a dense thicket of brushwood a quarter of a mile away to eat them undisturbed. The last victim had been taken six days previously and the local men were certain that the leopard was still hiding in the brush.

This time, Jim did decide to bait for the leopard with two young billy-goats.

During the first night, just before a rainstorm, the leopard had killed a goat, broken its tether and carried the carcass into the brushwood where Jim, come morning, decided it was not wise to attempt to follow the drag. Later that day, he did try to stalk the leopard – which had consumed most of the goat – and though he knew its whereabouts all the time from the behaviour of the birds in the brushwood he did not see it.

A drive was out of the question because of the danger to the beaters.

That night, Jim came down with malaria and spent the next twenty-four hours delirious. When he regained his strength on the third day, he went out to see what had become of the second goat, also tied out by his men during his illness. It had not been killed which meant that the leopard was now hungry. Jim at last set about baiting for the leopard and sitting up over the bait.

The trouble was that there were few trees into which he could climb. At last, he decided to sit on the trunk of an old oak tree that jutted out from a bank between two terraced hillside fields. He clambered on a thick but rotten branch – the only suitable one – fifteen feet above the lower terrace and had the tree trunk bound round with stout rope holding in place large bundles of blackthorn bushes. These not only protected Jim from behind but also gave him something to grip on to – the tree was devoid of hand-holds.

By five o'clock, the scene was set. Jim was as safe as he could expect to be on a rotten branch, with his coat collar turned up and his hat pulled well down against the thorns, his arms gripping some of the thorn branches that protruded forwards on each side of him. The goat was as insecure as it could be, staked out on the terraced field thirty yards in front of Jim. In order to improve his chance of a successful shot, Jim had armed himself with a twelve bore, double-barrelled shot gun, each of the two charges consisting of a black powder cartridge containing eight lead pellets each the size of a small pea. An Indian leopard is nothing like as big as a tiger – it is often not much larger than a very big dog – and does not need to be brought down with a single bullet.

To draw attention to the goat, the men sat about smoking and talking in the field but soon two birds gave away the leopard's approach and Jim signalled the men to go back to the village which they did with pleasure.

Nothing much happened. The goat bleated and faced the direction of the leopard. The sun went down. Dusk fell. The goat faced Jim and stopped bleating.

This puzzled him at first but was not to for long. There was a soft tug at the blackthorn shoots. The leopard was behind him, in the tree, and pulling at the thorn bundles with his teeth. Jim could not turn round to shoot. Peeved by the sturdy tying of the thorn branches, the leopard began to yank on them, so that Jim – struggling to keep his hold, grasp his gun and retain his balance – clouted his spine hard against the tree trunk. As this tug-of-war was going on, the leopard was growling so loudly that Jim's men up in the village could hear it. Each growl chilled his spine. Every now and then, the leopard was silent whilst trying to figure out how to get at Jim: it soon renewed its efforts.

Then there was a prolonged silence.

With a quick dash, the leopard made for the goat and swiftly killed it. By now, it was dark and Jim could see the goat only as a vague greyish blue. Aiming at where he thought the leopard would be, Jim fired. The report was answered by a growl of rage and there was a whitish flicker of belly fur as the leopard went over the bank to the next terrace down the hill.

More silence.

Jim called for his men, who came down the hillside with a group of twenty villagers, all armed with pine-twig torches. They cut the thorn bushes away and then Jim informed them that he had hit the leopard but that it might be alive still, down in the next open field.

With a promise of fearless and staunch co-operation, he set the men behind him in a line, their torches held high and together they walked carefully to the rim of the terrace. All was silent save for the hiss of the torches. They reached the dead goat. Twenty yards to go. The field below was being lit nearer and nearer to the terrace banking. When just a few feet of shadow remained, the leopard sprang on to the bank in full view of the men. It growled loudly as it leapt. The men, as one, turned and fled. In their confusion, some dropped their torches. But it did not matter. Jim hit the leopard in the chest with a charge of shot at a range of eighteen feet.

The men, shamed by their fear, were spared a castigation from Jim and together they all went up to the village with the man-eater suspended from a bamboo pole. The villagers rejoiced throughout the night whilst Jim returned to his bout of malaria.

So ended the first three man-eaters that Jim went after. He was pleased with himself at having shot two in the one year. Yet the fact remains that he did wait a long time after hearing of the animals' reigns of terror before he actually set about knocking them from their gory thrones.

9

A Time of Gradual Realisations

Jim resigned from the Naini Tal Municipal Board in 1910. He had not been able to attend meetings regularly and this upset him and irked some of his fellow councillors. He was too busy not only with the business of F. E. G. Mathews, which was in fact run by a manager and, later, Maggie and Mary Doyle, but also with his railway contract at Mokameh Ghat.

After the First World War, however, and Jim's giving up his contract with the railway, he settled more permanently in Naini Tal to run his business and extend it and to take a more active part in local life. His mortgage on the hardware firm settled, he dabbled in other fresh business ventures. During the Twenties, in addition to his farming in Africa, the Naini Tal store, estate agency, property dealing, contracting business and tenant farmholding in Choti Haldwani, he also established a brokerage business and was reputedly involved in setting up a local bank in Naini Tal for which he provided the land upon which the building was erected. This fact has never been substantiated, but it may be that the bank concerned was the one built behind the church of St John-in-the-Wilderness, although this was founded before the First World War. It failed and, after some years as a private residence, became a boarding house and subsequently The Swiss Hotel.

Mary Corbett was a woman for whom money was important. Very important, indeed. It did not only buy the necessities of life and the luxuries thereafter – although there were not many of those in Gurney House – nor did it merely buy security through investment or saving. It also bought position, respectability, recognition and social opportunity. She wanted this beyond everything else save her multitudinous family's welfare. To be accepted into the social whirl of Naini Tal was something paramount in her mind. She was domiciled and knew it and wanted to be rid of the stigma she felt it implied.

In the last years of her life, Mary Corbett was regarded as a part of the core of Naini Tal. Socially high-ranking in the church congregation, she was accepted but it had not always been so. The wife of the postmaster was hardly the wife of the brigadier, especially when the postmaster had previously been a non-commissioned soldier. Yet, as the decades passed, Mary Corbett became less associated with her husband and more associated with her family who had moved out into life to become doctors and engineers, a local businessman of some repute (and business acumen) and considerable courage. Even, by the closing decades of the nineteenth century, her eldest son Tom had a recognised position since he had taken over his father's job and built it up with efficiency and good administration. With the growth of Naini Tal, so grew the communications network of which Tom was the local controller.

Jim inherited, or was taught, the fact that money was all-important and talked. He was not a spendthrift by any means. He was generous and philanthropic but never riskily so: he did not part with what he could ill afford to lose. With his knowledge of financial matters swelling in him, he was soon to see the advantages of investment and, throughout his later life, he was shrewd and canny enough to spread his money about. The financial pitfalls and peaks of the economy of the western world made him aware of what could happen in the tiny world of Kumaon, the Naini Tal banks and the offices of his store and agency. He started, in the late Twenties, to salt money away in annuities for himself and Maggie, and for relatives to whom he felt the need to offer some security. Until just before his death, he continued to purchase such covenants and underwrite them in the names of nephews or cousins.

Regardless of his personal wealth, Jim always lived simply. Until his old age, he seldom wore a wristwatch except in Naini Tal and dressed most of the while for the jungle in shorts, knee-high socks, heavy shoes, a shirt and a 'bush' jacket. He wore an assortment of hats, though seldom a topee. When at Kaladhungi, he preferred to sleep in his tent rather than his bedroom and, in Naini Tal, he slept in the house but with the windows wide open regardless of the temperature outside. He did not own a radio until the Second World War and did not own a car as long as he lived in India. He did, on the other hand, own several pad elephants with their mahouts, a number of horses and ponies and a variety of *gharries*, carts and the like. So far as one can tell he did not fly before 1944 but preferred to travel by sea.

Of sea journeying, however, he did a good deal.

Throughout the Twenties, Jim travelled annually to Tanganyika and, in the last few years of the decade, to Kenya as well. He went there to look after the continuation of his interests in the land he shared with Percy Wyndham and to go on safari with his old friend. For a few months in the winter of every year, Jim took the train to Bombay and caught a steamer to Mombasa or Dar es Salaam. Once there, he boarded another train or hired a motor vehicle to take him to Arusha.

After a few days of rest in the brick-built house on the estate – of which Jim had proudly laid many of the bricks himself – the two men, with a few African guides and camp servants, set off into the bush.

In those days, before the massive agricultural programmes of immediately before and after the Second World War, Tanganyika was mostly virgin African grasslands. Unharmed by mankind, a huge wildlife population occupied it in harmony with the local tribes. The lion ruled supreme with no enemies other than the occasional Masai warrior-making, manhood-proving party and the increasingly present white man with his rifle. The wildebeest herds could number over one million animals. Elephants were common though already heavily hunted for their ivory. Rhinos were still abundant, hippos occupied all the permanent water (with crocodiles) and the antelope population numbers could only be quessed at.

Jim and Percy hunted to their hearts' content. They shot for the pot, for sport, for trophies. They tracked for the danger and the fun of the chase. Totally different rules applied in the grasslands of Africa. Lions did not behave like tigers: cheetahs were a new animal altogether: leopards lived in different sylvan environments in Africa and hunted in different ways – they even had different markings. And man-eating was virtually unknown.

It was these trips to Africa that first set Jim thinking about what, fifty years later, has come to be called 'conservation'. Riding for great distances through the tall grass on horseback or in a motor truck, camping under thorn-trees with the land around as flat as it could be –

certainly after the Siwalik Hills of Kumaon – Jim got to thinking. Once upon a time, India must have been like this . . .

Certainly, there was no shortage of game in the Kumaon hills. And yet there were pressures upon that game that were increasing by the year and Jim, spending some months away and in an utterly different place, was able to see what was going on with an objectivity that was perhaps lost on some of those back in India.

There was little to upset the balance of nature in Tanganyika at the time. Bush fires, started by lightning or other natural causes, did scorch the land yet this was not a destructive process but a regenerative one. Drought was nature's way of trimming the animal population – albeit vast – to manageable size. Few outside influences impinged upon the wildlife. Wildebeest were killed in minuscule numbers to provide tribesmen with meat, leather or blood for drinking: zebras were killed for their leather rather than their decorative skins: antelope were eaten. No one took more than they needed.

In India, he saw the opposite going on. There, he thought, the land was being exploited without due regard to the long-term future. Trees were not seen as a vital part of the ecology of the area – or the planet, as they now are, or should be – and were counted not in value to nature, but in rupees per trunk. Soil was not there to enrich the forest and provide for the animals but to extend the crop harvest. And the animals themselves were there for the sport of the upper classes (European or Indian) rather than the feeding of the locals who either did not eat meat or were cutting down the forest to feed or provide pasture for their own herds of domesticated animals and whereas the African bush soon recovered from natural devastation, in India this would not be the case. Once stripped of trees, the hills would remain barren.

Of course, this realisation did not come to Jim in a flash of inspiration. It came upon him gradually over the years. In the meantime, he continued to bring down his trophies with the pleasure of the hunter glistening in his eyes. Perhaps it is fair to say that Africa was a release for him in that he didn't feel so guilty shooting where there was such abundance. Certainly, he took a great pride in his African shooting, shipping the best head of antelope back to Naini Tal.

There is a conflict of ideals in Jim which he never truly resolved. On the one hand, he slowly became a fierce preserver of the natural world, fighting (literally, with his fists, on one occasion) on the behalf of beleaguered tigers and cheetal and tracts of virgin forest and yet, in

Africa, he took part in the beginning of a similar denudation of nature. He staunchly defended the jungles and yet he felled large areas of it to extend the farmlands of Choti Haldwani. He attacked environmental change for the sake of progress and yet he drained the *terai* for crops. He was heavily critical of those who shot for sport (particularly tigers) and yet he himself continued to organise tiger drives until the Second World War. He collected birds' eggs yet wanted to preserve the birdlife: he collected butterflies but did not, much to the chagrin of some of his friends, mount them properly for display or look after them in a worthy manner. His specimens lay pinned to their cork with their wings dropping, hiding their colours, and their fragile antennae soon snapped off.

The sum of it is that in Jim Corbett was the conflict of conservation. He was from an era that had no solid answers, only loud and vital questions. It is not right to criticise him for his apparent double standards for he was not a man who was in a position – geographically or historically – to fully assess what was going on. He was more an alarm trumpet sounding than a soldier fighting at the barricades. He was the one who alerted the guard of the future. It was hard for him to be rid of the habits of a lifetime. Posterity owes him a debt for having woken up consciences, even if his own was still just a little sleepy.

From 1919, Jim took an active part in city matters. His ill-attended membership of the town board ten years before was something he did not intend to repeat. One of his first acts after being voted on to the committee was to provide a civic amenity for Naini Tal. On the Flats at the head of the *tal*, where many gathered in the evenings and where the Europeans played polo from time to time, Jim paid for the construction of a bandstand on the water's edge. For this, he gave to the town the sum of seven thousand three hundred rupees. The bandstand cost four thousand rupees and the balance of the money was earmarked to provide a reading room for soldiers in the town. Whether or not this was set up is uncertain, but what is a certainty is that the bandstand was constructed and remains to this day as a very incongruous-looking structure indeed, much renovated, somewhat altered and painted in garish red, white and blue.

It would be unkind to imply that the bandstand bought Jim his place on the committee for he was already one of the town's most successful businessmen. The fact remains that, in the September of 1920, Jim took over the recently vacated vice-chairmanship of the municipal board from J. R. Muirhead who had replaced him in 1910.

The committee started on a programme of considerable development. House taxation was increased, which could not have pleased Jim, a small laboratory was set up to monitor the town's drinking water supply, a burning *ghat* was provided, trees were planted, drainage was improved and standards were set for traders in the bazaar. The committee met every month and Jim attended all but one meeting when he was away 'on business' in East Africa.

In his first few years on the board, nothing would keep him from the meetings and this leads to one of the most astonishing facts about Jim and his physical abilities. For some months of each year, Jim and Maggie lived in Kaladhungi. Jim, in order to attend meetings, would walk from Kaladhungi to Naini Tal, sit in committee and then walk home afterwards. This seems easy enough until one realises that Naini Tal is some five and a half thousand feet higher than Kaladhungi, that the mule and doolie track was unmetalled, that it was winter so the last thousand feet of the journey could take place in deep snow, that the way passed through tiger- and leopard-inhabited jungle and that the air in Naini Tal is much thinner than that lower down. Leaving just after breakfast, Jim was in Naini Tal by mid-morning for the beginning of business. He was home in time for supper.

Within three years, he was the senior vice-chairman and had set into plan his first conservationist ideas. In 1923, he passed the motion prohibiting night fishing for mahseer in Naini Tal lake, in order to preserve the stocks. (There is a local legend that Corbett first stocked the lake with these huge fish, but that is uncertain.) He was also intent on preserving the beauty of the town and made sure that planning requirements were strictly adhered to and inviolate.

Until 1926, Jim retained his senior vice-chairmanship and he regularly turned up at meetings not only of the general municipal board but also those of the finance, tolls and taxes and public works committees on all of which he was a keen and active member. From 1927 onwards, he was a less regular attender although he remained a fully participating member on the general municipal board until October, 1940.

During his twenty years of committee work, Jim brought about some important changes to Naini Tal. As a finance committee member, he successfully sought to reduce the impact of the Depression in the Thirties upon the town by cutting expenditure in an austerity drive and by limiting spending on capital projects. He framed and introduced by-laws for the use of bicycles in the town and unsuccessfully petitioned for the placing underground of the unsightly power cables that brought electricity to Naini Tal in the early Twenties. He had steps built at the Flats to make it more of a stadium for the town's sports. Extending his by-laws on night fishing, he had anglers' platforms constructed around the lake and designated these to be the only places from which fishing could be conducted at the reduced fee of one rupee rental per platform per month: he also restricted fishing on certain stretches of the bank on the grounds of breeding and public health. He championed the plight of the overworked pack mules, donkeys and ponies in the town and saw that they had at least one day's break from work per week. In 1938, Jim was one of those instrumental in establishing the town's publicity and development department which made the first moves towards making Naini Tal a tourist attraction.

This quite far-sighted consciousness of the tourist potential for Naini Tal – which, perhaps fortunately, has yet to be fully realised – brought about a desire to ensure that the town, already staggeringly beautiful, remained that way. To this end, Jim pioneered within the municipal board several environmental issues. The first of these was unsuccessful not because of local, but governmental, opposition.

Always aware of the wildlife of the town – bears and leopards would venture into the outskirts in the winter to forage or scavenge – Jim tried to get the whole town and its surrounding area designated a bird sanctuary. Rules on the killing of wild birds were drawn up but rejected by the central government in New Delhi which had legally made this sort of declaration void under the Wild Birds and Animals Protection Act of 1912. Jim was not, however, to be so readily distracted or put down. He set about protecting not so much the birds as their habitats and, through them, the habitats of the whole locality's animal life.

Whenever the opportunity arose, Jim would talk with those who held sway over the jungles and peoples of which he was so fond. District officials, police officers, forest officers and medical personnel were always questioned by him. He wanted to know as much as he could about their jobs, what they were doing and why. Forest officers in particular were sought out and asked about a wide variety of matters of forestry and land usage. Many of his friends and acquaintances were forest officers for it was to these men that he related: he hunted with them, fished with them, had to gain their permission to hunt or conduct a drive in a certain block of forest and it was to them that he reported any untoward activity he came upon in his wanderings. He spoke the same language as the forest officers who spent up to nine months a year in the forests, on tour, living in camps and surrounded by the jungle and its population. A good number of these forest officers and conservators, as they were known, were even more knowledgeable about the forests' ways than Jim. Some found him to be good company, some that he was ignorant in some aspects of jungle lore, some tolerated him and some disliked his meddling in their affairs. To a few he was an upstart but to most he was a concerned citizen eager to share in their protection of the forests.

They did not always see eye to eye. Jim was very critical of deforestation policies and the taking of trees for financial gain alone. He moaned about the fact that when native trees were felled they were not replaced with their own type of slow-growing plant but with faster growing, cash crop trees that would mature as sound timber in fewer years. He condemned thinning because it introduced lantana bushes into the forests, despite the fact that these have, in time, come to offer a new and secure habitat for many of the animals – especially birds – which Jim was eager to save.

He was unable to affect government policy on forestry but within Naini Tal he was able to be somewhat more effective. His initial move was to enforce the licensing and therefore control of goats. These creatures were used as pack animals as well as food and Jim was quick to note what damage the goats could do to the forest if they were turned into it to graze: this was brought home even more forcibly to him when several strayed into the large grounds of Mount Pleasant (the house in which Jim lived until 1934 when he moved into Gurney House with Maggie) and stripped bare in next to no time some of the cover near to the house to which barking deer came.

Mount Pleasant – an understatement of a name if ever there was one – stood on the upper slopes of Ayarpatha hill, to the south-west of the town and on its very fringes. The oak forests came right up to and surrounded the house and wild creatures abounded in its secluded grounds which Jim jealously guarded. The forests were, Jim knew, vital to the area. They not only gave sanctuary to wildlife but they protected the soil from leaching and the roots held the hills in place. The landslip of his youth had been partially caused by the removal of established trees to ensure a better panorama for the houses constructed above the town.

The public works committee, of which Jim was for some years

chairman, was responsible for the giving of permission for trees to be felled inside the town limits, which interestingly included some substantial tracts of forest. Lopping of branches was even forbidden without permission, which led to an altercation with one of the local Christian priests who wished to remove some boughs from trees below his mission sanatorium so that the patients could see a clock tower. Whenever felling was permitted, it was invariably accompanied by the statutory stipulation that the felled tree be replaced with at least one other of the same type which had to be protected and guaranteed to survive. The rules were strict and unswervingly applied.

In this way, through the committees and later by his position in society, Jim helped others to see and appreciate the value and fragility of their surroundings. Until the end of the Second World War, Naini Tal lived under the influence of Jim and his committee colleagues: since then, much of that which he and his European and Indian committeemen alike strove to preserve has gone. The hills around Naini Tal are today bare by comparison and the wildlife has largely vanished.

Life in Naini Tal was not all business and committees. As he grew older, Jim became more and more accepted as a person of considerable social position. Though he had never been shunned outright by the European population, he was often regarded as but a fringe member of society, especially before 1920 and his resignation from Mokamet Ghat. After the First World War, he was a more central figure in Naini Tal and his social position consolidated not only because he was now Captain Corbett (he was promoted to major in the reserves in 1931: his wartime promotion had seemingly been dropped or not ratified by the day of his demobilisation: perhaps it was only a temporary measure) but because attitudes were changing. The 'country-bottled' epithet was losing its cruel usage, more and more people realising that India was operated and ruled as much by the domiciled as by the expatriates. Despite this social relaxation of the rules, Jim never felt he had the freedom to mix to too great an extent. He had a wide circle of acquaintances, but only a small coterie of very close friends which included men and women from all ranks of life from the judiciary and district officer's department to the local headmen and farmers of villages all over Kumaon.

When he was not attending to business, the day-to-day running of F. E. G. Mathews remaining in the charge of Maggie and Mary Doyle, or visiting Tanganyika, Jim was enjoying himself. He played tennis passably well, billiards or snooker better thanks to Tom Kelly's tuition.

He hunted frequently and, when called upon, tracked down and killed man-eaters. He was an avid and expert fisherman who particularly enjoyed angling for mahseer, a submontane river fish that can reach massive proportions for a freshwater fish and can give considerable sport once hooked. At regular intervals, he went on fishing trips with friends or acquaintances, sometimes agreeing to go along as much as a guide or tracker as a fellow sportsman.

One such trip is well documented by an army officer, later a schoolmaster at Eton, Lionel Fortescue. Jim (accompanied by his faithful servant, Mothi Singh) and Fortescue (with his Indian servant, James) set off in September, 1921 on a fishing and shooting trip which Fortescue records in depth in his diary under the heading 'Expedition to Pangi & Chenab valley, Sept. 1921.'

How they first came into contact is not known, but it is most likely that Jim came across Fortescue in Naini Tal, either through a member of the club introducing them or by their meeting through matters military. Jim, for many years, was on the army soldiers' board, a charity looking after the welfare of ex-soldiers, particularly native ones.

They joined forces at Amritsar on 27 August and headed by train for Dalhousie where they arrived the following day. With coolies, mules and horses they then set off into the hills of what is today the Kashmiri-Indian border. They fished often, climbed to sixteen thousand feet and did some shooting, mostly for the pot. The weather was clear and the views of the western Himalayas beyond description: even Fortescue had difficulty writing accurately of their splendour. They struggled over rope bridges, of which Mothi Singh had such a fear that he insisted on being carried across by a goatherd who more normally transported his stock that way, up precipitous paths and across forested ridges. When they were not fishing, Jim hunted for he wanted a fine head of ibex.

By the end of September, they were back in Islamabad and heading for Srinagar in Kashmir where they arrived on the 29th. Going south from Srinagar, they headed for Riasi, fishing for trout and mahseer in the upper reaches of the Chenab, one of the main contributory rivers of the Indus. Their fishing here was better than previously encountered, despite some atrocious weather hitting them. They fished from the bank and used a large raft with which they shot some rapids. Moving in late October to Udhampur, they fished the Tawi river with much success.

On 5 November, Corbett left for home, Fortescue unable to persuade

Mothi Singh to stay with him to assist with a Madrasi servant who was stealing their food: Mothi Singh was, in Fortescue's words.

> 'a companionable little creature & very useful. His fidelity to Corbett is quite touching & is the only instance of a "devoted" servant I have yet seen.'

It appears that Jim let Fortescue down badly upon reaching Jammu for he was supposed to send supplies back but these arrived in Fortescue's camp without tea, butter and baking powder and with too little jam and calcium carbide – they used acetylene lamps in camp, the gas made by dripping water on the carbide and igniting it through a jet.

On the trip, Corbett's biggest fish was a 36-pound mahseer.

Such hunting or fishing trips were not uncommon in Jim's life, though few lasted as long as the one with Fortescue. It was in the year before the Pangi and Chenab trip that Jim had gone on the shooting journey to the upper branchings of the Sarda and Pindar rivers beyond Almora and Ranikhet, in the company of Robert Bellairs and, with a variety of friends or acquaintances, he had taken such expeditions on his short holidays from Mokamet Ghat for the whole twenty years he was working on the railways. It was on such an excursion with the noted *shikari* and game shot Eddie Knowles, in 1903, that he had first heard of the Champawat man-eater. Yet it was on his travels with Fortescue that one of Jim's subsequent major pastimes was first to appear.

Fortescue's diary entry for 9 September 1921 reads, rather disjointedly:

> 'In the evening we fitted up a dark room & I developed 3 rolls of film & Corbett. The exposures are all right but development without a red lamp in the dark is a troublesome and unsatisfactory process.'

The loss *en route* of a part of his developing tank did not make matters easier, either.

The missing words after the mention of Jim's name are most probably 'developed one (or some), too.' Jim had had his camera along on the journey, as well.

When Jim first purchased a camera is unknown. Photographs of the family exist from before the turn of the century but these were either large plate pictures or taken in a studio – in other words, they were the work of a Naini Tal photographer, most probably Lawrie or his company which Jim used for most of his still photography processing. From the immediate post-First World War years onwards the family album expanded rapidly and it seems likely Jim bought his first camera either in Britain on his way back to India or in Bombay upon his arrival.

Jim took to photography with the eagerness of a boy with a new and wonderful toy and, alongside shooting, it became one of his primary joys and involvements, the camera even eventually replacing the gun.

Although to discuss photography is to leap ahead through Jim's remaining years, it seems best to mention it now for with his growing interest in the camera came his growing interest in conservationism.

What has become of most of Jim's wildlife photographs is a mystery. He must, over the years, have taken hundreds if not thousands. His relatives, among whom his belongings are now scattered, have few. His own few surviving albums contain mostly snapshots of friends or large social gatherings – including tiger drives – held mostly in the 1930s. Lost are many of his original pictures of the man-eaters he killed, for he often photographed them either stretched out or skinned; one fascinating photograph does survive, however. It shows all the man-eaters' skins to date (circa 1935) arranged for a display in the garden of Gurney House.

Suggestions that Jim took to photography as a result of his friendship with A. W. (Ibby) and Jean Ibbotson or because he knew of the stunning night flash photography of tigers that was being conducted by F. W. Champion are without sound foundation even though Jim generously acknowledged Champion as one of the people to influence him in this way. Suggestions that Jean Ibbotson, who was an avid photographer, gave Jim his first camera, one of her own when it was replaced by a more up-to-date model, are groundless: he was definitely taking pictures before he knew either the Ibbotsons or Champion well, if not as seriously or purposefully as later. It is far more likely that he simply discovered the camera as did many people at the time when cameras were becoming more readily accessible to those who could afford them. They were modern and fashionable, one of the first instances of complex technology falling into the hands of the common man.

Certainly, part of the stimulus to go beyond taking mere snaps must have arisen from Jim's awareness of Champion's work in the early Twenties (which was published in 1927 in his seminal wildlife photography book, *With a Camera in Tiger-land*) and he was awed by what he saw and fascinated by the possibilities Champion was bringing to the fore. Yet the main drive turning Jim to photography was his conscious and increasing interest in the study of nature for its own sake and future, rather than the understanding of nature as a means towards a sporting kill.

Like many of Jim's acquaintances, F. W. Champion was a forest officer who, like his peers, was concerned not only with flora but fauna as well. He was wise – well before his contemporaries, including Jim – to the depredations of mankind upon the forests and the damage that could be done to a vast ecology. He was utterly at home in the forests of India and took to photography not merely as a scientific tool but as a means of explaining to the ignorant the immense beauty of such wild places. It became for him a series of challenges and the greatest of these was to capture the tiger, close-up, on film. This was easier said than done. Cameras, for all their apparent sophistication, were still cumbersome, awkward and restricted in range. Lenses were fixed and not inter-changeable. Telephoto lenses were unknown. If one wanted to get a close-up of a tiger, one had to get that close to the beast itself. What added to this impossible task was that tigers are solitary, very wary of mankind and seldom seen when the light is suitable. They appear at dawn and dusk and are nocturnally very active: in the daylight hours they are reclusive and well nigh invisible.

Champion overcame the tiger's reluctance to be snapped by erecting his camera along jungle tracks with a magnesium flashboard nearby. The camera and the primitive flash were activated when the tiger sprang a trip-wire. The photographic results were quite astounding and are amongst the best tiger photographs ever taken. Full frame portraits, tigers on kills (which were also wired), snarling, resting, startled tigers . . . Also, Champion did not keep to tigers. He photographed every animal he could from *machans*, from elephant and on foot – including tigers. The sadness is that this remarkable man, the father of wildlife photography, lived before the invention of colour film.

It was not long before Jim took his camera everywhere: his Indian bearers reported that he was seldom without it, even carrying a camera and a gun simultaneously. He captured on film as much of the fauna of Kumaon as he could but he did not leave it at that. He also photographed views that impressed him not merely for their beauty but also for their implications. He took pictures of forest fires, of people conducting a way of life now lost, of villages and rivers and haunted gorges: and he took family snapshots of Maggie, Mary Doyle, the house at Kaladhungi, his trophies . . . and here he came to appreciate a basic and very important advantage of the camera which he was to propound for the rest of his life.

His premise was that the photograph lasts for ever. Look after it, safely in a book or frame and protect the negative and whatever the picture holds is preserved for eternity. Trophies, on the other hand, rot or get dirty, lose their fur or gloss, smell musty, go mouldy and, within a few years, are only fit for the dustbin. By 1930, Jim was often heard to say that photographs were the best trophies – they kept and they did not entail the death of the subject. Why have a record head, with the longest antlers in the world, mounted on a wall when the photograph showed the same thing? Indeed, to get the picture, the photographer often had to be stealthier than the marksman for he had to get in closer.

A man always proud of his guns Jim became, from his mid-fifties, just as proud – if not more so – of his cameras. He updated his equipment regularly until 1937 when he bought his last camera: it served him very well until his death.

In the summer of that year, Jim went to Calcutta specifically to buy the latest equipment. What he bought was the Rolls Royce of cameras at the time. In the Photographic Stores and Agency Co., Ltd he purchased a Leica Model 3, one of the first of the 35mm. cameras. It had a black body with chrome trim and came with a template for cutting the film loading tongue and fitted in a three compartment, tan leather shoulder case. The lens was a Leitz Elmar 1 : 3.5 50mm. To operate it, one pulled it out and twisted it right to lock it. The camera had an exposure range of one second to one five-hundredth of a second. When Jim purchased the Ernst Leitz Wetzlar Hektor 1 : 1.9 7.3cm. telephoto lens, the universal viewfinder and the 5cm. expansion ring for close-up photography that were with the camera when he died and it was passed on to Ray Nestor one cannot tell.

Photography intrigued Jim but he was not to confine himself to still shots for long. Some time in 1928, he obtained a Bell & Howell 16mm. movie camera (then known by the trade name of Filmo) said to have been a gift from Lord Strathcona. Quite how Jim came to be so friendly with Strathcona is a mystery: they met through common acquaintances and had hunted for tiger together. Jim had been on *shikar* with Strathcona and had been the organiser of a drive for him or a party of *shikari* including him, but this does not account for why he should have given Jim, with such generosity, something as costly as a movie camera.

It did, however, open new possibilities for its receiver who quickly set about filming wildlife. He was probably the first film-maker to capture tigers on cine film.

Where still photography of tigers was very difficult, movie filming was exceptionally so. Although the cameras were driven by clockwork and were, therefore, at least no longer cranked by hand, they were fairly limited in their abilities. Lenses were unsophisticated and film by and large grainy and awkward to use. Above all, before each reel was exposed, the camera had to be wound up like a sitting room clock. They were also noisy.

After some not very successful attempts to shoot a variety of wildlife, including tigers – the verb 'shoot' now taking on a totally new meaning for him – Jim realised that there was only one way by which he could take cine film. It was impractical, if not impossible, to stalk the animals with the camera. Instead, the animals had to come to the camera. To this end, and anticipating the popular nature film-makers of half a century later, he 'constructed' a studio.

The Farm Yard was the section of jungle with which he was most familiar. He knew the game paths, wildlife (and human) inhabitants and terrain. He was thoroughly at home in it and had been so almost since infancy. Carefully choosing his site, by a typical boulder-strewn stream, he built a number of *machans* from which he could film the comings and goings of the animals as they came down to drink.

Up to a point, this was a very good idea. All the animals of the Farm Yard came to drink from the stream and Jim had specially built a small loose-stone weir so that the sound of the water running over it would to some extent mask the clatter of the film passing over the ratchets of the film gate inside the camera and of the rewinding. If the water was not loud enough he supplemented it with his own bird calls and insect noises.

It has been suggested that Jim did not arrange his outdoor studio until 1938, but in fact, although he might not have gone to the careful contrivance of fixing the noisy water until then, he was certainly filming there for many years previously. He was keen to film alone (as he was to shoot with a rifle) but he did show off his prize place to close friends as early as 1933 and he guarded it jealously against intrusion by hunter or poacher.

Despite his efforts though, Jim was still not getting tigers to pass through his lens. To get them, he took to using the same gimmicks to attract tigers to his viewfinder as he would to the foresight of his Rigby. He baited for them and he 'called them up'.

Baiting, already mentioned and often used by Jim in hunting man-eaters, entailed very securely staking out a bullock or goat and leaving it to be killed. Once killed, the tiger would stay in the close vicinity of his meal if he could not drag it away to a safe hiding place, out of sight of scavenging jackals and vultures. All that was needed was for the hunter turned cameraman and nature observer to sit in a *machan* and wait for the tiger to fancy sitting down to his food. Inevitably, this did not always work: the tiger saw or sensed Jim's presence and decided to leave well alone. When the tiger was that cagey, it was perhaps better to call it up, especially in the early months of the year when the usually solitary tigers come together to mate.

Calling up a tiger is an art in itself and it was one Jim could achieve with no small degree of accomplishment, having learnt the trick from friends in the forestry service.

To call up a tiger means to imitate another tiger so as to fool the intended beast into thinking that the false sound is not a man but a possible mate or territorial intruder. One needs to know the various calls of tigers and to distinguish between a lascivious mating growl and a get-thee-hence-from-my-area growl. Once the language was known, the imitation was acquired.

Tigers communicate by roaring over long distances (though not as commonly, loudly or vociferously as lions do), growling, quietly whining, hissing or spitting and purring. Indeed, apart from the roar, they have a vocabulary like a domestic cat's although somewhat amplified in volume if not in tone: for example, a tiger purring is not unlike a loud electric central heating pump at work.

To give some idea of what is involved in calling up a tiger, the following are the instructions on how to imitate a tiger's low growl: place the hands together in front of the mouth so that the palms are cupped to give a resonant hollow; press the nostrils half shut with the thumbs and take a deep breath; breathe out slowly through an open mouth, at the same time giving a deep-pitched and low cough-cum-hum-cum-belch well back in the throat – from the diaphragm as a singing tutor might demand; angle the hands to control volume and resonance. It takes practice but once mastered provides a very passable copy of a growl.

Over a kill or in the mating season, Jim would growl possessively or call enticingly, as the occasion demanded. He seldom failed to bring to himself the tiger or tigress he already knew to be in the area. The highlight of his tiger calling in this way is a quite amazing reel of black-and-white film – the fruition of ten years of filming, for it was shot in the spring of 1938 – showing seven tigers, including a white one, all present at once on a bank near to which are the remains of a buffalo.

Not all his filming was so deliberately 'planned': one film sequence he shot was obtained by sheer good fortune. It shows an intrepid and courageous goat seeing off the repeated attacks of a hungry leopard in a most nonchalant manner rich with humour and gay abandon.

The studio valley paid handsome dividends over and over again. Jim did not take his films for any reason other than to gain the utter pleasure of observing nature at her best and retaining it to show later to his friends. Filming was more rewarding and satisfying than shooting with bullets and Jim soon realised that the cine film not only gave him much pleasure but also showed to many others who could not go there just what the beauty of the jungles was like: with his films, he visited the schools of Naini Tal, hospital wards and small social gatherings and thereby spread the first lessons in the gospel of conservation.

What had begun as a hobby had extended into a lifetime of fascination. What made it also so appealing was the danger it carried and Jim did not escape mishaps.

Maggie reported after Jim's death that he always went unarmed to film in the studio and that he took great delight and infinite pains to achieve top quality results. He also took risks. She told her friend, Ruby Beyts, in notes about Jim's life that:

> 'He always sat in the same place, about eight feet from the ground on the branch of a very small tree under which the tigers had to pass on the way to the place where they fed. So as not to disturb them, Jim took up his position very early in the morning. By putting out his hand, he could have touched the tigers on their backs as they passed below him.'

This has to be taken with a liberal pinch of the salt of poetic licence. The tigers would hardly have approached along only one route and they certainly did not have a regular eating place: no tiger has that. And, though Jim may well have had a low seat – he was not averse to low *machans* or even to sitting on the ground unless in the province of a man-eater – most of his 'studio' movies suggest that the camera was at a higher elevation when the film was shot. Maggie, as the dutiful and loving sister, was making sure that posterity saw the most heroic aspects of her already quite remarkable brother: he did not really need her well-intentioned embellishments.

Whenever Jim was off on a hunting trip, be it with a gun or a camera and Maggie, who did go with him on occasion, could not join him, he always wrote home to her of his exploits. His photographic expedition letters to her illustrate his sheer enjoyment of photography and his love of the natural world. (See Appendix 3).

The risk of having the soles of his shoes polished by the back of a passing tiger was the least of the risks Jim ran in his filming. In the true spirit of nature film-makers, he would go to great lengths to secure the best footage and another of Maggie's anecdotes recalls how filming from a tree branch, rather than tracking and stalking, once nearly killed her brother:

'Early one afternoon, he set off hoping to get a picture of a tiger which he knew was in the jungle just beyond the canal (in The Farm Yard). Before he went, he told me to expect him back in time for tea. Some friends, who were expected for tea, duly arrived, and time went on as we sat chatting. The sun went down and I began to feel anxious as there was no sign of Jim. As darkness fell, my anxiety increased, and I wondered whether or not to institute a search. But knowing how Jim hated me for worrying about him, I hesitated to do this. The hours dragged by, when suddenly there was the sound of voices, a white face appeared at the window, the door was opened and Jim appeared supported by the two men who had accompanied him.'

(At this point it must be added that when Jim said he hunted or filmed alone, he meant without European company: he often took with him, unless stalking man-eaters, one or two Indian bearers or servants who would remain in the vicinity though seldom with Jim in his *machan*.)

'Barely able to stand, Jim collapsed on the sofa, obviously in great pain and hardly aware of what he was doing or saying. I at once realised that there was something seriously wrong when Jim, who was never in the habit of drinking alcohol, asked for whisky, which when brought, he drank at a gulp. When I asked him what had happened, Jim replied that he thought he had fallen from the aqueduct on the way home. This was not so, however. The two men who were with him told me that, according to Jim's instructions, they were waiting some way off from the tree in which Jim was sitting with his camera. After some hours, when there was obviously no hope of photography in the fading light, they saw Jim let down his camera by a string from the tree, and then they heard a great cry, and on running to the spot found Jim lying at the foot of the tree unable to move. They lifted him up and, supporting him on their shoulders, managed to bring him home.

'I had a bed brought into the drawing room for Jim, as he was in such great pain, and after a terrible night I set off in the early morning to go to the (forest *dak*) rest bungalow to ask some friends who were staying there for a few days to telephone for the doctor. This they did and after some hours the doctor arrived. On examination, Jim was found to have a broken back, severe concussion, and internal haemorrhage. As he was too ill to be moved to hospital, the doctor strapped him round and round with strapping, and we nursed him day and night. After some months, owing to Jim's amazing resilience, he recovered.'

During his time in bed, he was more at risk in the Kaladhungi house than he was in the forest: the chimney caught fire one night and the fire started to char the roof-beams before it was discovered.

Maggie mentioned no date for this accident and the authenticity of the story is dubious: there are no records of Jim being out of circulation for an entire winter, as this implies, and his doctor (no longer alive to verify the diagnosis) never mentioned the episode to his wife or daughter as he surely would have done. The local newspapers appear not to have reported the accident either, as they surely would have had they known of it.

What most likely happened was that Jim did fall from the tree but either slipped a disc or bruised or broke a few ribs. His being wound tightly in bandages certainly suggests the latter injuries. He certainly did not break his back which would have left him paralysed and a permanent cripple. (Maggie's wild exaggeration of Jim's injuries may have been coloured by her own childhood experiences: she once fell from a tree and did do some damage to her own spine which, though not deformed, did give her a stoop in old age.)

Had Jim been left in the forest without his servants to help him he would not necessarily have died but there is a likelihood that that would have been the outcome and it was not the only time that Jim was rescued or aided by his servants.

In the Corbett household there were always a fair number of servants. There was the *mali* (gardener), the *khansama* (cook), the *dhobi* (washerman), the *masalchee* (washer-upper and kitchen helper), a *mahout* (one per elephant when Jim kept elephants) and a *syce* (groom, one per horse when Jim kept a riding horse), a *buddli* or two (temporary servants) and, finally, Jim's bearer.

The bearer was not a *gun*-bearer but more a personal servant, a cross between an army batman and a butler. Jim had a number of these servants throughout his life and, as a butler might, they became close and loved (and loving) friends. Throughout his *shikar* stories, they occurred and re-occurred and he was never to speak ill of them.

The man who served him the longest was probably Mothi Singh who was not only a bearer but Jim's *shikari* as well, his hunting assistant, so to speak. He had entered Jim's life as a very young farmer in the countryside near Choti Haldwani and Jim had taken him on as his bearer. With Mothi Singh, he ranged the forests, went hunting and fishing and worked at Mokameh Ghat. A handsome man of high caste, he was.

'. . . keen and intelligent, gifted with good eyesight and hearing, could move through the jungles silently, and was as brave as a man could be.'

That Mothi Singh was devoted to Jim was recognised and marvelled at by Fortescue. It was a two-way devotion too, based not upon a servant/master relationship but upon mutual admiration and firm trust. It was with Mothi Singh that Jim hunted some of his earlier man-eaters and he was utterly reliant upon his bearer for not only his domestic arrangements 'in camp' but also for the organisation of beats and the provision of a gun at the right moment. On more than one occasion, Mothi Singh had gone in the early morning to find his master not knowing if he would discover him alive or partly eaten. To be bearer to a man like Jim was deemed an honour.

Jim always trained his personal servants very well. Maggie dealt similarly with the household servants. Visitors were seldom unimpressed.

When Mothi Singh died, his son Panwa stepped into his father's shoes. Whilst teaching Panwa his job, Jim saw him one day rest a rifle on the sandy bed of a dry nullah. Saying nothing at the time, Jim rattled the bolt and cleaned the mechanism with his handkerchief and walked on but, as they turned to head for Kaladhungi, Jim asked his future bearer to carry home a boulder he pointed to, saying that he needed it. The young man picked it up and carried it home where, on arrival, Jim told him to put it down and then reminded him, quietly, that one never rests a rifle on sand. It is an indication of the trust that his servants had in him that the man carried the rock unquestioning: it is an indication of the way in which Jim was venerated that the servant did not feel his trust had been compromised.

To list all Jim's faithful servants and to outline their contributions to his life and *shikar* experiences would be tedious but it is worthwhile to name a few.

Madho Singh accompanied Jim on most of his later man-eater hunts as well as ordinary *shikar*, angling and photography trips. He is often mentioned and, like Mothi Singh, often went to find his master with much apprehension in his heart. On some occasions, he was very close to the kill of a man-eater: in the case of the Chowgarh tigress, he was but yards away when Jim came upon the animal and shot it, in tortuously dangerous circumstances, at a range of eight feet. Having killed the creature, Jim stood still with delayed shock and as he

> '. . . lowered the point of the rifle on to my toes, Madho Singh, at a sign, came forward to relieve me of it, for very suddenly my legs appeared to be unable to support me . . .'

After that, they shared the honour – Jim, Madho Singh and another whom Jim had been forced to keep with him for to send them both back to the bungalow in that particular man-eater's territory would have been 'nothing short of murder' – of carrying the heavy carcass of the tigress up the hill.

Other servants include Ram Singh who was a bearer, a *khamsama* called Elahai and Bala Singh (he who died after believing evil spirits had entered his stomach to live there). And many more . . . They all receive a mention in Jim's stories in which they are all done justice.

Not only bearers held a close friendship with Jim. So too did local Indians of many positions from low caste members with menial jobs to *zemindars* (land owners), *tahsildars* (local tax collectors and men in positions of trust), *chokidars* (guards or caretakers), *patwaris* (village headmen and/or officials), lawyers, teachers, doctors and priests. Indeed, Jim's friendships cut across race, creed and caste.

As with his servants, these people featured prominently in his *shikar* stories: Badri who owned an apple orchard and the market garden at Mukteswar, the pundit who survived the Rudraprayag leopard, the priest at Dabidhura and sage of the god-protected tiger, Ram Saran the stationmaster. And Kunwar Singh.

It was Kunwar Singh who had taught Jim how to shoot with the Dease muzzle-loader, had (with brother Tom) given him his first instruction in jungle lore and who, many years later, had his life saved by his one-time acolyte.

In common with many local Indians, Kunwar Singh was in his later years addicted to opium and this, in combination with his already being weakened by malaria, almost killed him. The family were in preparation for mourning, the would-be corpse was gripping (as was the custom) the tail of a cow and a priest was sitting by the bed ringing his little brass bell and chanting. Jim drove them out, threw out the *ungheti* (brazier) that was smoking with burning cow-dung, the universal Indian fuel, and turned the cow loose. He then carried his jungle mentor outside, *charpoy* (bed) and all and gave him a long, loving and strict talking to. The old man pulled through because of Jim's help and because he told Kunwar Singh's son that if he returned in the morning and found the old man dead, he'd burn their house down. Kunwar Singh lived for another four years, frail but avoiding the poppy.

No mention of Jim's servants or friends would be complete without the inclusion of Bahadur Shah Khan. He was for more than thirty years the Muslim headman of Choti Haldwani.

Their relationship, which was the longest Jim had with any single Indian, was based not only upon friendship and respect but also upon business. It was through Bahadur that Jim had many of the day-to-day dealings with his villagers and through the headman that complaints were lodged and dealt with. However, within the locality of Kaladhungi, Bahadur also acted as a top bearer, *shikari* and even adviser.

The stories that involve the two are many. Before the First World War, Jim and Bahadur were walking along a path, the Indian having been at a partridge shoot with Jim and Percy Wyndham. Suddenly, ahead of them, they saw a leopard that was so big and magnificent that, with the sun behind him, Jim had thought at first he was a tiger. Bahadur claimed it was the biggest leopard in the *terai* and Jim decided to bag it as a trophy. As there were only the two of them present, Jim decided to flush the animal from a patch of twelve foot high elephant grass into which it had gone by burning it out. It was a method Jim was to find repugnant in later years, but early in the century he gave such an act no second thought.

They set about torching the grass and then, with Bahadur up a tree, Jim lay down on the track and put the .275 Rigby to his shoulder. Just as he was expecting to see the leopard break cover, he saw a bare foot standing by his head. He reached up and grabbed down a carter out looking for a stray buffalo, shouting at him to lie still and, to ensure that he did, throwing one leg over the startled man's prone body. The leopard shortly appeared dashing across the path and Jim fired, sure of a fatal hit by the way the animal flicked his tail upwards.

With the fire approaching, and grabbing the carter by the arm, Jim raced after the leopard and found it dead on the ground. So that the fire should not harm such a fine trophy, Jim took the carter's hand and closed it round the leopard's tail, his own holding the other's in place. Together they started to pull it away from the flames. As they pulled, the leopard looked over its shoulder and snarled. Jim had hit it in the neck and paralysed it. He did not put it out of its misery, however, but continued to make the carter pull the heavy animal away down the path. By the time they had gone fifty yards, the leopard was dead and the carter terrified out of his wits. The moment Jim released his hand, the man grabbed his turban off his head and fled, the material unwinding behind him.

It was with Bahadur that Jim hunted other tigers and leopards both with a gun and a camera and, in the late Thirties, it was he and Bahadur Shah Khan who executed some of the greatest tiger drives Jim ever planned and Kaladhungi ever saw when both he and his headman mixed with the highest in the land.

As the years of the 1930s passed, Jim began to feel disgruntled. He readily criticised forest officer friends for their policies or actions, he grew increasingly annoyed at what he saw as the rape of the wild places by European and Indian alike and he sensed an encroaching doomsday, even if he was unable to assess in what form it would manifest itself except that it would be without virgin forest and their most impressive occupant, the tiger. He felt increasingly ineffective. He wanted to halt or turn the tide of detrimental environmental change and he started to do what every true-born Englishman with a similar bee in his bonnet has always done in the same circumstances. He wrote to the newspapers.

As early as 1926, Jim had been writing to or for the newspapers. A letter to the *Pioneer* on 13 May of that year, from the Personal Assistant to the Raja of Rajgarh, asked for a report on the death of the Rudraprayag man-eating leopard which had been announced a few days before. On 15 May a brief report appeared to the effect that Captain Corbett had shot it on the night of 1 May: on 21 May, a congratulatory letter to Jim from G. B. Lambert, chief secretary to the provincial government, was printed. Yet, in fact, the India-wide interest in this man-eater had been aroused, in part, by Jim himself for, in the *Pioneer* of Boxing Day, 1925 there was printed a long article quoting Jim at length over his failure to kill the leopard in the October.

With his increasing indignation over deforestation and over-shooting, Jim started a campaign of writing to national newspapers sometimes using his own name and sometimes not.

The main published pieces show that Jim was an eager and competent author with a factual and precise yet modest prose style and an ability to thrill: his subject matter could hardly not excite a reader.

The *Hoghunters' Annual* of 1931 contains the first of Jim's tiger stories to appear in print. It was the tale of the hunting of the 'Pipal Pani tiger'. Not a man-eater, Jim went after it because it had been wounded by a local woodsman and he was afraid it would become one. Eventually, he shot it, saddened by subsequently discovering that the wound he thought would drive the tiger to take the easier prey of mankind was healed and not of any consequence. It was a huge tiger, too – ten feet three inches long and in its best winter coat. Jim noted the regret he felt looking down on the carcass. He also waved a red rag at the hunting fraternity bull by writing in the story:

'I make no apology to you, my reader, if you differ with me on the ethics of the much-debated subject of sitting up over kills. Some of my most pleasant *shikar* memories centre round the hour or two before sunset that I have spent in a tree over a natural kill, ranging from the time when, armed with a muzzleloader whipped round with brass wire to prevent the cracked barrel from bursting, I sat over a langur killed by a leopard, to a few days ago when, with the most modern rifle across my knees, I watched a tigress and her two full-grown cubs eat up the sambhar stag they had killed, and counted myself no poorer for not having secured a trophy.'

These were brave words in a magazine devoted to pigsticking and camping and edited by two noted hunters: Jim was definitely not a pigsticker (a sport whereby wild pigs were killed by lance from horse-back) but he was a camper in no uncertain terms and he was keen on that aspect of outdoor life. Camping brought one close to nature and Jim was, in fact, a member for many years of the Meerut Tent Club which was devoted to all outdoor pursuits and included pigsticking under its auspices. His admiration of Baden Powell was based upon a similar concept – the young, camping in the forests, would learn to love them.

In August, 1932, Jim published in the Naini Tal *Review of the Week* one of his most outspoken articles against those who would rape the land. Entitled 'Wild Life in the Village: An Appeal' (see Appendix 2), it was an impassioned plea for conservation, one of the first ever made.

Jim sought by his writings to give rise to controversy, but he failed. Few rose to the bait but some rallied to the call.

In 1931, Sir Malcolm Hailey was reappointed Governor of the United Provinces: he had first been appointed governor of the province in 1928. He was a man who believed in the same ideals of conservation as Jim and he agreed to be the patron of an association for the protection of wildlife in the United Provinces. Jim and an Oxford-educated Indian barrister, Hasan Abid Jafry, were appointed honorary secretaries. With these two men, Jim had a sound social as well as conservationist power working on his side. The governor was 'the Governor' and Jafry, a very astute and intelligent diplomat as well as a lawyer, was the political aide to the Raja of Mahmudabad. Jim was soon to move in exalted circles.

'The Association for the Preservation of Game in The United Provinces of India' developed into a grander organisation, 'The All India Conference for the Preservation of Wild Life'. Knowing full well that nothing was possible without good publicity and capturing the interest of the young, Jim obtained the approval of the provincial education department (they could hardly refuse him, considering his 'backers') to distribute any material issued and then, with Jafry as managing editor, and in collaboration with Randolph Morris, he inaugurated a magazine called *Indian Wild Life*.

The first issue, which appeared in July 1936, was a milestone in nature conservancy. Although it was implied that the magazine was a journal of nature study, its distinct editorial policy was protectionist. The front cover bore the corrupted proverb, 'A Bird in the Bush is Worth Two in the Hand'.

Jim's contribution, illustrated with his photograph of the tiger and the father of its final victim, was entitled 'The Terror That Walks By Night: an Episode of the Indian Jungles' and is the story of his hunting and successful killing of the Kanda man-eater in 1932. It is not a long story but it is exciting and unembellished unlike some of the other tales Jim was to write in his later years. Quite possibly, the Kanda piece was the first man-eater he put on written record. Certainly, it was, bar his quoted letter about the Rudraprayag leopard, his first published man-eater *shikar* story.

The next issue of the magazine contained the first blasts of anger. 'Wild Life in the Village: An Appeal' was reprinted preceded by a five-page article 'Written by the Editors' and called 'Wild Life in India'. The tone of this was set by the opening paragraph:

'Game Preservation wherever it may be undertaken embodies the same principle – the principle that, in order to afford game animals that peace and protection which will enable them to live and repro- duce their kind without damage to man, man should only be allowed to damage them under certain rules and should be restricted from ruthless destruction . . .'

What followed was a reasoned but emotional criticism of shooting laws and the need to establish a fund, raised from gun and hunting licences, to be used in conservation.

Three issues later, Jim published another attack, 'A Lost Paradise: Forest Fires in the Hills', which begins uncompromisingly with:

'"Stop! You fools. Stop!"'

which concerns forest burning and includes:

'When the tiger [sic] reached this pool the watching men saw she was carrying two small cubs.

'Crossing to the far side of the water she laid the cubs on the wet ground under an overhanging rock and turning – bounded back in the direction of the fire. Were the cubs she had rescued, one of which had a portion of its right hind leg burnt off, only a part of her young family and had the devoted mother gone back in the forlorn hope of saving the others?'

Not all the articles were written under real names. Some contributors wrote under pseudonyms, one of the most outspoken being 'Jungli' who was also a tiger expert. ('Jungli' was a derogatory term addressed to those who lived for the jungle and jungle sports). Obviously some were unwilling to attract the hostility arising from an unsavoury reputation amongst their peers.

The magazine ran to Volume IV, issue no. 2 before it folded: the initial volume contained five issues. It was published from Butler Palace, Lucknow at an annual subscription of four rupees. It was never an influential journal but it started a groundswell running.

There was no one event that convinced Jim that he should turn towards conservation. It was a gradual process of decision and despair but there was one particular day that more than helped to tip the balance away from slaughter in the name of sport. The story originates from the Reverend A. G. Atkins who was, for two years, minister of a church in Naini Tal. Walking down from one of the schools in Naini Tal towards the town, after attending one of Jim's naturalist talks, the priest asked Jim what had turned him into a photographer rather than a hunter. He related the story in an article for *The Hindustan Times* a year after Jim's death: Jim

'. . . had always been fond of *shikar* in the ordinary sense of the term, going out for hunting or shooting with not much thought of anything else but the fun and sport of it. He was known as a skilled jungle man and was often asked to lead parties out for a good shoot. One day he was out with three military officers in one of the lake and river areas of North India. They came upon a large batch of waterfowl, literally thousands of them. The officers began shooting; they went on and on, following and killing their game till they had killed over three hundred. They could not possibly carry them away for any use; it was simply unrestrained slaughter for the crude pleasure of it. Said Jim: "That sickened me and opened my eyes to what ordinary uninhibited hunting and shooting meant. I resolved from that time that I would use my jungle lore for a different kind of shooting, and in that way I began to take photographs of wild animals and jungle life. It requires much more of my skill and gives me an even greater thrill to get good pictures of my animals than when I used to hunt just to kill."'

How much truth lies in this statement is just a little suspect unless one accepts that it was the shooting for purely unbridled and lustful slaughter against which Jim turned. Until the start of the Second World War, he was still not totally against shooting. He took to the killing of man-eaters for humanitarian reasons – to protect humans and to put invariably senile or infirm tigers or leopards out of their misery – and he did withdraw, by and large, from shooting tigers himself. But he was not to withdraw from organising big tiger drives for the Viceregal parties and others of importance nor did he fail to attend the annual partridge conferences when the senior Indian Civil Service staff of the province met in the winter for a week or so of organised partridge shooting, in the evenings and between the drives of which much social and official business was conducted.

What Jim became was not a rabid and tunnel-visioned conservationist, an anti-blood-sport maniac, but a man with a balanced view of the difference between murder and killing. It is important to realise this stance in assessing his character and it is equally important to see his attitudes in the light of his times. Wildlife and its environments were not under the out-and-out attacks that they were to face in the next half century; in Jim's day, the attack was but beginning and was still slight, no matter how insidious or potentially threatening and harmful. His value lies not in his withdrawing from sport but from his view that killing (and environmental destruction) should be tempered with human sanity, natural consideration and an eye for the future. The terrible sorrow is that his warning or temperate approaches have been all but ignored.

Jim was the archetypal example of the hunter who still hunts, *but in moderation*, and obeys the laws of natural regeneration and justice. As a hunter he was a sort of conservationist – it was to his advantage to protect what he shot because if he over-shot or overkilled, his hunting would cease for the simple want of targets – but this is not easy for us to accept today when, because of those hunters unlike Jim Corbett, we regard hunters as killers, not guardians. Times have changed.

To spread the message of tolerant protectionism, and to show the intrinsic value of the forests and jungles for their own sakes, Jim took to lecturing on jungle lore and life. His lectures were illustrated initially with still photos and, later, with his movies and he talked not only of the animals but also of the humans of the forests. He spoke to schools and colleges, in hospitals and homes, to social societies and church groups throughout the United Provinces.

Few records exist of those talks, but those who attended them have never forgotten them. Jim would arrive in his usual clothes, making no concessions for occasion, and preferred to talk on what he called 'the jungle telegraph'. He discussed the various animals and how they communicated and he would then go in to a routine of what would happen as a tiger approached, mimicking the bird and animals calls of alarm, changing these as the threat of the tiger passed. Not unaware of the dramatic quality of his performance, Jim would then have the lights put out and would give a few distant tiger calls, explaining as he did them what they signified. With his audience alert, he would suggest that anyone with a weak heart or disposition should now leave – none did, of course – and then he would give a full-throated tiger's roar. The imitation was spine-chilling. The lights would be rekindled and Jim would end his lecture with a brief but potent homily on protecting the forests and forest creatures for the benefit of all.

Despite his views on killing for sport and his determination to bring the public to a point of conservation awareness, there was one period in the mid-Twenties when Jim put all this aside. He not only used his gun and jungle lore, but he also used all the other 'hunting' tricks he could lay his hands on and that included some of the dirtiest, most unsportsmanlike in the book.

10

The Rudraprayag Leopard

Seventy-five miles north-west of Naini Tal and in the neighbouring region of Garhwal, next to Kumaon, is the town of Rudraprayag, at the point where the routes to Kedarnath and Badrinath divide and the Alaknanda River is joined to the Mandakini. With such associations, it is obvious that Rudraprayag is of immense importance to the Hindus and their religion for it is at this town that the holy Ganges River proper begins, made up of the two rivers that come together there, after beginning at Kedarnath and Badrinath respectively. For many centuries, Rudraprayag has been a centre for pilgrimage and, even today, it is the last outpost of civilisation before the long trek to Kedarnath: there is only one other, smaller town before Badrinath, that of Karnaprayag.

The Alaknanda is a fast flowing, submontane river which has cut its way deeply into the mountainous terrain, giving rise to difficult and dangerous crossings for pilgrims. The countryside around is awesomely beautiful with the hilltops affording breathtaking views of the western end of the Himalayas only thirty miles away to the north.

Between Rudraprayag and Karnaprayag, a distance of about fifteen miles as the crow flies and twenty as the river runs, there were, in Jim's day, but three crossing points of the Alaknanda. One was a road suspension bridge at Rudraprayag itself and, two miles west of Karnaprayag, there was another bridge of a similar sort at a village called Chatwapipal. Equidistant between the two suspension bridges was a perilous rope bridge (a *jhula*) of the sort commonly found in either India or daredevil Hollywood films.

On both sides of the Alaknanda River, though somewhat more on the northern bank, from 1918 to 1926, there hunted a leopard which lived partly on animal and partly on human prey. Between 9 June 1918 and 14 April 1926, it accounted for the lives of 125 people, put terror into the hearts of all the 50,000 villagers living in a five hundred square mile area (for such was the enormous extent of the leopard's hunting territory), disrupted daily life and made the annual pilgrimage of 60,000 Hindus to their most sacred sites all the more dangerous. The leopard caused great concern to the provincial government and brought entreaties from villages leaders and holy men. For eight years, the animal made headlines in the press all over the world, gave rise to questions from Members of Parliament in Britain and was the quarry for a good number of hunters. Three hundred special gun licences were issued over and above the four thousand usually in force. A reward of ten thousand rupees was placed on the leopard's head and it was local legend that the ownership of two villages went with the cash sum. Special hunters were employed at high wages to track and kill the beast. Local troops, going home on leave, were permitted to take their guns with them. Army officers embarked upon the task. Drop-door traps, baited with goats, were set up on paths frequented by the leopard: leopards tend to keep to pathways because, being tree climbers, the pads on their feet are softer than those of, say, a tiger, which can walk over any reasonable terrain. Human and animal kills were laced with cyanide, arsenic and strychnine. Small primed grenades were planted in kills with the aim of exploding when the leopard bit into them, blowing the animal's jaw off: such abhorrent and diabolical methods had been used in the past. All this was to no avail.

Stories of the leopard's narrow escapes from being killed were numerous and mostly true. The governmental reports contain some of these accounts.

The leopard was caught, in one instance, in a baited door trap. The local Hindus, however, were afraid to kill it for fear that, in doing so, the evil spirit that dwelt in the leopard, believed by many to be that of a dead fakir, would escape and enter them. They sent for an Indian Christian, who lived thirty miles away, to come to kill it: whilst he was on his way, the leopard dug his way out of the trap.

Two young British officers, with a wise eye to the geographical spread of the kills, realised that the leopard must use the suspension bridges at Rudraprayag and Chatwapipal to cross from one bank of the river to the other: the animal would not be able to negotiate the *jhula* and would not be able – or would be reluctant – to swim the waters which are fast moving all through the year. For two months, every night, the two officers sat out on the towers that held the Rudraprayag bridge suspension cables, one at each end of the bridge. Their long sentry duty finally paid off: one night, the leopard crossed the river by their bridge. Waiting until it had reached mid-span, the first officer fired. The leopard dashed along the bridge towards the other officer who emptied his revolver at it. At first light, they climbed down and found blood the trail of which they followed up the hill on one side of the bridge. Convinced the wounds were fatal, the officers organised a huge beat to recover the carcass. No dead leopard was found although for the next six months no human kills were made.

On one occasion, the leopard was driven off a human kill and took refuge in a cave. Bravely, the crowd of men following it dragged heavy thorn bushes and rocks to the mouth of the cave and sealed the entrance. Then they called for what the report terms 'a man of influence'. He arrived to find the cave surrounded by a seething, curious and vengeful mob. The report stated that the man

'said scornfully there is no leopard in this cave and took the thorns off the cave. As he took the thorns up, the leopard suddenly rushed out of the cave and made his way safely through a crowd of some five hundred persons who had gathered there.'

After surviving tracking hunters, traps, poisoning (for the leopard did eat of laced corpses), imprisonment, a fusillade of rifle and pistol bullets and several attempts at drives, it was no wonder that the leopard became a creature of folklore. That it was the devil incarnate in league with the fakir and with considerable occult powers at its command seemed quite plainly obvious to everyone.

Jim's close friend William Ibbotson, with his wife Jean, had moved to Garhwal in 1925 where Ibby, as he was known, was promoted to Deputy Commissioner. Educated at King Edward's School, Birmingham and later at Pembroke College, Cambridge, Ibbotson had joined the Indian Civil Service in 1909, the year after going down from Cambridge. He had served with distinction in the First World War, attached to 17th

Cavalry and 18th Lancers with whom he had been awarded the Military Cross.

The relationship that existed between Jim and Ibby, who was ten years the younger, went back to before the latter's marriage in 1921 to the time of their joint bachelorhoods. As with his former friendship with Wyndham, their bond was forged by a love of hunting and angling allied to that of India. Each man had considerable admiration for the other and Ibby was the only man in Jim's life, other than Percy Wyndham, whom he would allow to accompany him on tiger hunts and the only one to go with him after man-eaters: they hunted for two man-eating tigers (at Chuka and Thak) together in 1938.

In some respects, Ibby was similar to Wyndham and one could see the attraction his personality held for Jim. An eccentric, he called himself one of the Seven Devils of the Indian Civil Service, he was loved and feared by the Indians under his command whom he protected and badgered with equal ardour and ferocity, was an expert horseman and farrier who made his own horseshoes, cut his own hair using two mirrors and whose hobby, even when sitting up in bed, was weaving rope. Referring to Ibby, Jim later wrote,

> 'Of all the men I have been on *shikar* with, Ibbotson is by far and away the best, for not only has he the heart of a lion, but he thinks of everything, and with it all is the most unselfish man that carries a gun.'

Ibbotson's first main task upon taking up his Garhwal appointment was to rid the area of the man-eating leopard. As he was a hunter of repute, this was an appropriate decision by his superiors. And Ibby had, on receiving his charge, instantly thought of his old *shikari* friend, Jim Corbett who was already known as a successful hunter of three man-eaters, one of them a leopard.

It was during the interval of a production of Gilbert and Sullivan's *The Yeomen of the Guard* at the Chalet Theatre in Naini Tal in the winter of 1925 that Jim first heard definite news of the leopard. He had known of its existence for some time – it had been newsworthy for six years – but had assumed that the leopard's days were numbered with the attention it was getting. Standing at the theatre bar, he overheard Michael Keene, the Chief Secretary to the United Provinces government, trying to convince a group of army officers and senior civil servants that they should have a crack at the animal. Their response was considered and not encouraging: no one wanted to tangle with what was by now a hardened and wily creature with a more than passing knowledge of humans, incredible stealth and a reputation for courage in the face of attack.

Despite not having shot a man-eater since his hunting of the Mukteswar tiger and the Panar leopard nearly sixteen years before, Jim felt he might make an attempt for what was now officially called the Rudraprayag Man-eating Leopard. He offered his services to Keene and was accepted: at the same time, Ibby wrote to Jim asking him to try for the man-eater.

By now, Jim was in his early fifties and Maggie was not at all eager to see him go off on such a hunt. She tried to persuade him against it, but was unsuccessful in her quest. With six Garhwali porters and his current trusted servant, Madho Singh, Jim set off for Rudraprayag.

Just before he reached the pilgrim town, a *sadhu* (priest) on his way to Badrinath had been taken from the centre of a party of twenty men sleeping on the veranda of a shop near Kamera, two miles from the Chatwapipal bridge. Ibbotson had been in the area, though on the opposite bank, beating a likely bit of cover and on hearing of the kill immediately crossed the river by the *jhula* with two hundred beaters. The *sadhu*'s body lay where it had been found, draped across a stone field wall with the lower portion consumed. Ibbotson immediately organised a massive drive of two thousand men with several other guns added to it. They beat for the leopard in the late afternoon but it was gone.

On the evening of his first day, Jim baited with two goats he bought in Rudraprayag. That night, one was killed by a leopard but not eaten by it. The next afternoon, at 3.00 p.m., Jim positioned himself in a tree overlooking the kill and waited. He sat there until 6.00 p.m.: no leopard appeared and none of the jungle animals informed him of the presence of a leopard. As evening began to approach, and knowing that to stay out for the night in man-eating leopard (rather than tiger) territory, even in a tree, was foolhardy in the extreme, he climbed down, severed the rope by which the bait had been tethered and, with the utmost caution and watching his back as well as his sides and front, went off to the forest bungalow in which he was staying. In the morning, returning to see if the goat had been touched, he found the pug marks of a big male leopard superimposed upon his own footsteps: the man-eater had stalked him on the way back the evening before, only his vigilance keeping it from killing him.

The next day, a human kill was reported. A pregnant woman, seated in the doorway of her house cleaning the evening meal food utensils, had been taken. Her husband called for her, then, knowing her to be lost, bolted his door. His neighbours, hearing him call for his wife and receiving no response, rapidly followed suit.

The woman was taken silently struggling to the end of the lane in her village before she was killed: she could not call out as the leopard had her by the throat as leopards invariably kill this way. Jim tracked the blood spoor to the body which was in a ravine at the end of a terraced hillside field. Forty yards away – too far for a good shot – was a stunted walnut in the bare branches of which was a hay rick. The rick itself was about six feet high with a space of four feet under it, between the lower branches of the tree and the ground. Hay ricks were (and still are) built this way in the mountains to keep them dry and aired, to prevent them slipping down the hillside and to keep them out of the reach of goats and the like.

Jim decided to sit up in this rick over the remains of the body which had been partially consumed. That it was half-hidden in the ravine implied that the leopard would return to it though he had the reputation of not coming back to a kill. The signature of the pug marks on a path nearby told Jim that it was the man-eater that had stalked him two nights earlier.

Jim set about in an unsportsmanlike manner to get the man-eater. It was the first of several such unsporting attempts. He attached his spare rifle and a shotgun to stakes and tripwired the path the leopard had used. He then climbed on to the hay rick, with his back to the tree to give himself protection as well as camouflage, and prepared to wait. His experience with the Panar leopard made him doubly wary but – as on the previous occasion – the tree to his back gave him confidence. The leopard would not be able to get him from behind, which was the usual direction of a leopard's approach.

Darkness fell as a storm came up and just as the first big drops fell, the leopard arrived. Rather than get wet, it sheltered under the straw of the rick six feet under Jim.

As a precaution against the night being black, Jim had placed a white stone by the body to act as a marker. The man-eater and the body would be obscured by the darkness but Jim knew where the leopard would lie in order to eat. As soon as he heard the sounds of it feasting, he could judge direction from the stone and get a reasoned shot in.

The rain had formed puddles. The leopard did not want to lie in one of these so it shifted its feeding position, obliterating the stone. Jim waited. The stone became visible: almost immediately there was the sound of the leopard coming in under the rick. Jim saw a light-coloured smudge pass under him. He lifted his rifle and held it steady on the marker: as soon as it disappeared, he would fire at it. Nothing happened. His arms ached under the weight of the rifle. He lowered it. The stone promptly disappeared again. This happened four times in two hours. On the last occasion, in desperation, Jim fired at the tan smudge at close range. The leopard fled into the night. In the morning, Jim discovered his bullet had missed the leopard's neck by a fraction – the shot had been so close it had shaved off hairs that were scattered on the damp earth. The frustrating night ended with Jim having the sorrow of seeing the victim's husband collect the pitiful remains of his spouse and displayed unborn child for cremation. It naturally hardened his feelings against the leopard.

For the following twenty nights, Jim sat on one of the towers of the Rudraprayag suspension bridge. He was certain the leopard had used this means of crossing the river after his narrow miss. The suspension bridge had been barred against the leopard by thorn bushes in order to restrict it to one bank of the Alaknanda, but these were removed for the duration of Jim's vigil. Perched precariously on the towers, pelted with rain and hail, buffeted and frozen by the wind whipping down the river valley, covered in the grease from the cables and stung by ants which actually ate raw bits of his skin, he saw nothing. Only one living creature crossed the bridge in twenty nights. It was a jackal.

Before long, Jim was to have another close encounter with the man-eater. One night, he and his men were camping under canvas and in the open air, in an enclosure made of thorn bushes through which the leopard would not venture and over which it could not leap. The defences, however, had a weak point. A tree leaned over the thorn barrier at one point.

In the night, Jim was woken by a crack in the tree which had been partly felled. He swung himself out of his tent cot and grabbed his rifle that had lain across him, safety catch off. A yard away lay Madho Singh, snoring. The Indian also woke up to see the leopard's face in the bright moonlight directly above his own and on the way down. He screamed.

Jim rocketed out of the tent to see the leopard bounding up a bank. Racing to the thorn 'gate', Jim ran out into the field in which they were camped. A jackal alarmed on the hill above.

Soon afterwards, a cow was killed by the leopard in a small hamlet half a mile away from where Jim had nicked the animal's neck. The leopard had entered a small house in which were kept some cows. It had killed one, dragged it to the door but finding itself unable to get its meal through the opening, had eaten it there. Ibby and Jim had themselves locked into the room for the night, incongruously eating sandwiches and drinking tea during the dark hours. The leopard, typically, did not return to the building although it was in the habit of regularly patrolling the village -- claw marks on all the house doors showed where it had tried to force entry to get at the occupants.

Two days later, another cow was killed in identical circumstances close to the bungalow in and around which Jim and the Ibbotsons were camping. Once again, nearby, there was a new, sixteen foot high hay rick on a two foot high platform. This was dismantled, moved nearer to the house and reassembled to look like a rick. In truth, it was a highly camouflaged, two storey *machan* made of wire netting, poles and rope. As dusk approached, Ibby sat on the top floor and Jim below him. Both made holes through which to shoot and settled down, incommunicado, to wait.

The moon rose brilliantly.

At 10.00 p.m., the leopard arrived and slid under the platform as he had done at the scene of the dead pregnant woman. At this moment, Ibby got cramp and moved slightly to ease the pain. A board creaked. The leopard flashed out of the shade of the platform and streaked up the hillside to the right, giving no chance of a shot.

Two nights later, a third cow was killed near the Rudraprayag bazaar but only after the leopard had spent an unfruitful hour trying to demolish the makeshift internal plank wall of the cow owner's house which separated the man's living quarters from the byre. It evidently preferred the cowherd to the cow.

By chance, the leopard dragged the cow off and ate a good portion of it in the open, in the middle of a stubble field. Twenty yards away from the carcass was another tree carrying in its topmost branches another rick. In this it was decided to sit again only this time the two hunters had another form of assistance which, under normal circumstances, would have filled both men with revulsion.

On quite a number of his attempts to bag the man-eater, Jim was accompanied by Ibby and, once, they thought they had it. It was this occasion that was the only time in his entire life when Jim resorted to the despicable.

From Moradabad, the government had sent Jim a gin trap. It weighed eighty pounds, was five feet long and had three-inch sharpened teeth on arms with a spread of two feet. It was activated by two springs, had a feather-sensitive treadplate and took the strength of two men to set. It was attached by a chain of half inch links and a three-inch diameter ring to a tough stake in the ground. They positioned it on the path leading to the kill and, to ensure the leopard walked through it, put small thorn bushes on either side to restrict his way.

Together, the two men climbed into the rick and hid themselves. It was one of the earliest occasions upon which Jim had an electric hunting light fixed to his rifle. Such things were not popular for they were heavy – small dry cell batteries were unknown in those days – and he was not happy with it. With the sky clouding over and moonrise three hours off, they waited. An hour after dark, the trap sprung. Angry roars ensued. Jim switched on the clumsy light and saw a leopard in the trap, thrashing about. He took a quick shot which missed the leopard and severed the half inch chain. Using a .450 weapon, it was hardly surprising at a range of less than sixty feet.

The leopard, caught by both forepaws in the gin, leapt down the field. Jim fired his left barrel at it. Ibby fired both his. They missed. Jim reloaded his gun in the process knocking the hunting lamp aside which now refused to work. Ibby pumped up the pressure lantern they had with them but a bigger menace was arising. Hearing four shots and being not a little optimistic, half the population of Rudraprayag started to come out of doors carrying pine torches and an assortment of lamps. Shouting for them to keep clear was useless. The hubbub they were making rendered the two hunters inaudible.

Climbing down, Jim and Ibby started to make their way across the field, Jim at the ready with his gun to his shoulder and with Ibby holding the lantern up over his head. Behind an outcrop of rock in the field was a depression and in it was the leopard. Jim shot it through the head at a range of less than ten feet.

Before them was a large male leopard. A study of its pads showed that it was the killer of the cow and would-be killer of the farmer. But Jim knew, somehow, that it was not the man-eater. He sensed that this was not the leopard that had eaten the pregnant woman and which he had so narrowly missed. The colour wasn't somehow right and the pugs were dissimilar.

The local Indians, however, were not so sceptical. The whole of Rudraprayag turned out to see the beast paraded down the main street in a torchlight procession to the bungalow.

Over a late dinner, Jim, Ibby and Jean argued the case over and over but no conclusion was reached. Over the next day, the belief swelled that the Ibbotsons were right and Jim wrong. This was the man-eater. To be on the safe side, though, precautions were to be maintained in the region and no jubilant telegram was to be sent to the provincial government.

All doubts were laid to rest two days later. Just as Jim was about to leave for home, the report came in that a young woman had been killed on the opposite bank of the river a mile from the Chatwapipal bridge.

The two men headed hot-foot for Chatwapipal and into an experience neither of them ever forgot. The details of the kill and what happened that night are best told in Jim's own laconic and thrillingly plain language:

'It had rained earlier in the evening and it was easy to reconstruct the scene. Shortly after the rain had stopped, the leopard, coming from the direction of the village, had crouched down behind a rock in the field, about thirty yards to the left front of the door. Here the leopard had lain for some time – possibly listening to the man and girl talking. When the girl opened the door she squatted down on the right-hand side of it, partly turning her back on the leopard. Creeping round the far side of the rock, he had covered the twenty yards separating him from the corner of the house with belly to ground, and creeping along close to the wall of the house, had caught the girl from behind and dragged her to the rock. Here, when she was dead, or possibly when the man called out in alarm, the leopard had picked her up, and holding her high, so that no mark of hand or foot showed on the soft newly ploughed ground, had carried her across one field, down a three-foot bank, and across another field, which ended in a twelve-foot drop on to a well-used footpath. Down this drop the leopard had sprung with the girl – who weighed about 150 pounds – in his mouth, and some idea of his strength will be realized from the fact that when he landed on the footpath he did not let any portion of her body come in contact with the ground.

'Crossing the footpath he had gone straight down the hill for half a mile, to the spot where he had undressed the girl, and, after eating a little of her, had left her lying in a little glade of emerald-green grass, under the shade of a tree roofed over with dense creepers.

'At about four o'clock, we went down to sit over the kill, taking the gasoline lamp and night-shooting light with us.

'It was reasonable to assume that the leopard had heard the noise the villagers made when searching for the girl and later when guarding the body, and that if he returned to the kill he would do so with great caution; so we decided not to sit near the kill, and selected a tree about sixty yards away on the hill overlooking the glade.

'This tree – a stunted oak – was growing out of the hill at almost a right angle, and, after we had hidden the gasoline lamp in a little hollow and covered it over with pine needles, Ibbotson took his seat in a fork of the tree from which he had a clear view of the kill, while I sat on the trunk with my back to him and facing the hill; Ibbotson was to take the shot, while I saw to our safety. As the shooting light was not functioning – possibly because the battery had faded out – our plan was to sit up as long as Ibbotson could see to shoot, and then, with the help of the gasoline lamp, get back to the village, where we hoped to find that our men had arrived from Rudraprayag.'

Their plans seemed sound and were considerably aided by the fact that Ibby had a telescopic sight on his rifle. This not only promised great accuracy over the distance to the girl's body but also added at least thirty minutes of light on to the day. The sun set and as it dipped behind the mountains, a kakar alarmed then ran down the hillside. It stood on a ridge for a while and barked and then made off, the sound of its calls fading. The leopard had arrived but was not to be fooled. The daylight thinned and the telescopic sight was made redundant.

Possibly it saw an outline of Ibbotson, for it had approached from a direction the hunters had not expected, but whether or not it did, the leopard started to head for their tree. Ibbotson took Jim's place and Jim climbed down and lit the petromax lamp which gave a brilliant white light. The leopard checked his advance and vanished.

Ibby took the petromax and led the way: Jim walked behind him, alert all round and with rifle at the ready. At this point, their well-conceived plan came horribly unstuck:

'Fifty yards from the tree, while climbing over a rock, Ibbotson slipped – the base of the lamp came in violent contact with the rock – and the mantle fell in dust to the bottom of the lamp. The streak of blue flame, directed from the nozzle on to the gasoline reservoir, gave sufficient light for us to see where to put our feet, but it was a question how long we would have even this much light. Ibbotson was of the opinion that he could carry the lamp for three minutes before it burst; three minutes to do a stiff climb of half a mile, over ground on which it was necessary to change direction every few steps to avoid huge rocks and thorn bushes, and possibly followed – actually followed, as we found later – by a man-eater, was a terrifying prospect.'

By sheer good fortune, they reached a farm and Jim kicked on the door to be let in. No one inside stirred. He rattled his matches and shouted that unless the door was opened immediately, he would set fire to the thatch. The door opened, Ibby and Jim fell in and slammed it shut behind themselves. Ibby promptly extinguished the now red-hot lamp which by now was dangerously near to exploding.

Hearing that their men had arrived at some buildings further along the hillside, they borrowed a guttering lantern with very little oil remaining in it and headed off once more into the night.

'More buffalo wallows and more sunken rocks; but with the glimmer of light to help us, we made good progress, and, finding the second lot of steps we had been instructed to climb, we mounted them and found ourselves in a long courtyard facing a row of two-storey buildings extending to the right and to the left, every door of which was fast shut, and not a glimmer of light showed anywhere.

'After calls to our men a door was opened, and climbing a short flight of stone steps we gained the verandah of the upper storey, where we found two adjoining rooms had been placed at the disposal of our men and ourselves. While the men were relieving us of the lamp and our rifles, a dog arrived from nowhere. He was just a friendly village pye, and after sniffing around our legs and wagging his tail, he went towards the steps up which we had just come. The next second, with a scream of fear followed by hysterical barking, he backed towards us with all his hair on end.

'The lantern we had been lent had died on us as we reached the courtyard, but our men had procured its twin brother, and

Ibbotson held it at all angles while I hurriedly reloaded my rifle, he could not get its light to illuminate the ground eight feet below.

'By watching the dog, it was possible to follow the movements of the leopard, and when the leopard had crossed the yard and gone down the steps leading to the footpath, the dog gradually stopped barking and lay down, intently watching in that direction, and growling at intervals.'

Two other attempts were made for the man-eater: the girl's body was impregnated with cyanide capsules – not a very pleasant task for Jim to do – but the leopard ignored her. A cow was killed soon after and the gin trap set. The leopard ate from the cow but avoided the gin. The cow was then poisoned but another leopard ate the meat and subsequently died. Again, the leopard followed Jim but didn't attack him.

After ten weeks of living with such experiences and 'adventures', Jim's nerves were ragged. He gave up and returned to Naini Tal in the autumn of 1925.

The following spring saw him back in Garhwal in the company of Madho Singh, and after the leopard once more. Ibby was unable to join him permanently but came and went as official business allowed. He was in the area when the leopard was finally killed.

For a fortnight, the man-eater had been operating near a village called Golabrai where it had, over the years, taken the lives of three humans. One of these had been a woman whom the leopard had taken in a most awesome and gruesome manner. At Golabrai there was a pilgrim shelter and the leopard had, one night, carefully walked over *fifty* sleeping pilgrims to kill a woman whom it had then carried back over the pilgrims, waking only one of them by scratching the sleeper's foot: the woken pilgrim thought he had been stung by something and went back to sleep. Also at Golabrai lived one of the few people whom the leopard had attacked but who had survived despite having had his neck pierced through to the windpipe by the leopard. He had kicked the animal off himself by placing his feet on its belly and heaving. Badly mauled, he was taken to the cottage hospital in Rudraprayag and lived.

Jim worked out that the leopard used the Golabrai to Rudraprayag road about once every five days. If he sat up over the road for ten days, he might get a shot at it. Ibby agreed on the condition that, if Jim failed this time, he would withdraw and the field would be open again for all hunters: Jim had, as before, made the stipulation that he was to be the only hunter operating.

One hundred yards from the pilgrim shelter and fifty yards below the house of the pundit – the man who had survived the leopard – there stood a mango tree and, in this, a *machan* was constructed. In the centre of the road underneath the tree was tethered a white goat with a bell round its neck. For ten nights, nothing happened except that, on the first night, a barking deer alarmed. Jim knew the leopard was still in the vicinity for it had killed a goat and a sheep during the ten days. It also broke down the door of a house but failed to kill an occupant as an inner door held up to its onslaught of clawing and rattling.

Ibbotson had, in his official capacity, advertised widely for other hunters to take up the challenge. None had come forward. On the morning of the eleventh day, Jim and Ibby sat to discuss the future. Both had pressing business elsewhere – Ibbotson was needed in his head-quarters at Pauri and Jim's farm in Africa was in urgent need of his presence which he had already delayed for three months in order to have this final attempt. They were therefore faced with two alternatives: first, to leave Garhwal once more at the mercy of the leopard and secondly, for Ibby to apply for leave and for Jim to cancel his voyage to Tanganyika – and both of them carry on with their hunting.

It was decided to defer the decision until the following day and Jim climbed, at dusk, into the mango tree. It was the evening of 1 May 1926.

Before this, however, the magic was done. A crowd of pilgrims had gathered by the tree to watch two snakes fighting in the field down the hill. They went down to see what was going on and found the two snakes: Ibby killed one and the second reptile escaped down a hole. The spell was broken.

The scene was set. In the pilgrim shelter, really just a roof on wooden and stone pillars, were one hundred and fifty Hindus on their way to Kedarnath. One hundred yards off, by the road, was a thorn enclosure enclosing a shepherd and his large flock of sheep and goats. The moon was waning and the early part of the night was in darkness.

The pilgrims were as much of a bait as the tethered goat that was asleep in the road. At 9.00 p.m., a pilgrim foolishly left the shelter with a lantern, crossed the road, relieved himself and returned to his fellows, putting out the lantern. A few minutes later, the shepherd's dogs started clamorously barking. The leopard had been attracted by the pilgrim and was heading down the road. At first, the dogs barked towards the road but they soon changed and barked at Jim's mango tree. The leopard had by now seen the goat and was using the tree as cover to stalk it. The night was pitch-black and the goat, although white and only twenty feet away, was invisible. Jim closed his eyes and concentrated on his hearing, praying that the leopard would go for the goat and not the pilgrims.

Minutes passed and nothing happened. Jim, by ear, aimed his rifle at the goat. Suddenly, there was a rush from beneath him. The goat's bell rang. Jim snapped on an electric torch he had tied to the rifle. In the weak beam he saw that the rifle was pointing straight at the shoulder of a leopard. He fired. The torch went out almost instantly but not before Jim saw the leopard jump over the goat and head off down the hillside towards where the snakes had been fighting.

The pundit riskily opened his door and called from his house but Jim made no reply. The man closed his door quickly. As he shut it, Jim thought he heard a gurgling noise. The pilgrims stirred but soon went back to sleep. The goat, unharmed, started to browse on some grass provided for it.

It was about 10.00 p.m. when Jim had fired. With nothing to do now until moonrise, he sat and listened and smoked.

By 3.00 a.m., the moon was up. Jim climbed as high in the mango tree as he could and as far out along its branches as he dared, to try and gain a better view of the hillside below but he was still restricted. With the dawn, he left the tree, the goat bleating a morning welcome and found a wide blood streak on the rocks by the side of the road. From its thickness and width, he knew his shot had been lethal. He jumped down into the field and, fifty yards away, found the dead leopard, which had slipped into a hollow in the ground. He was crouched with his lower jaw resting on the rim of the hollow. The devil of the Garhwal was done for but

'. . . here was no fiend, who, while watching me through the long night hours, had rocked and rolled with silent fiendish laughter at my vain attempts to outwit him . . .' Jim wrote. 'Here was only an old leopard, who differed from others of his kind in that his muzzle was grey and his lips lacked whiskers; the best-hated and most-feared animal in all India . . .'

The goat was returned to its owner from whom Jim had purchased it. The man bought it a brass collar and it was a major source of his income for the rest of its life. Ibbotson literally danced with joy. The killing of a snake, albeit not by Jim, had turned the magical tables.

On examination, Jim determined the following facts and noted them down:

Measurements

Length, between pegs	7 feet, six inches
Length, over curves	7 feet, 10 inches

Note: These measurements were taken after the leopard had been dead twelve hours.

Description

Colour	Light straw
Hair	Short and brittle
Whiskers	None
Teeth	Worn and discoloured, one canine tooth broken
Tongue and mouth	Black

Wounds

One fresh bullet wound in the right shoulder.

One old bullet wound in pad of left hind foot, and part of one toe and one claw missing from the same foot.

Several deep and partly healed cuts on head.

One deep and partly healed cut on right hind leg.

Several partly healed cuts on tail.

One partly healed wound on stifle of left hind leg.

(The fresh wounds had been gained in a fight with another leopard which Jim had witnessed some weeks before. The missing toe and claw were the result of the two army officers' hail of bullets on the Rudraprayag suspension bridge.) The curiosity was that the animal's mouth was black. Leopards usually have pink mouths. Jim hazarded the guess that this one was discoloured by the poisons it had swallowed.

That day the word spread faster than fire. By nightfall, and long after it, for the roads were now safe, thousands of people flocked to see the man-eater that had terrorised their lives or killed and eaten their friends and relatives.

Within a few days, Jim returned to Naini Tal and then left for four months in Tanganyika. The job was – at last – well done and he was well pleased.

So ended Jim's fourth man-eater hunt. It made him doubly famous and, beneath the mango tree was erected a painted sign, based upon a photograph, which bore a vague resemblance to Jim and the leopard. It read:

'Here . . . ! JIM CORBETT shot dead man-eating leopard of – Rudraprayag in May, 1926'

The man-eating leopard of Rudraprayag was far from being his last such exploit.

In April 1929, he shot the Talla Des man-eater, being nearly permanently deafened during the hunt by an abscess in his ear which burst as he was stalking the tigress. He was in hospital in Lahore for three months afterwards. On 11 April of the next year, he killed the Chowgarh tigress, a particularly daring and skilful animal who hunted humans with her cub, a unique occurrence: he had previously shot the cub.

During the Thirties, he shot another four man-eating tigers or tigresses – named after the places near which they were shot: Mohan (shot near Kartkanoula; May 1933[?]: no date is certain but Jim stayed in the Kanda forest bungalow from 29 November 1932 until 20 May 1933 and this suggests that he was, during this winter, hunting the Mohan animal for Kartkanoula is not too distant from Kanda and the bungalow there is the nearest that would have been convenient), Kanda (near Kanda; July, 1932), Chuka (April 1938), Thak (near Chuka; November 1938).

Quite possibly, Jim shot other man-eaters as well as these which were his renowned kills. In 1933, local Indians believed that he had shot a man-eating leopard at Nagpur and used this act to try and persuade him to rid them of their own local enemy. Certainly, after the Second World War, aged 71, he shot his last man-eater in the Ladhya valley. This was an easy kill, but for a man of his age some feat.

Despite the fact that she was very confident of Jim's abilities to hunt and track tigers and live safely in the jungle, Maggie was aware that man-eaters were extraordinarily artful and devious and, for this reason, she was always more than a little anxious when her brother was off hunting one. Jim, however, kept her informed about his activities and sent her regular letters whenever he could.

On 17 May 1928, Jim wrote from Dalkania that he was after two

man-eaters. It is more than likely that the animals he was after were the
Chowgarh tigress and her cub. Although he wrote in later life that he did
not set off after them until February 1929: he was not always accurate
about his dates. His letter, sent presumably after he shot the cub, shows
how much he kept Maggie in the picture:

'The remaining man-eater does not appear to be able to kill without
the help of her companion. Two women she has caught lately both
got away with terribly wounded heads, I am doctoring them and think
one will live. I had a shot at the tiger last night but it was pitch dark
and I missed – my torch is about used up. I expect the tiger will move
to some other part of the Patti(?) now and she won't be inclined to kill
a Katra (bullock) again and as she can't kill humans and won't
show up in the day I am afraid it will be next to impossible to bag
her.'

Another longer letter Maggie received was written on 19 July 1932
from the bungalow at Kanda and concerned Jim's shooting of the
man-eater there:

'I was only able to send you a few lines on the 16th for the reason that
the dak runner, who is an old man and has to do 14 miles every day of
his life, was waiting for my letter. So I was unable to give you any
particulars about the killing of the tiger and am doing so now. This
was the way of it. The tiger killed a katra on the 13th. The following
day I walked up to the kill, very carefully, and got quite close to the
tiger. Unfortunately there was a big tree covered with maldhan
creepers between us, and keeping behind the tree, we went up the hill
and I got my first glimpse of him as he was disappearing into a nala
(nullah). Just a glimpse and no more but as there was a chance of his
being the man-eater I took a shot. He was going up hill at an angle to
me and the bullet passed under his chest, hit his left elbow, carried on
and hit a rock and burst back catching him a terrific blow on the front
of the jaw. Both very painful places to be hit in, but only painful and
no more. He came crashing and bellowing down the hill, with, I
thought, a broken back, but recovered himself before he got down to
me and went crashing on across the side of the hill. As he disappeared
there was an extra loud crash and an avalanche of rocks went
smashing down the hill. Bakhtar and another man who were with me,

jumped and danced about saying "*Sher mur gia, sher mur gia*". But I was not so sure, and when I examined his tracks, which I eventually followed for half a mile and where he had been when I fired, I knew he had been struck by the back blast of the bullet in the face, but did not know that he had also received a terrific blow on his left funny bone. Well, that was the last I saw of the tiger that day. The following morning when I went to have a look at the kill, I heard the tiger calling not far from where I had tracked him to the previous day. I tried calling him up but he refused to come, so at 4 p.m. I selected a tree and sat up about half way between where he had called and the kill, which by the way he had returned to the previous night. There were a lot of his pug marks in the bed of the ravine and I expected him to go to the kill that way and selected my tree accordingly. At dusk I heard the kill being dragged followed by the sound of crunching bones. He had got to it without passing me and there was nothing to be done but sit tight and hope for the best. The crunching stopped after a bit, a langur called and when it was quite dark the tiger came down the hill, not directly from the direction of the kill, and came up to the tree I was sitting in. My back was to the trunk of the tree and as he came I quickly turned round in case he tried to climb the tree, which, however, he did not try to do. I did not hear him again at the kill but several times during the night he came and had a close look at me. (I was about a hundred yards below the kill.)

I had instructed Bakhtar to bring a cup of tea for me in the morning (I was sitting two miles from the bungalow) and to coo-ee to me from the ridge to let me know he had arrived. If I answered with a leopard call he was to come straight down to me, and if I did not answer he was to divide his party and come down on either side of the ravine throwing stones into it. Well, I heard him call some time after it had got light, probably about 6 a.m. or 6.10, and a minute or two later I caught sight of the tiger making off across the hill to my left front. It wasn't too good a shot, and I had been sitting up for 14 or more hours with my eyes wide open, however I took the shot and the tiger to my joy came straight for my tree and I finished him off at the foot of it. Both shots, I afterwards found, were beautifully placed. At the request of the villagers I allowed the tiger to be carried up to the nearest village about 1/4 of a mile away and after taking 40 feet of pictures I skinned him. His mouth, both forepaws and fore arms were full of porcupine quills. He also had a broken foot but it was an old wound and would have had nothing to do with his turning a man-eater.

If the tiger that kept on visiting me at night was the same animal that I shot, then the addition of the porcupine quills makes it almost certain that I have accounted for the man-eater. The last two human kills on the 23rd and 26th of March took place in the ravines on either side of the one in which I shot the tiger. There may, of course, have been two tigers in the ravine that night, possible but not probable. The villagers tell me that after Herbert(?) sat over a human kill, he told them that the tiger was very big; again, the chowkidar (sic) of this bungalow who for years was chaprassi to Burke and Whitehead (forest officers), told me on my arrival that he had gone with rescue parties to several human kills and in each case had seen the prints of a large male tiger. The animal I shot was a male about 9.8 or 9.10.'

A more moving and terse correspondence was sent the next day in the form of a telegram postmarked 20 July 1932. It was written on buff telegraph paper. Sent from Ramnagar, it read:

'TO: Corbett Gurney House Naini Tal
All well home tomorrow Tiger is dead Jim'

Whatever became of the cine film Jim took of the tiger is unknown, another example of a vital and fascinating historical record of his life being lost.

When writing the story up a few years later, Jim gave this episode a very much more exciting and heroic telling with the tiger finally hit as he was about to spring at Jim: the animal bounced off the tree and went tumbling down the hillside, staining the tree and a number of puddles with his blood. Then he vanished from sight to be found dead, later, in a pool of water.

Although most associated with the killing of man-eaters, Jim was not the only hunter who removed these pests from the Kumaon hills. The region was bedevilled by the creatures for years – until the Fifties, in fact – and forest officers in particular were known for their killing of human predators. For example, J. E. Carrington-Turner and Francis ('Henry') Ford-Robertson both killed a number of man-eaters: Robert Bellairs, after the First World War and before going off to manage Jim's farm in Tanganyika, had hunted the man-eating tigress at Gwaldam.

A variety of explanations were given for the plenitude of man-eaters, the most plausible being suggested by J. E. Carrington-Turner, a younger contemporary of Jim's who joined the Indian Forest Service in 1912 and who wrote and published his memoirs, *Man-eaters and Memories* in 1959, four years after Jim's death. He noted that most man-eaters, especially tigers, operated at altitudes higher than four thousand feet which was certainly true of most of Jim's man-eaters – his Mukteswar tigress was killed at the altitude of about five thousand feet. Carrington-Turner believed that the man-eaters were driven higher up the mountains by competition from younger tigers living in the more natural tiger country of the lower hill slopes and plains. It is a convincing theory: at higher altitudes there was less game and yet still human activity. The tigers, to stave off hunger, turned to humans and their domestic stock. Yet he also believed that scarcity of game, due to environmental and habitat destruction, was the prime reason over and above infirmity or senility. Man, in short, brought man-eaters upon himself.

It was Jim though, above all others, who became known as the man-eater hunter. This was due to his having killed so many, some of them internationally infamous, his conservationist attitudes and, later, his authorship.

Critic, Conservationist and Lieutenant Colonel

When Mary Corbett, Jim's mother, died on 16 May 1924, a large proportion of the European population of Naini Tal mourned. She was one of the oldest inhabitants and virtually a founding member of the town. Her position in local society was well entrenched and her loss was more than noticed. Her funeral was a grand affair and she was interred near to Christopher William. That she lived to be nearly ninety was a wonder and she was a local character simply because of her inordinately unusual longevity: life at an altitude and in the harshness of India had strengthened her.

For Jim, Maggie and Mary Doyle, the death of their mother was expected but nevertheless a terrible shock. Her mere presence had been enough to give them security and stability even into middle age when they no longer needed it.

After the funeral, life returned to normal for the family. Jim still lived in his own house, Mount Pleasant. Maggie and Mary Doyle inherited Gurney House and continued to live there. Winters were spent in the house at Kaladhungi and Jim made his annual trips to Tanganyika or off hunting. Maggie and Mary Doyle kept the family business going, the latter having been running her mother's house agency for some years.

For Jim, however, although he was much saddened by his mother's death, there was a slight change in the air. He might now be free to marry even though he was nearly fifty. It would not have been too unusual: European men in India, because of their work and the way in which they lived, often married late and then to women a good deal younger than themselves. Whenever an eligible woman had appeared on the scene, and Jim had shown even the most diffident or distantly romantic interest, his mother had seen to it that the possibility of a match was out of the question. As she grew older, so Maggie accepted the same role of match-breaker. She, like her mother, had a vested interest in Jim's bachelorship.

Not long after his mother's death – within months, in fact – Jim fell deeply in love with a young woman in her late teens. Her name was Helen. She was the sister-in-law of one of his forest officer friends and was out in India for a prolonged holiday with her parents. To say that Jim sought her company would be an understatement. He was smitten by her. She was beautiful, young, accomplished and flattered that an older man, and one of position within the Naini Tal society, was so keen on her. He courted her but with little hope, arriving at whichever house she was playing tennis or having tea in order to escort her home walking all the way by the side of her pony. She was much too young, not yet nineteen, and although she appreciated his advances, she did not feel able to return the love he offered. Nevertheless, Jim sought permission to ask for her hand in marriage but both his friends and the parents of the girl, who were on holiday with her, were totally against it. The couple came from utterly different worlds.

Saddened by these rebuffs, Jim withdrew but was not to forget the young woman: in 1928, he made his next trip to Britain by way of the Ibbotsons in Kenya. He took the voyage partly to see and go fishing with Percy Wyndham, who had a farm in Cumberland, but also to try a final time for the young lady's hand. Though he told Maggie that he did not want to make the journey, he had this other motive in mind which he was not prepared to divulge to her. He went to see Helen in Edinburgh but arrived only to discover that she was soon to be married.

It must have been a painful journey for Jim's stopover in Kenya would have doubly reinforced for him the sorrow he must have felt at not achieving a wife for he had had, for some years, a more than passing love affair with Jean Ibbotson. She was a very pretty and lively woman, with fashionable tastes and a degree of style who was spoilt by her husband who, like Jim, was much older than she. Whether her husband knew of the affair and thereby condoned it or not, is unknown but certainly, whenever Ibbotson was away on governmental business, secret billets-doux passed between Jim and his friend's wife, these often carried not by domestic servants but more usually in the hands of the children of other

employees. It was additionally tacitly understood that when Jim visited
Jean Ibbotson, he would leave his hat on a chair or table on the veranda
of the house and this was taken as a signal that no-one – neither visitor
nor servant – was to interrupt them. Needless to say, Maggie was
privately outraged by these goings-on, not so much for their immorality
or impropriety but because of the threat they implied to her own
security.

It is sad that Jim could not permanently find for himself a woman like
Jean Ibbotson. She was outward-looking and outward-going, lived the
life of the jungle, was an excellent shot and enjoyed the occasional
hunting trip. She was adept at jungle lore, in which craft Jim was her
tutor, and an avid photographer and supporter of nature. Once more,
because of his family, he had to accept the position of second-best as a
lover conducting merely a very secretive affair.

Jean Ibbotson's influence over Jim, for as long as she and her husband
lived in Kumaon, was great. It is only speculation to believe that she was
a moving power behind Jim's growing interest in conservation but that
she had a hand it in – through photography, perhaps – is more than
likely.

With Helen, however, his last chance at his own unhampered,
romantic happiness was over. He would now have to be content with a
sister, a half-sister and a wife that was India.

Whilst in London on this trip, he again lost his way but did not use
junglecraft to regain it. He wrote home on 29 July 1928:

. . . 'The thing that has struck me most in England is the orderliness,
good fellowship of the British people and the absence of pomp and
show. I lost myself the night I arrived, and it took me three hours to
find the hotel I was staying at. [Thomas] Cooks man at Victoria
directed the taxi driver to an hotel and in the evening I went out to get
some dinner and crossing many streets and dodging motor cars, I got
mixed up when I wanted to get back. I could not remember all the
turnings I had taken and as I did not know the name of the hotel I had
the time of my life finding my way home. The police here are awfully
good and do their best to help anyone. The people in the street too
are very obliging and go out of their way to direct one.'

His being a local businessman and landowner with a great reputation
as a *shikari* and the fact that he had killed three man-eaters, albeit some

years back, gave Jim an entrée into society and his friendships swelled. Through Wyndham and Ibby, not to mention his forest officer acquaintances, he met many others all of whom he impressed with his gentleness, candour, humanity and jungle lore.

He loved children and was befriended by many, not least the three daughters of Joseph (later Sir Joseph) Clay, the deputy commissioner for Naini Tal from 1925, who was to become Chief Secretary to the provincial government and later its Finance Minister.

Whenever they were in Naini Tal the Clays rented a house from Jim or Mary Doyle and were very friendly with them. Jim was a frequent visitor at their rented homes and they visited him as often, either in Naini Tal or Kaladhungi where they fed the Corbetts' pet cheetal, spent Christmas helping with the distribution of sweets to the Choti Haldwani children, listened to Jim's jungle and ghost tales, picnicked with him and hunted with him.

Perhaps the best insights into the Corbetts' everyday life come now from Audrey Baylis, the elder of Clay's three daughters who was, unusually, governess-educated in India by her father rather than being sent 'home' to school. She was subsequently to marry a civil servant and judge and spend much of her life before 1948 in northern India. Her anecdotes of the Corbetts are many, starting in 1923, and including her going tiger and leopard hunting with him, her father and a Major Mallock in the Christmas week of 1927.

It was a week of some excitement. Joseph Clay shot a leopard on 23 December; on the 28th, Clay came near to meeting his maker. They were all out shooting beaten peafowl when the beaters brought up a tiger. The tiger, appearing from nowhere, leapt out of the cover ten yards from Clay who, seated on a rock in a river-bed, jumped to his feet and started to make off: then he tripped and fell flat on his face. All thought the tiger had hit him. Lashing its tail and growling loudly with its ears flattened, the tiger then bounded towards the children and Mallock who had his gun to his shoulder and was covering the tiger but waiting for Jim to give the command to fire. The tiger stopped, went to where Clay had been sitting and then bounded into the jungle. Jim had shouted 'Don't shoot! Don't shoot!' but Mallock had not heard him. Jim said afterwards that he knew the tiger but had expected it to be some miles away in its customary territory.

On another occasion, the Clays had come across a single-tusked rogue elephant near Tanakpur which had scared them and, on reporting it to Jim, he put it to the back of his mind. In 1928, whilst the Clay family were 'on leave' in Britain, he shot it. From the elephant, he kept the tusk that was a permanent feature of Gurney House and one of Jim's conversation pieces: he asked first-time guests to assess its weight.

The Corbetts' life was domestically peaceful when Jim was not in Africa or hunting. From almond trees in the garden at Kaladhungi, Maggie made her own marzipan and almond cakes and, with 'wild' sugar and honey she made very sweet toffees and fudges. Her cheese loaf was much admired and envied, too. Jim played tennis and cricket and attended garden (as opposed to cocktail) parties. He sang and played the piano and guitar and went to the theatre and entertained friends to tea and dinner. He gave his lectures and showed his films. In short, he lived a split life – on the one hand a domesticated, business-man's existence with a house-proud sister and, on the other, one of great excitement and travelling.

It has been said of Jim that he was an outsider to the European community, only allowed into it when his services for a shoot or in the killing of a man-eater were required. This is not true for the years after about 1910. In his younger years, it was certainly the case that Jim was an observer rather than a participant in European society. This was due partly to the structure of that society but also partly to the fact that he was seldom present. Naini Tal saw him infrequently until after the First World War, by which time not only had society altered but Jim had risen as a businessman, *shikari* and ex-soldier with an officer's rank. It is therefore unfair to both him and the Europeans to say that the class snobbery of the last decade of the nineteenth century still operated. As regards Indians, Jim was popular with many of them, but hated by a few of position, especially those working towards Indian independence, who disliked his attitudes and saw in him a threat. He was, if anything, too popular. He not only killed man-eaters and ran a model village but he was also on the board of the association that looked after the welfare of Indian ex-servicemen and, in this role, he was (to the independence struggle) embarrassingly just, kind and understanding.

When Jim made friends, he did so in a considered manner. Known to many people, he was a private man and chose his close friends with care. Once into his small circle, one was cherished and loved, helped and advised. When the youngest of the Clay girls was tragically killed in a horrendous accidental fall down a mountainside near Naini Tal in 1946, it was Jim who wrote her long obituary in the *Pioneer* newspaper in touching, glowing and yet genuine terms.

In return, the Corbetts' friends were as loyal and as helpful. Though Jim was seldom in need of assistance, Maggie often was, especially of the more womanly variety. She was not a woman of the world and once Jim began, especially from the late Twenties onwards, to move in exalted circles, she was to find herself a bit out of her depth. Like her brother, she was mousily quiet, appeared shy and lived in a similarly simple way. Their cooking was done over charcoal braziers even after the arrival of electricity in Naini Tal and their material demands were few. She dressed usually in a 'tweedy' manner with a skirt, blouse and jumper: her shoes were invariably heavy and practical brogues that she had made to measure by a Chinese cobbler in Naini Tal. From time to time, she was persuaded (with difficulty) by the wives of friends of Jim to purchase and put on a 'party' dress to visit the Governor's house or, later, the Viceroy either on tour or in Delhi, but even then she was most reluctant to wear delicate shoes. To her, shoes were for walking and not for show.

Moving into the higher brackets of society had Jim organising shoots. When he began this activity is uncertain. By 1925, he was already arranging shoots for civil service friends and he controlled the beating at the annual partridge conferences, but the first drive he conducted for a pukka sahib, a VIP, was at Christmas, 1929 when he arranged a tiger shoot for the then governor of the province, Sir Malcolm Hailey.

This took place in the jungles near Kaladhungi and included a part of the Farm Yard. It was a successful drive and at least one tiger was shot, and several leopards. For Jim it was an added opportunity for him to indulge himself in his hobby of photographer – and the new branch of it, home movie making.

The Thirties were an exciting time for Jim. He shot man-eaters, involved himself in council and conservation matters, sat on committees, hunted though with less enthusiasm than before, photographed and travelled. He also started to write.

In fact, Jim had begun to write in the early Twenties. He had first committed to paper his jungle stories to send them to a number of Indian journals and to *Blackwood's*, the magazine back in Britain that was for nearly a century one of the best literary journals in the world and the best organ for short prose. (Ironically, Major Mallock had written up the episode of Joseph Clay and the driven tiger and published this in *Blackwood's*, with the names altered, in 1929.)

Jim's submissions were rejected.

The reasons for this are hard to judge. He was a competent writer, if somewhat stiff of style as his letters show, and what he was writing about was good copy. Probably, he was rejected on the same grounds as many an emerging author: he was unknown, with no background and so he was turned down as a matter of course.

When his work started to appear in the pages of *Indian Wild Life* and elsewhere, he felt spurred on but still did not take writing at all seriously. He saw it more as a means of evangelising his beliefs in the cause of conservation. Entertaining or educating anyone other than his friends or acquaintances did not enter his mind.

He had become less interested in his business affairs by the mid-Thirties. He was, after all, now sixty years old, at an age when most men retired from work if indeed they had not retired earlier: the retirement age in the Indian government was fifty-five. He did not sell out from F. E. G. Mathews & Co. until the Second World War, but he left the running of it more and more to Maggie and a manager. He concentrated on his hunting of man-eaters, his photography and his future.

The growing independence movement in India worried him. When Gandhi was arrested in the spring of 1930, at the same time as a number of leading Congress Party members, and there was a good deal of civil unrest, Jim saw the first faint scratchings of the writing on the wall. As he had foreseen the corruption and the end of the forests and jungles so also he began to envisage an Indian India. It concerned him deeply. He knew in his heart of hearts that the European's days in India were numbered.

To protect and provide for himself and Maggie in their old age he started to sell his properties, bit by bit, in the early Thirties. With the money so raised, he bought annuities and life insurance policies. The rest he invested wisely or presented to dear friends and relatives.

Always a generous man, Jim gave away much during his lifetime. Ray Nestor, who had been one of the two Nestor children Mary Corbett had raised, wanted to be an engineer but the First World War intervened. Ray Nestor signed up for military service but had to buy his own uniform: Jim gave his father fifty pounds with which to buy it. Later, when Ray Nestor went to live in Kenya, Jim gave him a Churchill shotgun, one of the best makes available. As a child, he had also given Ray his little guitar.

Despite his generosity, Jim was a clever investor, not a spendthrift or one to risk money. His care with cash he inherited from his mother. He entered into investment transactions with a number of people through his own share dealings: his clients or partners included not only friends but also some very powerful men including the Maharaja of Jaipur. Needless to say, his successes brought him jealousy from some quarters but he had the sense of humour to ignore it.

The success of Jim's Christmas hunt for Hailey brought him a close ally and not only in the conservationist cause. Together they often fished in the *tal* at Naini Tal and in the surrounding lakes lower down, especially Bhim Tal. One of their favourite spots, however, was on the Ramganga river west of Ramnagar and south of Kanda, where Jim had shot the man-eater in 1932.

The Ramganga was fast flowing and, in the spring when the water was low before the beginning of the thaw in the mountains, the fishing was superb. Their favourite sport was the mahseer but they also fished for trout, trying to take both fish on a fly – which is possible with the former but requires immense skill – or with a more easily used spoon or spinner. Not only was the fishing good, so was the scenery and the wildlife. The forests were largely unobliterated and forestry activity had been restricted. Tigers and leopards were commonplace and the deer population substantial. The rivers were well stocked with muggers (marsh crocodiles) and otters, and the birdlife was immensely rich and varied.

It was as a result of fishing trips that Hailey, prodded by Corbett and advised by the forest officers, started to think about setting up the area as a wildlife preserve.

Such an idea was not very common. The big game reserves of Africa were still largely undreamed of and those reserves that did exist in India were for the protection of game for hunting rather than simply for its own good. To press the cause and give added weight to Hailey's idea there was held in London, in 1933, a wildlife convention which outlined the needs for reserves as well as starting to define hunting and trading laws for wild animals.

In 1934, over three hundred square kilometres of the forests in the Ramganga river valley area were deemed to be a sanctuary in which all hunting was prohibited for five years. In the following year the United Provinces National Parks Bill was approved and the reserve established on a permanent basis. It was named after Hailey. The idea was that the area should be kept free of as much human interference as possible so that the tiger in particular might breed and then be used to stock other parts of India where it was becoming noticeably thinner on the ground. That the idea of restocking was related to the same principle of fish restocking – so that people could kill them rather than simply guard them for their own intrinsic worth – was put aside.

Jim was pleased in the extreme. Whilst accepting that the Hailey tigers would be used to swell hunting stocks, to which idea he was not fully (but was partially) party, he also knew that this was the beginning of conservation proper.

Although many believe it to be so, it was not Jim who was the first proponent of such a reserve. Two forest officers, E. R. Stevens and his successor, E. A. Smythies, had proposed a sanctuary themselves in 1916 and 1917 respectively but Percy Wyndham had turned down the plans. He had seen no need for it. By chance, Smythies knew Corbett well for they had hunted together near Kaladhungi on several occasions and the two of them worked with Hailey as advisers on the setting up of the reserve.

Smythies' wife is also worthy of remembrance. A noted tiger hunter and *shikari*, she has to her credit the distinction of being the only person to be attacked by a tiger whilst in a tree. She was sitting in a high *machan* in the forests near Tanakpur when a tiger spied her and, enraged, attempted to climb up to get at her. The animal was very nearly successful, reaching to only a few feet below the platform. Mrs Smythies put the gun between her legs and, at point-blank range, fired into the tiger's mouth. Blood fountained up and over her. The tiger fell out of the tree – to be killed by her husband shooting from another *machan* – and she followed it, knocked aside by the recoil of the rifle. A small obelisk now marks the spot of her narrow escape and a rare instance of a tree-climbing, attacking tiger.

When Sir Malcolm Hailey, who was a forceful and charismatic man, left his post there was a move by some officials to reduce the size of the reserve but they were unsuccessful. It was not shrunk for forty years when a vast dam was built across the Ramganga at the southern end of the reserve which took away forty-six square kilometres of land. Luckily, the government of India saw fit to redress this loss most generously and the area today is nearly five hundred and thirty square kilometres. Hailey's name has gone, too. The reserve, operated jointly by the state government and the Project Tiger organisation, is today the Corbett National Park, one of the very few remaining places on earth where the tigers are truly wild in their own natural environment – elusive, wily and exquisitely beautiful forest-dwellers who cannot be approached except on elephant and then only by good fortune. Jeeps and minibuses and the paraphernalia of tourism so common to other Indian wildlife reserves, not to mention the African ones, are absent from what is universally known simply as 'Corbett'. There are, bar one in-and-out route, no roads. The tigers are breeding very successfully as a result. Jim would love it.

The establishment of the reserve gave Jim something else. It gave him a place in which to photograph although he seems seldom to have visited it with this in mind. F. W. Champion was reputed to have taken a lot of his famous tiger and wildlife photographs in the area but Jim preferred to film in localities with which he was more familiar and which were nearer to home. He was getting older.

The aged Mary Doyle in Naini Tal was, by the mid-Thirties, causing some concern and not a little embarrassment to both Jim and Maggie.

She was for all her life a diminutive and dumpy little woman who wore dowdy clothes and, in old age, a sort-of billycock hat. She was austere but greatly admired or respected by all who knew her.

Now in her eighties, she was going senile. After a lifetime of stern and pious religiosity, abstinence from sin (and men) and a strict moral outlook, she started to give under the pressures. Her mother had quite clearly warned her against sinning and men in particular and her attitudes towards the opposite sex are summed up by a remark made over Christmas dinner in 1927. It was suggested that Joseph Clay and their guest, Major Mallock, should kiss Maggie and Mary Doyle under the mistletoe: Mary Doyle's prim and sharp reply to this was, 'Once a young man tried to kiss me under the mistletoe. But *never again*!'

As her mind lost concentration and her senility increased, she took – as do many of a like upbringing – to casting off her inhibitions. In her case, this meant casting off all her clothing and walking stark naked from Gurney House down into the town of Naini Tal. More often than not the servants, who were instructed to keep an eagle eye on her, restrained her and brought her back to the house before she had gone a hundred yards but there were a few occasions when she gave them the slip and reached the bazaar. Quite how the Indian population regarded her is open to speculation. Jim and Maggie were mortified. After several of these escapades, they faced up to the fact that Mary Doyle was no longer able to live at home. They arranged for her to go into a convent, into the care of the nuns and there she remained until her death in 1940. She must have been one of the last survivors of the Indian Mutiny.

Hailey was not the only governor or VIP for whom Jim arranged a tiger shoot. After Hailey had gone from the province, Jim was 'inherited' by his successors, Hallett and Haig. And it was through organising shoots for these people that his reputation grew as a *shikari* of not only inordinate skill and native ability but also care.

Whenever Jim agreed to set up a shoot, all the details were left to him. It was he who arranged clearance with forest officers for the beating of certain blocks of forest – all forests and jungles were divided into administrative blocks – and gathered the beaters, elephants and mahouts. He also spied out the land beforehand, ascertained where the animals were, not just the tigers, and decided for which tigers the men were to beat. He established camp sites, laid on services and settled with local inhabitants for anything that might concern them. (Had he done all this in Africa instead of India, he could have run a substantial safari business. And, later on, he did.)

There were several motives in Jim's mind when setting up such grand *bundobasts* or hunting extravaganzas. (*'Bundobast'* meant 'to tie up loose ends': Jim did). He wanted to mix in the upper circles of society and to maintain his well- and long-earned position there and he enjoyed the company of those whom he met who, conversely, found pleasure in his company. Yet he also wanted to keep an eye on what was done.

Many of the drives in the period immediately after the First World War were simply matters of deciding on a tract of forest to be beaten, beating it and shooting what came out at the end. Seasonal rules were obeyed and the like, but not much else. Jim himself had seen tigresses, their teats heavy with milk, shot and knew that that implied cubs starving to death. When he could, he would seek these cubs out and arrange for them to go to 'safe' homes – usually in private ownership or the breeding zoos such as the one in Lucknow – but it was of course best to avoid such tragedies. Even cubs themselves were brought down by the guns from time to time.

By running the whole shooting match – a cliché that was not lost on Jim himself – he could to some extent control what was killed. He saw to it, whenever he could, that the tigers shot were either already troublesome (perhaps as cattle killers) or well past their prime: in this way, he managed to divert the hunts from being straight slaughter to a form of semi-controlled culling. He knew that, if he declined to organise such events, they would still go ahead and perhaps at the hands of less conservation-conscious *shikaris*. In truth, he was reluctant to be left out, too.

On many of these drives, he did not shoot himself. He took along his Rigby in case he was needed to save a situation or kill a tiger that was wounded, but he did not shoot for sport. Instead, he took along his movie and still cameras and the pictures he took are now of considerable historical interest: some of his cine films are lodged with the British National Film Archive or, in worse condition, the Natural History Museum in London's South Kensington.

Jim's ultimate shoots were arranged for the highest in the land, the Viceroy himself.

The Viceroy with whom Jim became close friends almost from his taking up the post in 1936, was the Marquess of Linlithgow, one of the best of India's viceroys and the one who faced her most challenging years from 1936 to 1943.

It was through his writing that Linlithgow came to know of Corbett, though not through his conservationist magazine articles and editorship but from his first attempt at a book, a copy of which the Viceroy was shown when visiting the Governor of the United Provinces. Linlithgow, liking the book's idealistic bent as well as its excitements, asked for a copy which was tantamount to a royal command. Jim sent one.

Linlithgow was a sportsman and nature lover through and through. His ideal relaxation was to be in a camp in the forests, surrounded by wild life. He was a keen fisherman and it was through fishing that he and Jim came to know each other well. It was inevitable that when Linlithgow wanted to have a jungle holiday, to fish and hold a series of tiger drives – as he did several times annually, until the Second World War, almost as an obligatory part of his viceregal position – he asked for Jim to run them and suggest where they might take place. He recommended Kaladhungi and the first took place in the March of 1937.

Of course, Jim was as pleased as Punch and thrilled to the core. So were the local Indians around Kaladhungi where these drives were sometimes held. To be able to have anything to do with such a mighty affair was honour indeed. To arrange the details, Jim would go down to Delhi and stay in 'The Viceroy's House', a gross misnomer for the largest and grandest palace ever built. He avoided social gatherings there (as did Maggie on the few occasions when she accompanied him) but would take in a little bird shooting. With the Linlithgows alone, he was at ease, joining in after-dinner snooker and conversation but always in his shy way which was never clumsy or gauche and appealed to many who met him in Delhi as modestly charming.

His sense of humour was much appreciated by Linlithgow and his children and, with them, Jim was often enough at ease to be more himself than perhaps he was with most others: he joked and was good company. His lack of flamboyance and mannerism, his simplicity, no doubt made him a welcome change from most of those with whom the Viceroy had to deal.

In camp, however, Jim was the undisputed master. It was not that he impressed himself upon the proceedings. It was just that he was accepted as such and that was that. If it involved hunting, it was his affair.

The drives consisted of both shooting from *machans* and *ghooming*, shooting from elephant back: at the largest drive in September, 1937, sixteen elephants were used. On occasion during that month, Jim would take Linlithgow's son, John, and a friend shooting on foot. To Lord John Hope, as he then was before receiving his own title of Lord Glendevon of Midhope, freshly down from Oxford and a keen athlete and lover of the outdoors, Jim was a hero in the flesh. Uncannily, he called to tigers and was answered, could tell where a tiger would appear and was able to name and explain the actions of all the animals around them. He was a patient teacher, too. With quiet skill, he advised and guided the Viceroy's son and had enough confidence in him to allow him to stalk a tiger on foot.

The drives caused Jim and his villagers, who acted as beaters and guides, much worry. It was important etiquette that the first tiger be shot by the Viceroy himself otherwise, as Jim told one of his beating groups, 'My name will be mud, not just here but in England.' Panwan Gusain, who still lives patriarchally in Jim's village of Choti Haldwani, in a Corbett house surrounded by the next three generations of his family, bearing Jim's fear in mind, caused the Viceroy to shoot the first tiger by ruining the shot of a general in the viceregal entourage who was about to shoot first. After the beat, the general and Jim had a private slanging match which the latter, it would seem, won. The general was much put out for the rest of the Viceroy's holiday. Jim was not to be toyed with . . .

Lord John Hope was able, though, to catch Jim out on several occasions. By now Jim's senses were, albeit slightly, beginning to fail him.

One night in camp in September, 1937, Jim shone his torch on a pair of eyes in the darkness which he claimed was a leopard: closer investigation proved it to be an owl. Hunting from a line of elephants one day, a wild boar rushed out of the cover and Jim shot at it for the beaters' and mahouts' pot. He missed it quite plainly – John Hope saw the dust spurt up a good six feet behind the pig – but refused to admit the miss until some time had been spent searching for the blood trail or the pig's remains.

Again, there was an occasion when John Hope and a friend, for a student-like prank, 'made' a trail of pugmarks in the dust with their fingers and knuckles, not a difficult task if the uninitiated are those to be fooled. They showed this to Jim who became quietly excited and started to track it, only to lose it. He believed he was on the track of a tiger. After a while, the two young men owned up to their mischief. Jim was not angry – he never showed a temper – but he made it quite plain that he was exceedingly displeased.

The friendship that arose between Jim and the Viceroy was not just a meeting of two like minds that would fade with time. It was a lasting friendship and resulted in Jim and Maggie being invited to stay often in Delhi or in Simla. In the latter case this led to Jim receiving an invitation to go bird shooting as a private guest of the Maharaja of Patiala. Long after both Jim and Linlithgow had left India, they continued to remain in touch and on one occasion in the Fifties, Jim visited the former viceroy at his family seat in Scotland. Jim fished for salmon and they shot grouse which sport excited Jim with all the fervour he had always shown for something new. How good he was in his mid-seventies at hitting flying grouse is not recorded but he admitted to a friend he found it thrilling and very difficult indeed. The last photograph taken of Linlithgow before his death was a group portrait in which were gathered the Marquess and Lady Linlithgow, Jim and Maggie.

Some time around 1933, Jim started once more to take an interest in writing down the stories of some of his adventures. His failure to be published had not dampened his desire to get into print and, of course, he realised the power that the page was able to exert for conservation. He was also keen to have some sort of record in writing of his adventures: as early as April, 1930, on the day he shot it, he had written to Maggie about the Chowgarh man-eater saying that the facts had to be kept straight for:

'. . . from scraps of conversation I heard before dinner, the story, although only three hours old, is already distorted, and will be un-recognisable by the time it gets to Naini, per the bearer of this.'

With writing in mind, and believing that his previous rejections had been due to his poor literary skills, he started to show his writing to an acquaintance in Naini Tal, an officer in the education service by the name of Major White. White was constructively critical and Jim was eager to accept whatever guidance he could from his teacher who judged his writing 'incoherent and puncture-less in style'. Despite these acts of help, though, Jim was still not committed to publishing his writings but was simply recording his adventures and experiences for posterity.

It was at Government House, Naini Tal, that he was finally pushed into constructing more than a random collection of thoughts. The Governor at the time was Sir 'Harry' Haig who had replaced Sir Malcolm Hailey in 1934 and, one evening at dinner, Jim found himself seated next to an inquisitive lady. What happened thereafter was later outlined by Jim in a telegram to his American publishers on the occasion of the appearance of his first book in the USA, possibly one of the longest and costliest cables every sent. Sent on 1 April 1946, it reads in part:

'At dinner Government house one night Lady sitting next to me who had recently come from an outlying district of Kumaon asked me to fill in some blanks in story she had got from local inhabitants about one of my hunting experiences. After dinner my hostess informed me she overheard part of my conversation at table, and asked if I had committed any of my jungle experiences to paper. When I pleaded "not guilty" she surprised me by asking if it had ever occurred to me how intensely selfish it was of me not having done so. Before I said goodnight she had extracted a promise that I would write up some of my jungle experiences so that as she put it – "Others besides those who sat next to me at table, could enjoy them." For many days I avoided the good lady, then day came, as such days always do come when attempt is being made to shirk a job when it was necessary for me to meet her again and knowing what her first question would be I took a sheet of paper and wrote title of story on it, under title wrote "chapter one", then took Robin who you will meet in my book out for a run.

'On arrival Government House that evening pleasure my hostess expressed when, in answering to her question I told her I had made a start, so shamed me I then and there resolved to write up some of my experiences even if no-one ever took trouble to read them.'

Of course, there are some half-truths here. Jim was indeed 'guilty' of having written some material: he was just not guilty of having sold it. And yet it is fair to say that he did not really see the true worth or potential of his writing until after he had sold his first trade book to the Oxford University Press who were his sole publishers in his own lifetime. It is also interesting to look at the turn of phrase in which the cable is couched: 'in answering to her question' and 'then and there' are both very Indianesque ways of speaking and indicate what all of his friends remember most about his quiet voice – he had a distinct if not exaggerated 'chi-chi' accent, halfway between the 'Welsh' accent of the Indians and the accent of plain English.

Thanks to the persistence of Lady Violet Haig, Jim started to write.

Whatever his thoughts about any potential readership, Jim's first stories were highly entertaining and thrilling. He worked on – or brushed up – seven pieces, including 'Wild Life in the Village: An Appeal', and put them together in a collection. The other six were a hotch-potch: the story of the Pipal Pani tiger, an angling tale called 'The Fish of my Dreams', 'A Lost Paradise' and 'The Terror that Walks by Night' (both later reprinted in *Indian Wild Life*), a short piece entitled 'Purna Giri and its Mysterious Lights', which is a recalling of the supernatural event to which Jim was a witness, and a long and spine-chilling account of the hunt for the Chowgarh tigress and her cub.

Never having kept a diary or notes, Jim relied for his stories upon what he said were metaphorical 'photographs' in his memory and actual ones in his albums. The work done, he took the stories to an acquaintance in Naini Tal who operated the London Press, a small printing works. Never having printed a whole book, the printer was faced with quite a problem but agreed to do the job a page at a time which was all his font of type could run to: page by page, Jim and Maggie proof-read and corrected or changed the text before it was finally run off. The print was then broken up and re-used for the next page. After four months, Jim had his first book.

Entitled *Jungle Stories*, it was 104 pages long and was bound in a brown manilla paperback-type cover of the paper more usually used to wrap parcels and was stitched with twine at the spine. The front cover was printed in gold and read 'Jungle Stories': beneath was added with typical business acumen, 'all rights reserved' and 'By Jim Corbett'. The text paper was cream. One hundred copies were printed. What came next Jim mentions in his epic telegram:

'Retaining one copy I started to distribute the other copies among friends, but owing demand for additional copies for relatives in other parts of the world I was only able to give 75 friends copies. Those copies drifted from hand to hand until majority had been read to death, and concerted demand was then made for me to publish my stories in regular book form, but before I was able to make a start, Hitler started on his land collecting tour . . .'

A reprint was impossible because the type had been dismantled as the book was made. Copies are now, inevitably, highly-sought-after collectors' items.

It was this book that Linlithgow had requested.

In the meantime, of course, Jim did publish in *Indian Wild Life* and a few other places, but that was all. With the exception of conservationist blastings, he wrote few more stories and not because of the outbreak of war but simply because he did not feel the urge to write.

His life returned to the normal round of socialising, organising the occasional drive, fishing and walking, minding his investments and taking photographs. Throughout their lives, he and Maggie had walked a great deal for the pleasure of the activity. If one considers the land in which they lived, one can understand why: mountain paths with some of the most beautiful alpine views in the world, small lakes sheltering in forests, jungle rich with bird life but, as he was continually aware, becoming less populated by bigger game. And he fished, his favourite lake spots being opposite Smugglers' Rock and by the bandstand on the *tal* at Naini Tal and at Bhim Tal, a lake to the east. When fishing, he was usually accompanied by one of his dogs.

As soon as the Second World War broke out, Jim offered his services. He was in his mid-sixties and could hardly have hoped for a services posting despite the fact that he was a major in the reserves. He was turned down. Undaunted, he joined and was made vice-president of a soldiers' board, a charity which looked after the welfare of the families of native troops on active service. This kept him very busy and gave him the feeling that he was, at least, helping the war effort by proxy if not by direct action.

In 1940, however, on his own admission by lying over his age and subtracting ten years, he obtained what he called a 'war job' and spent two years doing much the same as he had in the First World War – recruiting for a pioneer corps. This time he did not command it in action although he nearly lost his life as a consequence. Crossing the Sarda River near Tanakpur the dug-out in which he was travelling capsized and he was tossed into the water. At his age he was no longer a strong swimmer and he almost drowned.

Jim carried on this war work for two years before falling dangerously ill with tick typhus, possibly aggravated by his enforced swim in the Sarda. He was confined to hospital for three months firstly in Agra though, later, he was moved to the Ramsey hospital in Naini Tal. He entered hospital weighing twelve and a half stone and left weighing seven and was told that he would spend the rest of his life in a wheelchair. For a man like Jim, that was a living death sentence and he was damned if that was going to be the way the future was for him.

Returning home, he vowed that he would not be a cripple. He forced himself to walk, to live actively. He exercised daily and, although for the rest of his life his usually unhurried but long and steady stride was to become shorter, slower, and a little more halting, it did not seize up. He also spent the year of 1943 exercising his mind. He wrote.

Whilst he had been forcing himself to recovery, the Japanese had invaded South-East Asia and the Allies were preparing to drive them out. Late in 1943, seeking further service, Jim again approached the army and they saw in him just what they wanted – an adviser. By February, 1944, Jim had spoken with General Frank Moore, the commander of 39th Training Division and was recommissioned as a lieutenant-colonel and appointed a senior instructor in junglecraft. He was posted to and based on Chhindwara in Central Provinces (now Madhya Pradesh) with the brief to lecture to soldiers heading for the jungles of Burma on jungle survival and lore. Jim was in his element.

His lectures were varied. He dealt with animal (and human) tracking and methods of snaring small mammals for food. He gave a course in edible and inedible plants and how to obtain clean water, how to make smokeless fires in wet habitats and brew tea over them without a metal pan and how to find and gather wild honey without being stung. He studied and explained how to differentiate poisonous snakes from the rest and which were edible. He taught herbal, 'natural' medicine and how to make bird calls with reed pipes that could be translated into a 'natural' message system. He allayed fears in British and American troops for whom the jungle was as much of an enemy, in their own minds, as were the Japanese. Jim was able to show how this was not so. To his students, he seemed almost wizard-like, a cross between, as one of them put it after his death, a magician and a master-detective.

Not one to be left out of the farcicality of warfare, he advised on one occasion that soldiers be issued with silk stockings. Jim reasoned that these would be more than useful in the Burmese jungles as the permanently wet vegetation was alive with leeches and leeches cannot get a grip through silk mesh. Leech-borne diseases would be minimal-ised, secondary infections greatly reduced and the soldiers would be more comfortable in the knowledge that the bloodsuckers would leave them be. No record exists of the replies this suggestion received. As, for a part of his advisory term, Jim trained some of Orde Wingate's 'Chindits', one can perhaps imagine the response. (Jim never met the legendary Wingate, but their paths had crossed long before for Wingate was born on 26 February 1903 in a house called Montrose in Naini Tal, for which Mary Corbett was the agent.)

For all his junglewise knowledge, Jim was still fascinated by civilis-ation which aroused the curiosity by which he always lived. What took his eye in the army was his first encounter with a '24-hour compo pack', a balanced food supply that was supposed to last a day and came packed flat and tightly into an aluminium tin. Jim handled the processed foodstuffs with 'the excitement of a schoolboy' but he did not eat it. He amused or impressed some of his fellow officers by his habit of drinking a sip from some of the most stagnant jungle ponds he came across in order to maintain his immunity to the germs that lurked therein.

He also kept clear of some ponds: once, when driving with a fellow officer in a jeep, on a baking hot day, the officer stopped their vehicle by a rare jungle pool and announced that he was going to dip himself into it to cool off. Jim would not join him. The officer, as he divested himself of his uniform, asked why he would not. Jim's reply was that the pond was the only one for miles and was, therefore, most likely the lodging place of the area's largest Indian python. The officer smartly replaced his clothes and, wondering whether or not he had just been 'had' – for Jim was smiling quietly to himself – they drove on.

Although based in Chhindwara, Jim travelled widely around India to military bases. He conducted courses in Bhopal and went to Assam on at least one occasion. He also crossed into Burma in the late March of 1944, soon after he was commissioned, where he spent a month studying the flora and fauna of the Burmese jungles which were very different from his familiar Indian forests. The difference was so great that it amazed him. Whilst in Burma, he was befriended by a number of American airmen who not only gave him lifts in their aircraft but also tried to persuade him to take an illegal 'rest and recreation' hop over to the USA to see what America was like. He reluctantly had to decline but he did accept a lift back from Burma to Agra which thrilled him.

In September, 1945 with the war over, Jim returned home weakened by malaria to find Maggie similarly suffering. They nursed each other and pondered their future. India was nearing her independence and Jim was more than a little apprehensive about their future. He had though, the year before, embarked upon a new profession. He was now not only a published author, but a bestselling one into the bargain.

Author and Africa

By August, 1943, Jim had completed his book. It was, as he put it, an 'enlarged manuscript copy of jungle stories', although in fact the book as it stood was much different. With the exception of Maggie's help in reading the text and Lord Linlithgow's in checking for errors, Jim wrote the whole book himself. When it was finished, as the long telegram outlines:

> 'I offered it as a free gift to St Dunstan's and in doing so exhibited my total ignorance of all matters connected with publication and books, for this most estimable institution had no funds to speculate with.'

It was his intention that the book – entitled *Jungle Stories*, like its forerunner – should be published by St Dunstan's, a recently inaugurated charity set up to benefit and help those Indian servicemen blinded on active service. He had thought that they would merely print some hundreds of copies as he had of his first book, selling them to make a minimal profit to marginally swell the charity coffers. (Eventually, they were given a part of the royalty of the first edition.)

What happened next was that Jim showed the manuscript to a friend who had published a book but whose advice was not encouraging:

> 'After skimming through pages of my manuscript his verdict was that he did not think any publishing house would look at it, unless I was prepared to indemnify against all loss resulting from publication.

With visions of spending my days indemnifying publishers for vast losses I thanked my friend for his advice, and brought the manuscript home.'

Fortunately, Jim did not let matters rest there. Either he was eager to try and sell the book because he had faith in it, or because he wanted to help St Dunstan's still with it, or because he was simply bull-headed: whichever was the case, when he reached home he and Maggie

'. . . talked the matter over that night and as there appeared to be no risk in obtaining a publisher's opinion, I wrote next day to Bombay branch of the Oxford University Press, giving them brief outline of my stories and asking if they were prepared to help me. By return of post I received a request for manuscript.'

Within a month, the Oxford University Press made an offer for the book but suggested that the title was too bland. They suggested calling the book, *Man-Eaters of Kumaon.*

Jim accepted after being persuaded by Lord Linlithgow, when staying with the Viceroy in Delhi in October, 1943, to agree to this title. Sir Maurice Hallett wrote the introduction and Linlithgow the foreword. Jim added an author's note to set the background and give his opinions and theories on man-eaters, the majesty of tigers and their plight. (This small but very important and much quoted essay appears in the appendix on page 253.)

The book was published in August, 1944 in hardback. It cost five rupees. (In Naini Tal, it cost five and half rupees. The Modern Book depot, the bookstore on The Mall in the town, added half a rupee for freight.) The endpapers carried a map of the Kumaon region and the book included nine photographs of which four were out-cuts from some of Jim's cine films including the 'studio' valley sequence of many tigers gathered at once. One was a portrait of Corbett in his late forties. The publisher's editor found little need to edit the text other than to excise repetitions. The conversational style and sense of almost journalistic reportage building to a climax – just as hunts do in any case with the hunter and the quarry converging for the kill – were the stuff of popular literary success.

The contents consisted of the stories of the Chowgarh tigers, the Pipal Pani tiger, the Kanda man-eater (an extended version of the short story entitled 'The Terror That Walks By Night') and the angling tale 'Fish of My Dreams' from *Jungle Stories*. To these were added the stories of the Champawat, Mohan and Thak man-eaters, the shooting of a record 'trophy' tiger known as the 'Bachelor of Powalgarh', a two-page essay about filming tigers entitled 'Just Tigers' in which Jim acknowledged his debt to Champion as one of the spurs goading him to photographing rather than killing big game and a short piece about Robin.

From his earliest exploits with Magog, Jim had always kept a dog as well as an assortment of pets including a cheetal buck called Jonathan and birds, which he began to care for in his railway forest clearing days. His most remembered and loved pet was, however, Robin.

A cocker spaniel (for the greater part) and originally named Pincha, Jim purchased Robin at the age of three months for fifteen rupees. He was the runt of his litter but he was to accompany his master on some of his greatest hunts.

Jim taught the dog to obey, to heed commands, not to be gun-shy, to retrieve game birds and generally how to behave in the jungle. He taught the dog also to stand in the pocket of his shooting jacket, with its front paws over his arm in such a way that Jim could still shoot. The dog did not move in this position for it knew not to spoil the aim.

Robin's greatest moment came when he and Jim hunted the 'Bachelor of Powalgarh' and it was the dog (as well as Maggie) that brought the tiger home. A brave dog, Robin was the predecessor of David who went with Jim after his last tiger and, when he died, he was buried in an elaborate grave in the garden at Kaladhungi.

Robin not only gives some interesting background to Jim's hunting but also to his writing. When Robin died is not known exactly but he was in his prime in 1930 and yet, in his story of Robin in *Man-eaters of Kumaon*, Jim comments on the fact that the dog died whilst he was writing the piece. This may be artistic licence seeking a sentimental reader but if it is not, it sets this fragment as having been written well before 1943 and possibly as early as 1935 and the writing of *Jungle Stories*.

In September, 1945, a second edition was published in Madras by the Oxford University Press. The following year it was published in Great Britain and the USA with all the razzamatazz associated with a best-seller. In New York a tiger cub, one of a pair flown up from a zoo in Florida, pug-autographed copies at a reception in the Hotel Pierre.

Bookstore windows put on major displays with luminously printed tiger posters and, ironically, pegged out tiger skins. Within four years, it was translated into nine languages (including Czech and Finnish) as well as six Indian dialects. It remained in print, either in hard- or paperback, for thirty years. By May, 1946, over half a million copies were in print and the book was to sell more than four million copies world-wide by 1980.

Man-Eaters of Kumaon received considerable critical acclaim on both sides of the Atlantic, was an American book club choice and an instant success. Sadly, none of the editions other than the Indian ones included the cine film out-cuts: the 1952 British edition was superbly illustrated by Raymond Sheppard, in *Boy's Own*, true ripping-yarn fashion but at the expense this time of all Jim's photographs.

In Naini Tal, Jim became a focus of attention and not all of it was local. He suffered the inevitable fan mail that writers could ruefully expect in those days. Dowagers wrote to him with effusive congratulations and proclamations of marriage both veiled and direct. Other Corbetts sought to prove their blood relationship. Letters offered to send him memoirs, more stories (some of the ignorant believed that his tales were fictional!), ephemera ... one offered to send him a live replacement for Robin. In March 1946, Jim was asked to sell the film rights.

Universal Pictures bought the rights. The producers were Monty Shaff and Frank P. Rosenburg. A scriptwriting team of Alden Nash, Richard G. Hubler, Jeanne Bartlett and Lewis Meltzer were set to work and produced a screenplay of which Jim approved but it involved location shooting and this was refused – much to Jim's annoyance – by the Government of India. Eventually, the film was shot entirely in Hollywood under the direction of Byron Haskin and released in 1948 under the title, *Man-eater of Kumaon*. Starring Sabu, Wendell Corey, Joy Ann Page, Morris Carnovsky and Argentina Brunetti, it was an unmitigated cinematic disaster. What had started out as a series of true *shikar* stories with a conservationist undertone ended up as a commercial movie about an American hunter who wounded a tiger and was finally killed by it. It bore as much resemblance to the original book as it did to the Bible. Jim saw it once. He said that the best actor was the tiger.

With the war over, Jim in the meantime being promoted to colonel, he returned to his old life in Naini Tal and Kaladhungi. He walked through Choti Haldwani in the evenings, chatted to 'his' villagers and continued to act as the dispenser of justice and fair play. Linlithgow had long since left India and his successor, Lord Wavell, had used Jim to organise one tiger drive at Christmas, 1946. It was to be his last proper drive. Although he was requested to help with others, and he did, they were not serious affairs and little was shot: certainly, no tigers were killed.

In his journal, Wavell wrote that Jim:

'was running the shoot with Yakub Khan and some of the Bodyguard. His talk on tigers and jungle life is of extraordinary interest, and I wish I could have had more of it. He has rather pessimistic views on the future of tigers; he put the present tiger population of India at 3000 to 4000 (I was rather surprised at the smallness of this estimate) and that in many parts of India tigers will become almost extinct in the next 10 or 15 years; his chief reason is that Indian politicians are no sportsmen and tigers have no votes, while the right to a gun licence will go with a vote.'

It was a simplistic and naïve view but not without foundation. Jim could see or feel that India was going to change beyond all recognition. The politics would alter, the British would gradually go (for he was fully aware of Wavell's intention to let independence come as a gradual process of 'indianisation' such as was already well under way in both government and commerce) and the countryside would change. He had seen the last process taking place over his own lifetime. What had been tracts of mountainous near-virgin forest in the first twenty years of the century was now irrigated, drained, terraced and fertilised farmland. Where cheetal had roamed and tigers had roared goats now nibbled and cows and bullocks walked ploddingly by, safely guarded by Hinduism. Forest tracks had grown to be motor roads that were, with the end of the war, being paved with bricks and metalled.

Now into retirement – for he had withdrawn almost entirely from business holdings in Naini Tal by the end of 1941 – Jim was called upon, for the last time, to shoot a man-eater. It was taking human life in the Ladhya valley, not far from Thak where Jim had successfully called to task the Thak man-eater in 1938. Maggie was most anxious that he should not go but Jim felt obliged to do so. He went and killed the animal, which was in a sorry state and required little of his earlier expertise to stalk and track: or so he claimed. He also shot an alleged cattle-killing tiger in the trees behind the ruins of Arundel.

What often happened was that villagers from near and far would come to Jim to ask him to rid them of a cattle-killer. Jim's usual response was not to reach for his Rigby or the .275 Westley Richards he had bought as a treat for himself from Mantons in the mid-1930s, the same gunsmiths from whom Hewett had bought the Rigby nearly forty years before, but for his wallet. He would rather pay compensation for the dead cows than shoot the tiger, being only too well aware that the tiger was eating cows because there was nothing else left to eat save humans and their domestic stock.

In this instance, in 1946, the villager who complained was from the locality of Kaladhungi and he would not be fobbed off with cash. Jim refused to shoot the tiger. The villager then stood outside the gates to the Kaladhungi house and waved his shotgun in the air whilst telling Jim exactly what he thought of him and like-minded photographers. He then headed for the scene of the latest kill in order to shoot the tiger over it. Jim followed the man, called up the tiger and shot it. He said at the time that he regretted not having had his Leica with him, but it also made him very sad.

By late 1946, Jim was sick of heart. His forests had been decimated, the tigers that he loved were nearing extinction (his estimate to Wavell was only 1500 animals short of the truth), the morality of the world was changing. The politics of India were becoming complex, anti-British and worrying. That independence was inevitable was not what worried Jim and Maggie. Their concern was what life would be like for them after the transfer of power and sovereignty.

Lord Mountbatten was now in India as the Viceroy, with instructions to withdraw the British. His deep friendship with Nehru worried many of the domiciled British Raj and the speed with which the day of independence was approaching filled them with dread. As it drew nearer still, and bloodshed on the railways began, with political or sectarian murder rife in the land, apprehension escalated. Jim and Maggie thought over their future very seriously indeed.

They were caught on the horns of a painful dilemma. India was their home. Jim had travelled a good deal overseas but had always returned to the land of his birth. Both his birth and Maggie's. They were British but they were third generation Indians, too. Many expatriates were leaving but most were heading for their roots in Britain. Some of course made for the other colonies but they still had those ties with 'Home' to which they could run if the going got tough elsewhere in the diminishing Empire. For Jim and Maggie, Naini Tal and Kaladhungi were their roots. Indeed, Maggie knew nowhere else. She had been to Delhi, to Simla, to Lucknow, to Mokamet Ghat all those many decades before, but no further afield. She had never seen a large lake, let alone the ocean.

What were they to do?

To remain in India was definitely not an option. Jim was positive of that. He commented to several friends and relations that, when India gained her independence, the likes of himself and Maggie would become very much second-class citizens.

After much discussion, during which Maggie tried to argue against leaving, Jim ended the matter by saying with finality, 'We must simply go. Now really, under no circumstances can we stay on in India because we will simply become bottom of the queue.'

There was only one place to which they could go and that was East Africa.

Wyndham had long since left, settling for the last years of his life back in Britain. Jim was no longer the owner of a farm in Tanganyika. However, in Kenya, he had many contacts. His eldest brother Tom had a son, also named Tom and a much decorated and famous lieutenant-general who had been a leading officer in the Second World War. Commander of the 4th Corps in Iraq in 1942, he had been chosen by Auchinleck as his Chief of General Staff in Cairo, a post he held with distinction and honour until Churchill and the war cabinet removed Auchinleck from his command. (It was through Lt-Gen Tom Corbett, via Auchinleck, that Wavell, as Viceroy, came to know of Jim.)

Not only was Tom, another namesake of the family hero, in Kenya. So, too, was Ray Nestor, the son of Jim's sister Harriet, who had spent part of his childhood with the Corbetts in Gurney House. Brother Christopher's daughter also lived there. It seemed sensible to go there so Jim started to make plans, almost in secret.

In the meantime, he was writing his second book. After the meteoric success of *Man-Eaters of Kumaon*, the Oxford University Press were anxious for a follow-up and Jim provided this: it was to be possibly his best book but the least known of all of them.

Published in 1948, it was the story of the Rudraprayag man-eater. Whereas his first book had been dedicated to the gallant soldiers, sailors and airmen of the united nations who during 1939–1945 lost their sight in the service of their country the second, *The Man-Eating Leopard of Rudraprayag*, was dedicated to the victims of the animal itself.

The book is a powerful and sustained narrative. Where others of Jim's books were written as short stories or in an anecdotal manner, the Rudraprayag leopard is dealt with as a continuous plot. It is fascinating not only for its tale but also for the detail into which it goes. There are many moving, pathetic and very absorbing sections but what strikes the reader throughout is the immense humanity of the author and, through him, of Ibbotson. The painstaking and prolonged hunt is brought to a climax all the more effective for the fact that it is truth. A fiction writer would have to work hard to maintain such heightened and methodically deliberate tension. Once more, the book was published with Jim's photos which had been criticised by one reviewer of his first book as amateurish. Indeed, they were but this added to their attraction and efficacy. And, once again, the book had a conservationist undertone.

The Man-Eating Leopard of Rudraprayag sold very well indeed and went to a number of editions but it did not have the sustained success of its predecessor. It is interesting to remember that, whilst writing the book, Jim had to break off to deal with the pitiful specimen of a man-eater in the Ladhya valley.

By the time the book was in print, Jim had left India for good.

As Indian independence drew ever closer, rumours started to fly. The anti-British feelings that had been whipped up in India in 1942 had rekindled the flame of those distant memories of the Indian Mutiny which were ever tiny embers in the recesses of the minds of the domiciled Europeans. A new 'mutiny' in the guise of national freedom was positively feared: British women would be raped, their menfolk murdered, their homes burnt. Businesses would be nationalised or transferred to Indian ownership, foreigners expelled or deported. For Jim and Maggie, elderly and who had lost relatives in 1857, this was more terrifying than any tiger. It was history turning nearly full circle. Expatriate friends no doubt fuelled the couple's fears with their talk of the likely collapse of India after the sudden withdrawal of the British machinery of government: Mountbatten's haste to declare independence was blamed for this being a possibility.

Jim's comment to his sister about their position at the bottom of the queue was reinforced in his comments to Indian friends. He was afraid that, with independence and the absence of the British Raj, they would be alone with no one to care for them. He told his friends that there would be no one to bury them when they died.

His fears must have been partly groundless. He had enemies, it was true, but the overwhelming love the villagers of Kaladhungi held for both Jim and Maggie would have protected them. The hillfolk of Kumaon would never have forgotten his hunting to save them from the devils disguised as tigers and leopards. He would, it is certain, have lost his patriarchal position as the *sahib* of Choti Haldwani and this may have been of concern to him. Perhaps he remembered, as did so many colonials when their powers were about to be removed, the number of 'heads he had banged and arses he had kicked'. Despite this, Jim had little to fear.

Underlying it all, though, was the fear that spread beyond the political situation, the fear that two elderly folk inevitably have when they get older after a lifetime of love and companionship. It was the terror of being alone and Maggie summed it up years later:

'After independence came in India and our British friends were leaving, we began to realise that it would be very difficult for us to remain, especially as when the time came for one of us to be taken, the contemplation of the other having to live on alone in Gurney House, our home for nearly all the years of our lives and so full of memories, could not be faced.

'We, therefore, decided very reluctantly to leave. Our choice of destination fell on Kenya, the reason being that Jim knew the country, and we felt the conditions of life there would be much like those we had been used to in India. Jim had a very serious illness the last year we were in India. We had been on a fishing trip to the Kosi and Ramganga . . . and while there Jim was suddenly taken ill with a very high temperature and had to be taken to the Ramsay Hospital, where he was found to be suffering from both benign and malignant malaria. After a day or two in hospital, he also developed pneumonia and was so ill that the doctors despaired of his life.'

He was a month in hospital and gradually recovered with the help of the new wonder-drug, penicillin, though his lungs were weak for the rest of his life and prevented him from taking a holiday in the Seychelles in the November of 1949. This illness, however, had made up Maggie's mind for her.

There were those who tried to persuade Jim to stay. He was invited on to committees but he declined the offers although he maintained his place on the soldiers' board which had led to his most coveted official honour; Jim was made a member of the Order of The British Empire.

Through his long life, he had been variously decorated. He had received the Volunteer decoration in 1920 for his fighting in the First World War. In 1928, the Kaisar-i-Hind gold medal was given to him. It was a very prestigious award given usually for services to India: he had more than earned it by killing the Rudraprayag leopard. In 1942, he was awarded his OBE and, in 1946, he received his last honour, the uncommon and seldom awarded CIE or Companion of the Indian Empire.

The citation for his OBE read:

'Major James Edward Corbett, O.B.E.
'You have set a fine example in the United Provinces as an enlightened land-holder who always has the interests of his tenants at heart. Your exploits in ridding the countryside of man-eating carnivora are almost legendary. You commanded a Labour Battalion in France in the last war, and in 1940 you were appointed as Deputy Vice-President of the Soldiers' Board in the Meerut Division, in which capacity your unrivalled experience of the countryside has been of considerable value both to the Civil and Military authorities in maintaining touch with soldiers' families and in recruitment. You at present hold the important post of Commandant of the Civil Pioneer Force in the Province and your services have throughout been of unusual merit. I have pleasure in investing you with the insignia of an Officer of the Most Excellent Order of the British Empire.'

Just as with Jim's first public honour, the engraved plate on his Rigby .275, the authorities got his Christian names wrong.

Gurney House was put up for sale, fully furnished. It was sold on 21 November 1947 to Mrs Verma who was also offered the house at Kaladhungi but declined it. No buyer could be found for Kaladhungi and Jim left a power of attorney for its sale: it eventually sold for a mere two thousand rupees though Jim later tried to buy it back to have it converted into a village community centre but was unsuccessful. He released all his tenants and made them their own masters but he continued to pay the annual land tax on Choti Haldwani until his death – Maggie kept it on until she died. Jim and Maggie also maintained their bank account in Naini Tal: it was too great a tug to cast themselves totally adrift. In their deepest hearts they obviously wanted to keep their roots even if they knew they could never return to them.

Nine days after Gurney House was sold, they left. Maggie later told Ruby Beyts:

> 'The morning we were due to leave, we looked across the waters of the lake, which was indescribably beautiful-in the early morning light. Our servants did not make our departure any easier as they stood with tears trickling down their cheeks as we moved down the hill from the house we knew we should never see again.'

In Choti Haldwani, the villagers did not know the exact date of Carpet Sahib's departure. Jim kept it secret for the pain of leaving especially them was too much to bear. They were hurt by his secrecy: they wanted to give him a correct send-off.

They went via Lucknow to Bombay and boarded the *SS Aronda* bound for Mombasa. As far as Lucknow, they were accompanied by Jim's last bearer, Ram Singh: there had been talk of a band of men taking the journey to Bombay with them to protect them. Standing in the crowds on the station platform in Lucknow, Ram Singh cried as the train pulled out. He received a plot of land in Kaladhungi and a bank standing order of ten rupees a month until Jim's death. He soon sold the land and returned to Garhwal. With Jim gone, there was nothing left for him.

Maggie was fascinated by the crossing to the African coast. Jim was mildly sea-sick. Their ship docked in Mombasa on 15 December and they went by train to Nairobi. They stayed a short while with Ibby (by now Sir William Ibbotson) and Jean Ibbotson who lived at Karen, near Nairobi.

Their plan was not to remain with the Ibbotsons but, after resting from their journey, to move to join Ray Nestor and his wife on their 640-acre coffee farm near Kipkaren where the Nestors had specially built a detached cottage for them. It was not a large building, but it was sufficient. Jim and Maggie stayed with them for several weeks but Maggie hated it. The farm was isolated, living conditions comparatively primitive without indoor sanitation or running water, the landscape was alien and Maggie felt that she wanted to be nearer to the centre of things. She also wanted more creature comforts and said so quite forcibly to the

Nestors who were understandably taken aback: they had expected the two of them to be somewhat more imbued with the pioneer spirit.

For his part, Jim was prepared to live near the Nestors or Tom Corbett and he was embarrassed by Maggie's blunt refusal to accept such obvious and considerable generosity. He bought Ray Nestor a much-needed water pump for his farm and he insisted he pay for half of the costs of building the cottage. When Ray Nestor sold his farm in 1949, Jim asked him to move to Nyeri, if necessary with him buying the Nestors another farm there. They refused.

Jim then decided that, rather than stay with the Nestors, he would move to Tom Corbett's farm at Mweiga where he would – for Maggie, who was becoming increasingly homesick and disillusioned – build a replica of Gurney House in which to live. They went to Tom Corbett's farm, into which Jim, along with Ruby Beyts's husband, had previously invested some money, but again Maggie decided that it was too remote and primitive. They also began to realise that they were not as young as they might be.

At last, they settled at the Outspan Hotel in Nyeri where they rented the *banda* (small cottage), Paxtu, formerly occupied by Lord Baden-Powell whom they both greatly admired. It was to be their last home.

The hotel was very beautifully situated with fine gardens and a superb view of Mount Kenya. The view was, for Maggie, a poor substitute for the panorama of the Himalayas from Snow View, above Naini Tal, but it would do.

When they moved into the Outspan Hotel, Jim was still frail from his bout of pneumonia and he had been weakened by the malaria that had run in him for most of life. The tick typhus he had contracted in the war had not helped. He walked more slowly now, had a cough from time to time and yet he was still very active. He took photographs and cine films of African wildlife, travelling as far as Uganda in search of subjects, fed the birds on the veranda of their *banda* and began to build about himself a social life once more. He missed the social whirl to which he had grown accustomed in India, even if he had preferred to keep to the edge of it. He took his holidays at the Hotel Sinbad at Malindi, on the Kenyan coast north of Mombasa where, in an idyllic setting, he fished off the beach and coral reef. Jim also ventured into the romantic ruins of Gedi, a city visited by Vasco da Gama and lost in the coastal jungle: it was the haunt of some almost extinct and beautiful butterflies.

Being still a man with an eye for business, he and three friends (including Ibby) invested, late in 1948, in a safari company called 'Safariland' which had been started in the early part of the century. It opened up a whole new vista to Jim who wrote of the firm in a letter:

'My only object in joining the company was to discourage killing and encourage photography. From the day we took over, the company has been booming and we have more applicants than we can deal with. People come to us from all parts of the world and this necessitates our employing men who know a number of languages. We have a fleet of cars and lorries – we are permitted to purchase all the transport we need – hundreds of tents and tent equipment, and we employ twenty White Hunters and an office staff of five Europeans. In addition to several parties now in the field we are handling the Metro-Goldwyn-Mayer party of fifty-three who arrived a week ago from Hollywood to make a film which will be released under the title of King Solomon's Mines. This party will be with us for thirteen weeks and before they leave another party of fifty Americans will arrive by air to take pictures of wild life. Yesterday I was asked by the Kenya Director of Information if I would help the Hollywood party by making animal calls for their film. He also asked me if I would sell the coloured films I recently took of elephants in Uganda. My throat is too old now to make animal calls, and never having made any money from my pictures I am not going to start now. However, if after attending the cinema show I am giving here on 31st. of this month (October, 1949) the Hollywood people think my films will be of any use to them, I will give them to them . . .'

He did not. No doubt he viewed the antics of Hollywood with more than a little caution after the disaster of the film of his own book.

He also purchased annuities for relatives. To get about, Jim bought a Citröen car and they lived comfortably not only from their investments but also from the royalties of the two books.

Not all went well, though. In 1950, Maggie fell from a chair whilst hanging a picture and broke her hip. She spent some months in hospital in Nyeri where Jim visited her daily. She miraculously pulled through. Jim periodically suffered from recurring malaria.

Another undercurrent started to disrupt their lives. With India having gained her independence, other colonies started to demand a similar freedom. In Kenya, this was resisted by the authorities and the Mau Mau terrorist 'army' gathered momentum. Centred on the Kikuyu tribe, it had its loose headquarters in the Aberdare forests near Nyeri. Outlying farms were attacked, Europeans and the African servants murdered and travel became risky. Although far more Africans than Europeans were killed by the Mau Mau, the freedom fight incorporating a liberal amount of tribal as well as racial hatred, the air of living in a terrorist war zone was oppressive. For the Corbetts, it looked as if they had avoided the second Indian Mutiny only to be caught up in the first African one.

In 1951 and again in 1953, Jim and Maggie visited Britain. They stayed with Lord and Lady Linlithgow on the first trip and with Robin and Jean Hood, their old friends from the civil service in India by now retired to Edinburgh. They stopped also with the Nestors who had retired to England. Maggie's eyesight was failing and she was operated upon for a cataract at Moorfields Eye Hospital in London on their second visit. Jim also met his publisher.

Geoffrey Cumberlege was by now the publisher of the Oxford University Press and he became a dear friend to Jim and Maggie. Their relationship started as an author-publisher friendship does but they soon discovered that they had much in common. Cumberlege also wanted another book.

Almost since the day they had quit India, Jim was toying with the idea of returning for a visit. He wrote to Indian friends that he was looking forward to it and to friends in Britain that he was anticipating it. Nothing came of it. Money was not an obstacle: Jim and Maggie had planned several times to holiday in the Seychelles. The obstacles of ill-health – his own as well as that of his sister – and the apprehension of finding India to be too changed prevented Jim from making the journey. He was just as apprehensive about how he might feel on such a journey home.

Almost as an act of catharsis, his third book was not about man-eaters and hunting but about the country and the people he loved.

My India was published in 1952 and has remained in print in that country ever since. Reverting to the style of *Man-Eaters of Kumaon*, the book is a series of anecdotal essays about Indians whom he knew and admired, about village life and about his life on the railways. The stories span all of Jim's adult life and praise the steadfast grit of the common Indian. Rich with humour, pathos and humanity laced with excitement, the tales are rich evocations of Indian rural life viewed from an unusual standpoint. In writing the book, Jim had placed himself not as an observer, a member of the detached ruling class, nor as an utter confidant of the villagers of whom he wrote but as one somehow in between. He had seen his subjects with sympathy and objectivity but had nevertheless closely related to them. In some instances, he showed his own generosity of spirit (as well as of wallet) towards the Indians but never with any sense of immodesty or pride. As with his *shikar* stories, he simply stated the facts without apportioning any praise to himself or blame to others.

Though not intended as an historical document – Jim states as much in his long dedication to the book – he offers the book in memory of 'the poor of India' by which he meant all but ten per cent of the population and those amidst whom he lived his life. *My India* is very much a statement of its and its author's times. The administration of law, the problems of money-lenders, of disease and opium addiction, life in Choti Haldwani (including a humorous but dangerous episode with a wild pig) and Mokameh Ghat, the bravery of two men facing a tiger, the hunting of the dacoit, Sultana and the awesome tangle of everyday red tape (which Jim abhorred) all came under his scrutiny. Few books have given such an insight into the common lot in British-ruled India.

The book was not as successful as the others but it did expand Jim's authorship. He gained new readers from it who were not at first attracted by the bravery or bravado of shooting animals no matter how dangerous and philanthropic the acts might be.

The *shikari* had turned author in no uncertain way but writing was never a serious job to Jim. He did not discipline himself to write but produced whenever and wherever the whim caught up with him. Nevertheless, both he and Maggie welcomed the income that it brought them and this no doubt eased their minds a good deal.

Life in the Outspan Hotel was agreeable. Jim and Maggie became close friends of the proprietor and they enjoyed living in a place full of wildlife. The Aberdare forests were only a few miles away and Jim did not have to drive far in the Citroën in order to see and film wild elephants on the edge of the cover. Game was plentiful still and, if anything, appeared more so for the occasional bombing of the forests by RAF Lancaster bombers, to flush out terrorist gangs, brought some of the deep forest creatures to the rim. This upset Jim greatly but he made the most of it with his camera. With the car, he also drove into various game parks on photographic trips.

Even in their home, they encouraged creatures to come near to 'Paxtu,' just as Jim had all those years before at Mount Pleasant with the kakar. Maggie told Ruby Beyts that

> 'We lived very happily in this charming cottage and gradually made the garden into a small bird sanctuary. Some of the birds became so tame as to feed out of our hands. Jim counted twenty six varieties of birds, attracted not only by the food we gave them, but also by a lovely little pond at the foot of the veranda steps in which they could bathe.'

Paxtu had a deep and wide veranda upon which Jim and Maggie spent most of their days, living in much the same manner as they had in India where the veranda was considered an added room rather than simply a place to sit. The *banda* was furnished with their own possessions. They had their own African servants but Jim did not attempt to learn Swahili as he had Hindustani and the Kumaon dialects. He made do with the basics.

Jim's fourth book appeared in October 1953. Entitled *Jungle Lore*, it was a rich book about life in the jungles, his own childhood and how he came to hunt in as well as love the natural world, tiger-hunting and -beating and, again, life in India. The book was well-timed. Biographical interest in Jim had been aroused by his first two books and *Jungle Lore* provided some of the answers.

It was a mixed book, not as well planned as it might have been. It had its strong conservationist bent and it covered some fascinating areas of jungle life and study, but it was something of a disunited book with no aim to it. Despite its literary faults, it was immediately popular and a reprint was issued within four weeks of initial publication.

Jim was never a literary writer. He did not seek to be one. He wrote simply to entertain and educate, preaching his philosophy of live and let live, of natural justice and simplistic morality. After the years of the Second World War, this was very much admired and needed.

With his fifth book, Jim returned to the successful formula of his first. Its original title *More Man-Eaters* was changed to *The Temple Tiger* and it appeared in October 1954, to be promptly reprinted. It repeated the success of *Man-Eaters of Kumaon* and whereas the last two books had not contained photographs, *The Temple Tiger* did and, as with the first book, a newer edition in 1957 omitted the pictures and was illustrated by Raymond Sheppard.

The title story, 'The Temple Tiger', is the tale of the tiger Jim attempted to shoot when out after the Panar man-eating leopard but which he was unsuccessful in bagging because it had supernatural protection. It is a thrilling, *shikar* narrative with Jim getting in a number of shots but failing to even graze the tiger. To this tale Jim added the stories of the hunting of the Mukteswar, Chuka and Talla Des man-eating tigers and the Panar man-eating leopard. A brief epilogue gives instructions to the intrepid so that they might visit the places mentioned in the book in order to verify the facts of what Jim admits, especially in relation to the Talla Des man-eater, are almost beyond belief.

There were sceptics he had to appease. Some of his stories, especially the one referring to the killing of the second Chowgarh tigress, seem far-fetched in the extreme. To give Jim the benefit of the doubt, he may have used artistic licence in embellishing the stories, as would many another professional writer.

The Chowgarh tigress seems the most incredible. Jim, stalking the man-eater, sensed its arrival as he and his men were tying out a buffalo. Setting off after the tigress, Jim stopped in a ravine (in which were the quarry's pug marks) to collect two unusual nightjar's eggs for his collection, which he nestled in moss in the cup of his left hand. In the other was his .275 rifle, just given to him by Madho Singh, held diagonally across his chest. Thus encumbered, he went on. Rounding a rock, he came face to face with the tigress lying on the sandy ground ready to spring and eight feet from him. Jim froze. He then gradually moved the rifle down to point at the tigress, moving his hand along to the trigger. His other hand was redundant and still held the eggs. At last, by moving very slowly so as not to alarm the man-eater, the rifle was pointing at the tigress, Jim's arm now outstretched so as to clear the stock from his hip: he was holding the rifle in the manner of a pistol. Assuming the gun to be pointing at the man-eater's head, he fired. Luckily, the safety catch had been in the 'off' position. The tigress was dead.

This really is a good deal to believe. To accept the tale, one has to believe that Jim was stupid enough to collect the eggs (why not get them later?) when stalking a man-eater he knew to be in the vicinity and that he was unprofessional enough to walk with the safety catch 'off'. The rifle he used was the .275 Rigby. It is not a heavy weapon but it would require considerable strength to do with it what Jim claims even with the adrenalin flowing to bolster the muscles. More than a pinch of meta-phorical salt is perhaps required. (I have attempted the same action with the very same gun: even with my own gun- and archery-toughened wrists, I cannot achieve this movement. Phil Berry, a hunting acquaintance, has however initiated the action successfully.)

Interestingly, a letter written on the evening of the kill to Maggie back home in Naini Tal differs from the published version and is more closely truthful and to the point:

'Just a line to let you know that I shot the man-eater at 5 this evening. I will tell you all about it when I get home. It will take a couple of days to dry the skin and if to-day is Friday, as Gunga Ram says it is, I will start on Monday and be home on Tuesday night – but don't worry if I fail to turn up on Tuesday. I might be delayed over the skin. It has taken some getting and I don't want to risk its getting spoilt.'

What followed had none of the drama of the published story and deviates from it quite considerably. Jim continued:

'. . . At three o'clock this afternoon I set out to tie a katra up at Saryapani where I have been tying up since 31st. On the way out I changed my mind and instead of going to Saryapani turned down the forest track with the intention of tying the katra up where the Chamoli boy was killed on the 25th February. Most of the jungle had been burnt but about a half a mile down the track I came on a nice bit of green grass on which several sambhar were feeding. It looked as good a place as any so I made the men (I had three with me) collect a few bundles of oak leaves, and before leaving the katra I made a man go up a tree growing on the edge of the Khud and call, as they do here when out with cattle. I, in the meantime, stood on a projecting rock near by and once I thought I heard a movement down below me but could not be sure. Anyway the men had heard nothing so we left the katra, to go up the zig zag track to Dharampani where the Vivians and I had sat one evening looking down the valley. After going a few yards I came to a deep nala. As it looked a likely place for tracks I climbed down into it and found the tracks of the man-eater. The tracks were old, possibly made by the tiger when going away after eating out Vivian's katra. Anyway I decided to go down the nala and look for tracks where it joined the main ravine. The going was bad over huge rocks and in one place I wanted a free hand. By the way, I have forgotten to mention that I picked up two nightjar's eggs close to where the katra was tied so I handed the rifle over to Madho Singh. I got down alright and as Madho Singh joined me he put the rifle into my right hand, I had the eggs in the other, and whispered that some animal had growled like a pig or a bear, he was not sure which. The nala was very narrow just here, and to our right and overhanging us was an enormous rock the top of which was about 8 feet above our heads. At the lower end of the rock the bed of the nala was on a level with the banks. I tip-toed forward without making a sound and as I cleared the rock I looked over my right shoulder and – looked straight into the tiger's face. She flattened down her ears and bared her teeth and slipped forward but by then I had slipped the safety over and the bullet went through her heart. It was all over in a heart beat and the tiger was dead as nails. I am glad I got her like this – no sitting up and no fuss. She was just what I expected her to be – old and thin; cracked pads and teeth worn down to the gums, but her coat, on the whole, is not bad. I told Vivian last year that she was 8–4. I might be an inch out – not more. I did not break the eggs and the Nightjar was glad to get them back.'

Compare this with a fragment of the eventual telling:

'. . . to get it to bear on the tigress the muzzle would have to be swung round three-quarters of a circle.

'The movement of swinging round the rifle, with one hand, was begun very slowly, and hardly perceptibly, and when a quarter of a circle had been made, the stock came in contact with my right side. It was now necessary to extend my arm, and as the stock cleared my side, the swing was very slowly continued. My arm was now at full stretch and the weight of the rifle was beginning to tell. Only a little further now for the muzzle to go, and the tigress – who had not once taken her eyes off mine – was still looking up at me . . .

'How long it took the rifle to make the three-quarters circle I am not in a position to say. To me . . . it appeared that my arm was paralysed, and that the swing would never be completed.'

So much for the kill being over in a heart beat.

Justified criticisms were levelled at Jim and one has to accept that he did overwrite but he did not do this for the sake of self-promotion but just to give a better read.

Few opportunities exist now to prove or disprove his claims. Those who were present are most of them long since dead and, on the stalk, Jim was more often than not alone. One has to rely on his basic trustworthiness and the last of his traceable surviving man-eater skins.

This is the pelt of the first Chowgarh tigress, the cub of the one shot in such unbelievable circumstances. In his narrative, Jim mentions killing the animal with a single shot and, from his description of the way the tigress reacted to the shot, it was obvious he hit her well: the skin has but one bullet hole on the topmost corner of the right shoulder, by the hackles. The elevation of his shot as related in the story is correct for this kind of wound. The bullet hole is a neat round one. On the left hind leg there is another, jagged hole. The bullet shattered the animal's spine and passed on through her, disformed. From the range mentioned, this is more than likely. Furthermore, Jim mentions in the story that he had to skin the tigress with a penknife: the skin is very tattily cut and mounted on sections of brown bear hide – very soon afterwards Jim killed a bear with an axe.

An interesting aside to the tale of the Chowgarh tigress comes from Norah Vivian, the wife of Graham ('Ham') Vivian the District Commissioner. On the night of 21 March 1930, the Vivians had been, according to Jim, staying in the Kala Agar forest bungalow and were sitting on the veranda having tea when a woman was killed within two hundred yards. Vivian grabbed his rifle and followed the drag marks to the body.

Norah Vivian recalled the whole episode in 1984:

'We got there (Kala Agar) and were resting in camp – my husband was shaving – when there were great shouts outside. A woman had just been taken from a party of grasscutters a few hundred yards up the hill. She was up a rhododendron tree, cutting fodder branches, about six feet up. The tigress crept up and swept her legs from under her, knocked her down and crushed her skull. She was a young girl or woman, and was lying in grass in the open. My husband got permission – religious reasons – to sit up over the kill. He sat in a nearby tree for the rest of that day and all night. Nothing. At 5 a.m. dawn, I walked to him with a cocked rifle. Got him down. We sent a note to Jim. The next night we sat up again over a young bullock – the woman was taken for her funeral. We saw a bear, but not the tiger – we were not mistaken in this as Jim writes.' She added, 'He was wrong in the story – it makes a better tale, doesn't it?'

Norah Vivian was a good friend of both Jim and Maggie and her comments are not malicious. Indeed, when Jim finally shot the tigress on the afternoon of 11 April, he cut out from the tigress's neck, when skinning her, one of the 'lucky' floating bones that Indians regard as the ultimate talisman against tiger attack and, having this mounted in gold, gave it to Norah some time later as a scarf pin.

What was more, Norah Vivian was an expert *shikari* herself and a crack shot who certainly knew a bear from a tiger. But Jim wrote in his story:

'There was no moon, and just as daylight was fading out and nearby objects becoming indistinct, they first heard, and then saw, an animal coming up to the kill which, in the uncertain light, they mistook for a bear.'

Jim did not arrive until forty-eight hours later so how could he have assessed accurately the spoor marks of a bear on such ground?

'The details and dates in his stories are sometimes questionable,' Norah Vivian reported. 'Even the Chowgarh tigress story is not exactly as it was. He was not careful over some details.'

Jim was not a charlatan. He did not seek glory nor to be what he was not. He was simply an expert and courageous hunter turned conservator turned popular author who, determined to give his readers their money's worth along with a modicum of conservationist evangelising, twisted just a few little facts that his memory had already partially corrupted. His books are none the worse for it and, as they imply, he was undoubtedly regarded by many, from humble villagers to District Commissioners like Ham Vivian, as the Authority on the hunting of Indian big game in the mountains of the north.

The Outspan Hotel had an added attraction for Jim which he must have seen as the ultimate in luxury *machans*. It was called Treetops.

Eric and Lady Bettie Sherbrooke Walker, who owned the Outspan Hotel, had built what amounted to a unique game observation platform some miles away on the edge of the forests. Constructed over thirty feet up in the branches of a massive ficus tree and reached by a stout but uneven ladder, it consisted of a rough and ready tree house with an extensive observation platform overlooking a water hole and a saltlick. On three sides were jungle and on the fourth a long grass glade. To this clearing, about a hundred yards wide and two hundred and fifty long, came a huge assortment of game. Would-be photographers and tourists could visit Treetops for a day or a night, or both.

The accommodation was spartan: a dining room with a wood-burning stove, three bedrooms, a chemical toilet, a tiny room for the resident hunter-cum-guard, a room for the staff and the long viewing balcony equipped with comfortably padded seats. To reach the place, one had to walk through the bush for a little over two miles, chaperoned by an armed hunter.

The wildlife was the attraction, and millionaires, film stars and wealthy tourists went there. Jim, too, often visited Treetops either as an honorary guide or as a member of the photographing public. His nephew, Tom Corbett, was one of the semi-resident hunters.

In the February of 1952, the then Princess Elizabeth and her husband Prince Philip, Duke of Edinburgh, paid a state visit to Kenya and spent some of their stay at the Royal Lodge at Sagana, twenty miles from Nyeri. A number of engagements were arranged in the locality including a polo match at Nyeri and a trip to Treetops.

On 4 February, Prince Philip had played in a polo match eight miles from Nyeri to which both Jim and Maggie had gone, but not as spectators.

For Jim, the chance to be so close to royalty was as much of a thrill as being close to a tiger, if not more so. His life had been at times ruled by patriotism and this was the culmination of all his patriotic fervour.

The polo ground was, in Jim's opinion, a risky venue for the visiting royalty. Mau Mau terrorists were known to operate in the area and Jim noted with a *shikari*'s eyes that the ground was surrounded on three sides by forest and tall tropical grasses. Worse still, the ground was approached by a gully that began in the forest. Had he been a Mau Mau member, he would easily have been able to get close enough for a safe shot.

Before the match, Jim drove in the Citroën to a bridge that spanned the gully and went down into it. A careful study of the ground showed no human footprints. He and Maggie then parked their car close to the bridge and watched the gully for the duration of the polo game. It was a brave but foolish thing to do. Had the terrorists decided on an attack –

which was unlikely in the face of the considerable security presence – they would have been foiled and would certainly have killed two Europeans in a conveniently isolated car in lieu of the bigger targets.

The next day, Jim received a note from an aide to the Princess requesting that he join her at Treetops that afternoon. He could hardly refuse but he also certainly would never have considered doing so.

Reaching Treetops ahead of the royal party, Jim waited anxiously as he saw a herd of elephant drawing nearer. Finally, the small party arrived and the Princess fearlessly walked to the ladder ten yards from the nearest elephant and, giving Jim her handbag and camera, climbed the steps. The rest of the party followed. Jim was full of admiration for this young woman's act of bravery.

During afternoon tea and the evening's dinner, Jim talked with Prince Philip about the Abominable Snowman and helped the Princess to recognise animals as they appeared. When the royal party retired for the night, Jim sat himself on the top of the ladder, wrapped in his army blanket, a rifle across his lap, and kept an all-night vigil.

Provisions for Treetops were hauled up by a rope which hung down near to where Jim had set himself on sentry duty. In the middle of the night, it was suddenly, very gently, agitated. Jim, expecting a man to appear below him, readied himself. The rope again trembled but no one rose up it. Most probably, it was a leopard attracted to the clearing.

The Princess left the following morning at ten o'clock, after breakfast, filled with the thrill of the game watching.

During that night, King George VI died.

The register which was kept of animals seen was given to Jim to complete for that momentous night. He wrote up the report, ending it:

'For the first time in the history of the world a young girl climbed into a tree one day a Princess, and after having what she described as her most thrilling experience she climbed down from the tree the next day a Queen . . .'

His pride at having guarded the Queen as she acceded to the throne was something he never forgot and he wrote of it in a small book, *Tree Tops* which he completed early in 1955. Oxford University Press published it later that year with an introduction by Lord Hailey and more drawings by Raymond Sheppard. It was Jim's last book.

By now, Jim was frail. He had not been in good health since moving to

Nyeri. The town is situated at an altitude of nearly three thousand feet and the pneumonia from which Jim had suffered in 1947 had left lesions on his lungs which his cigarette smoking continuously irritated. He coughed badly and had difficulty breathing at that altitude, especially in the dry season when the air was laden with dust. Maggie suggested a number of times that they move again, but Jim saw no point in it: 'One has to live somewhere,' was his reply to these suggestions.

Several times between 1949 and 1955, he was kept in hospital suffering from bronchitis and, on the morning of 19 April 1955, Jim suffered a severe heart attack. He was rushed to the small hospital in Nyeri in great pain and died later that day. He was buried in the churchyard of St Peter's Church in Nyeri near to the tomb of Lord Baden-Powell. His last words to Maggie were:

'Always be brave, and try and make the world a happier place for others to live in.'

The words summed up his life.

Envoi

After his death was reported, most of the major British and American newspapers carried obituaries and memorials. The most pertinent appeared in *The Times* during the following month. One was from Lord Willingdon, who wrote:

'May I please be given space to pay a tribute from the Fauna Preservation Society to the memory of the late Colonel Jim Corbett. Not only had Corbett an unsurpassed knowledge of the jungles of northern India, but nobody cared more than he for the animals which lived therein. Moreover, as our members well know, nobody could plead more effectively for their preservation.'

The most moving tribute came from an anonymous correspondent:

'A friend writes:
    May I try, on behalf of some who knew him well, to add a few personal notes to your most worthy obituary notice of Jim Corbett? He was a great man. Not only was he a genius in the ways of the jungle, as millions who have read his books can tell, but he also had in him the depth and the gentleness that go with the best sort of greatness. With it all went, too, the quietest and softest of voices, which was a joy to listen to whether it was telling you a story about a tiger in the past or instructing you how to tackle one in a few minutes' time. His sense of duty and unselfishness was paramount, alike to his country in war as to the villagers of his Kumaon hills in peace – how these adored him and how they must be grieving at his passing.
    'Just before the war Jim gave me a copy of his original *Jungle Stories* and on the flyleaf he wrote the words "To remind you of the jungles in which you and I have spent many happy days together". Those

days were to me, as were similar days to my family, as happy as any I will ever know. Their essence is as fresh and compelling as if it had been of yesterday. The earth heavy with dew in the early morning, turning so soon to dry dust under the risen sun; the swish of the grass as the elephants ambled slowly through it; the scarlet of the samal tree blossoms and the gleam of the flame of the forest; the beauty of the birds around you; that fugitive glimpse of the striped back sliding noiselessly away before you; then the peaceful evening in Jim's company as you sat in the night air free from the smell of paraffin lamps in the tent.

'All this and much more, made magic by the presence of this man, comes welling up now. We shall never forget him, nor will the passage of the years ever dim our love for this "verray parfit, gentil knyght."'

The friend was John Hope, the viceroy's son.

The success of Jim's books continued and his fame spread. The Indian Government, in Jim's honour, renamed the Hailey National Park as the Corbett National Park in 1957. The house at Kaladhungi was repainted and eventually became a Corbett museum. The World Wildlife Fund (under the Duke of Edinburgh's patronage) sponsored the Project Tiger concern to save the tiger from extinction and the Corbett National Park is one of the chosen areas for positive – and, as it has turned out, highly successful – conservation. Interest in Jim Corbett grew.

With the changes in the world since Jim's death, wildlife conservation has become a major international concern. The indiscriminate killing of whales for pet-food, the destruction of environments and the inessential encroaching of land development and agriculture upon virgin areas have justly become powerful social, moral and political issues. It is in no small part due to Jim that such issues have reached the awareness of the public. Through his attitudes, his bestselling books, his criticism of both the British and subsequent Indian governments of India, his alliance with such people as Lord Hailey and by his embryonic conservationist mutterings in *Indian Wild Life* half a century ago, he has earned a great debt from the world after his death.

As John Hope, now Lord Glendevon, hoped in his letter to *The Times*, Jim Corbett has not been forgotten. More importantly, what he stood for has been remembered and his lessons, up to a point, are being heeded.

MAN-EATERS OF KUMAON: AUTHOR'S NOTE

As many of the stories in this book are about man-eating tigers, it is perhaps desirable to explain why these animals develop man-eating tendencies.

A man-eating tiger is a tiger that has been compelled, through stress of circumstances beyond its control, to adopt a diet alien to it. The stress of circumstances is, in nine times out of ten, wounds, and in the tenth case old age.[1] The wound that has caused a particular tiger to take to man-eating might be the result of a carelessly fired shot and failure to follow up and recover the wounded animal, or be the result of the tiger having lost his temper when killing a porcupine. Human beings are not the natural prey of tigers, and it is only when tigers have been incapacitated through wounds or old age that, in order to live, they are compelled to take to a diet of human flesh.

A tiger when killing its natural prey, which it does either by stalking or lying in wait for it, depends for the success of its attack on its speed and, to a lesser extent, on the condition of its teeth and claws. When, therefore, a tiger is suffering from one or more painful wounds, or when its teeth are missing or defective and its claws worn down, and it is unable to catch the animals it has been accustomed to eating, it is driven by necessity to killing human beings. The changeover from animal to human flesh is, I believe, in most cases accidental. As an illustration of what I mean by 'accidental' I quote the case of the Mukteswar man-eating tigress. This tigress, a comparatively young animal, in an encounter with a porcupine, lost an eye and got some fifty quills, varying in length from one to nine inches, embedded in the arm and under the pad of her right foreleg. Several of these quills after striking a bone had doubled back in the form of a U, the point and the broken-off end being quite close together. Suppurating sores formed where she endeavoured to extract the quills with her teeth, and while she was lying up in a thick patch of grass, starving and licking her wounds, a woman

---

1 Since Corbett wrote this, there has been established an eleventh case. It is that of the tiger dispossessed of his natural environment either by human habitation or, in the case of successful tiger reserves, increasing numbers of tigers in an inadequate territorial area and which, forced to exist in a locality in which natural food is in very short supply [or totally absent] takes to killing domestic stock or humans.

selected this particular patch of grass to cut as fodder for her cattle. At first the tigress took no notice, but when the woman had cut the grass right up to where she was lying the tigress struck once, the blow crushing the woman's skull. Death was instantaneous, for, when found the following day, she was grasping her sickle with her hand and holding a tuft of grass, which she was about to cut when struck, with the other. Leaving the woman lying where she had fallen, the tigress limped off for a distance of over a mile and took refuge in a little hollow under a fallen tree. Two days later a man came to chip firewood off this fallen tree, and the tigress who was lying on the far side killed him. The man fell across the tree, and as he had removed his coat and shirt, and the tigress had clawed his back when killing him, it is possible that the smell of the blood trickling down his body as he hung across the bole of the tree first gave her the idea that he was something that she could satisfy her hunger with. However that may be, before leaving him she ate a small portion from his back. A day later she killed her third victim deliberately, and without having received any provocation. Thereafter she became an established man-eater and had killed twenty-four people before she was finally accounted for.

A tiger on a fresh kill, or a wounded tiger, or a tigress with small cubs, will occasionally kill human beings who disturb them; but these tigers cannot by any stretch of the imagination be termed man-eaters, though they are often so called. Personally, I would give a tiger the benefit of the doubt once, and once again, before classing it as a man-eater, and whenever possible I would subject the alleged victim to a post-mortem before letting the kill go down on the records as the kill of a tiger or a leopard, as the case might be. This subject of post-mortems of human beings alleged to have been killed by either tigers or leopards or, in the plains, by wolves or hyenas, is of great importance, for, though I refrain from giving instances, I know of cases where deaths have wrongly been ascribed to carnivora.

It is a popular fallacy that *all* man-eaters are old and mangy, the mange being attributed to the excess of salt in human flesh. I am not competent to give any opinion on the relative quantity of salt in human or animal flesh; but I can, and do, assert that a diet of human flesh, so far from having an injurious effect on the coat of man-eaters, has quite the opposite effect, for all the man-eaters I have seen have had remarkably fine coats.

Another popular belief in connection with man-eaters is that the cubs of these animals automatically become man-eaters. This is quite a reasonable supposition; but it is not borne out by actual facts, and the reason why the cubs of a man-eater do not themselves become man-eaters, is that human beings are not the natural prey of tigers, or of leopards.

A cub will eat whatever its mother provides, and I have even known of tiger cubs assisting their mothers to kill human beings; but I do not know of a single instance of a cub, after it had left the protection of its parent, or after that parent had been killed, taking to killing human beings.[2]

In the case of human beings killed by carnivora, the doubt is often expressed as to whether the animal responsible for the kill is a tiger or leopard. As a general rule – to which I have seen no exceptions – tigers are responsible for all kills that take place in daylight, and leopards are responsible for all kills that take place in the dark. Both animals are semi-nocturnal forest-dwellers, have much the same habits, employ similar methods of killing, and are both capable of carrying their human victims for long distances. It would be natural, therefore, to expect them to hunt at the same hours; and that they do not do so is due to the difference in courage of the two animals. When a tiger becomes a man-eater it loses all fear of human beings and, as human beings move about more freely in the day than they do at night, it is able to secure its victims during daylight hours and there is no necessity for it to visit their habitations at night. A leopard, on the other hand, even after it has killed scores of human beings, never loses its fear of man; and as it is unwilling to face up to human beings in daylight, it secures its victims when they are moving about at night, or by breaking into their houses at night. Owing to these characteristics of the two animals, namely, that one loses its fear of human beings and kills in the daylight, while the other retains its fear and kills in the dark, man-eating tigers are easier to shoot than man-eating leopards.

The frequency with which a man-eating tiger kills depends on (a) the supply of natural food in the area in which it is operating; (b) the nature of the disability which has caused it to become a man-eater; and (c) whether it is a male or a female with cubs.

Those of us who lack the opportunity of forming our own opinion on any particular subject are apt to accept the opinions of others, and in no case is this more apparent than in the case of tigers – here I do not refer to man-eaters in particular, but to tigers in general. The author who first used the words 'as cruel as a tiger' and 'as bloodthirsty as a tiger', when attempting to emphasise the evil character of the villain of his piece, not only showed a lamentable ignorance of the animal he defamed, but coined phrases which have come into universal circulation, and which are mainly responsible for the wrong opinion of tigers held by all except that very small proportion of the public who have the opportunity of forming their own opinions.

When I see the expression 'as cruel as a tiger' and 'as bloodthirsty as a tiger' in print, I think of a small boy armed with an old muzzle-loading gun – the right barrel of which was split for six inches of its length, and the stock and barrels of which were kept from falling apart by lashings of brass wire – wandering through the jungles of the *terai* and *bhabar* in the days when there were ten tigers to every one that now survives; sleeping anywhere he happened to be when night came on, with a small fire to give him company and warmth; wakened at intervals by

2   cf. the Chowgarh tigress.

the calling of tigers, sometimes in the distance, at other times near at hand; throwing another stick on the fire and turning over and continuing his interrupted sleep without one thought of unease; knowing from his own short experience and from what others, who like himself had spent their days in the jungles, had told him, that a tiger, unless molested, would do him no harm; or during daylight hours avoiding any tiger he saw, and when that was not possible, standing perfectly still until it had passed and gone, before continuing on his way. And I think of him on one occasion stalking half a dozen jungle fowl that were feeding in the open, and on creeping up to a plum bush and standing up to peer over, the bush heaving and a tiger walking out on the far side and, on clearing the bush, turning round and looking at the boy with an expression on its face which said as clearly as any words, 'Hello, kid, what the hell are you doing here?' and, receiving no answer, turning around and walking away very slowly without once looking back. And then again I think of the tens of thousands of men, women, and children who, while working in the forests or cutting grass or collecting dry sticks pass day after day close to where tigers are lying up and who, when they return safely to their homes, do not even know that they have been under the observation of this so-called 'cruel' and 'bloodthirsty' animal.

Half a century has rolled by since the day the tiger walked out of the plum bush, the latter thirty-two years of which have been spent in the more or less regular pursuit of man-eaters; and though sights have been seen which would have caused a stone to weep, I have not seen a case where a tiger has been deliberately cruel or where it has been bloodthirsty to the extent that it has killed, without provocation, more than it has needed to satisfy its hunger or the hunger of its cubs.

A tiger's function in the scheme of things is to help maintain the balance in nature and if, on rare occasions, when driven by dire necessity, he kills a human being or when his natural food has been exterminated by man he kills two per cent of the cattle he is alleged to have killed, it is not fair that for these acts a whole species should be branded as being cruel and bloodthirsty.

Sportsmen are admittedly conservative, the reason being that it has taken them years to form their opinions, and as each individual has a different point of view, it is only natural that opinions should differ on minor, or even in some cases on major, points, and for this reason I do not flatter myself that all the opinions I have expressed will meet with universal agreement.

There is, however, one point on which I am convinced all sportsmen – no matter whether their viewpoint has been a platform on a tree, the back of an elephant or their own feet – will agree with me, and that is, that the tiger is a large-hearted gentleman with boundless courage and that when he is exterminated – as exterminated he will be unless public opinion rallies to his support – India will be the poorer by having lost the finest of her fauna.

Leopards, unlike tigers, are to a certain extent scavengers and become man-eaters by acquiring a taste for human flesh when unrestricted slaughter of game has deprived them of their natural food.

The dwellers in our hills are predominantly Hindus, and as such cremate their dead. The cremation invariably takes place on the bank of a stream or river in order that the ashes may be washed down into the Ganges and eventually into the sea. As most of the villages are situated high up on the hills, while the streams or rivers are in many cases away down in the valleys, it will be realized that a funeral entails a considerable tax on the man-power of a small community when, in addition to the carrying party, labour has to be provided to collect and carry the fuel needed for the cremation. In normal times these rites are carried out very effectively; but when disease in epidemic form sweeps through the hills and the inhabitants die faster than they can be disposed of, a very simple rite, which consists of placing a live coal in the mouth of the deceased, is performed in the village and the body is then carried to the edge of the hill and cast into the valley below.

A leopard, in an area in which his natural food is scarce, finding these bodies, very soon acquires a taste for human flesh, and when the disease dies down and normal conditions are established, he very naturally, on finding his food supply cut off, takes to killing human beings.

Of the two man-eating leopards of Kumaon, which between them killed five hundred and twenty-five human beings, one[3] followed on the heels of a very severe outbreak of cholera, while the other[4] followed the mysterious disease which swept through India in 1918 and was called 'war fever'.

3   the Panar man-eating leopard.
4   the Rudraprayag man-eating leopard.

WILD LIFE IN THE VILLAGE: AN APPEAL

(from *Indian Wild Life*, vol. I, no. 2: 1936)

It was a small village of some 16 ploughs differing in no respect from hundreds of similar villages, scattered throughout the length of the tract along the Bhabar. Originally the village had been surrounded by tree jungle intercepted with grass, and in this virgin jungle lived all the numerous denizens of the wild. To protect their crops the villagers erected thorn fences round their fields. As an additional safeguard a member of the depressed class was encouraged to settle in the village whose duty it was to watch the crops at night and see they were not damaged by stray cattle or wild animals. Owing to the abundance of game tigers did not interfere with the village cattle and I cannot remember a single case of cow or bullock having been killed by a tiger. In the course of time, a great change took place not only in the villagers themselves but also in the jungle surrounding the village. Hindus who formerly looked upon the taking of life as against their religious principles were now clamouring for gun licences and were competing with each other in the indiscriminate slaughter of game. As profits from the sale of game increased field work was neglected and land began to go out of cultivation. Simultaneously, lantana, introduced into Haldwani as a pot plant, started to kill out the grass and basonta until the village was surrounded with a dense growth of this obnoxious weed. Government now stepped in and at great expense built a pucca wall all round the village. The building of this wall freed the villagers from the necessity of erecting fences and watching their crops and gave them more time to devote to the killing of game. This heavy and unrestricted shooting of deer had the inevitable consequence of disturbing the balance in nature with the result that tigers and leopards, that had hitherto lived on game, were now forced to live on the village cattle. One morning in May of the present year[1] I arrived in the village and pitched my tent in a little clearing just outside the cultivated land. News of my arrival soon spread through the village and in a short time a dozen men were squatting in front of my tent. One

---

1 Not 1936: this essay appeared originally in 'Review of the Week' (Naini Tal) in 1932. The year in question is more likely to be 1931 or 1932.

and all had the same tale to tell. A tiger had taken up its quarters in the lantana and in the course of two years, had killed 150 head of cattle and unless it was destroyed the village would have to be abandoned. While the men were pouring out their tale of woe I observed a pair of vultures circling low over a narrow stretch of lantana running between the village wall and the public road. The two vultures were soon joined by others; so picking up a rifle I set off to investigate. Progress through the lantana was difficult but with the aid of a good hunting knife a way was eventually cut and the remains of a horse killed the previous day found. There were plenty of pug marks round the kill, little of which remained, and it was easy to locate the tiger from his low continuous growling but impossible to see him in the dense cover. Returning to the road which was only 40 yards from the kill and little used at this time of the year, I concealed myself behind a bush in the hope that the tiger would follow me to see if I had left the locality, quite a natural thing for it to do. Half an hour later the tiger walked out on to the road and gave me an easy shot as he stood facing me. That evening after I had skinned the tiger – he was a very old animal and I took four old bullets and nine pellets of buck-shot out of him – I called the villagers together and made an appeal to them on behalf of the few remaining deer in the jungle. On the opposite side of the village from my camp, irrigation water had been allowed to flow into the jungle. Over this water *machans* had been built in the trees and in these *machans* men sat through the heat of the day, and all night on moon-lit nights, and shot down animals that came to drink. There was no other water within miles and if a thirst-maddened animal avoided one *machan*, it fell victim to the man in the next. I told the villagers that God had given water free for all, and that it was a shameful thing for man to sit over the water God had provided and shoot His creatures when they came to drink. To do this was to lower themselves below a corpse-eating hyaena, for even he, the lowest of all creation, did not lie in wait to kill defenceless animals while they were drinking. The men listened to me in silence and when I had done, said they had not looked at the matter in this light, and they promised that they would take down the *machans* they had erected and in future would not molest the animals that came to the vicinity of the village to drink. I stayed in the locality several weeks, taking bird and animal pictures, and am glad to say the men kept their promise. I believe that much of the slaughter of deer that is daily taking place throughout the length and breadth of the Bhabar and Terai would cease if an appeal was made to the better feelings of men. I do not exaggerate the damage that is being done to our fauna by shooting over water.

Let me give you but one instance. An acquaintance of mine living in a village in the Bhabar adjoining my own, in one hot season, over one small pool of water shot, with a single barrel muzzle-loading gun, 60 head of cheetal and sambhar which he sold in a near-by bazaar at the rate of Rs. 5 per cheetal and Rs. 10 per sambhar. It is no exaggeration to say that the banks of every little stream and every pool of water in the vicinity of Bhabar villages are soaked with the blood of animals that never took toll of a single blade of the villagers' crops. I assert without fear of contradiction that for every shot fired on cultivated land from guns provided for crop protection, a hundred shots are fired in the jungle over water. Pigs and neelgai[2] are the only wild animals that damage the crops in the Bhabar to any extent, and to keep them out of cultivated land Government has expended lakhs of rupees in building pucca walls. It is asserted that in recent years tigers have increased. With this assertion I do not agree. It is a fact that more cattle are being killed every year, this is not due to the tigers having increased but due to the balance of nature having been disturbed by the unrestricted slaughter of game, and also to some extent to tigers having been driven out of their natural haunts where they were seldom or never seen by man, by the activities of the Forest Department. A country's fauna is a sacred trust, and I appeal to you not to betray your trust. Shooting over water, shooting over salt-licks, natural and artificial, shooting birds in the close season and when roosting at night, encouraging permit-holders to shoot hinds, fencing off of large areas of forest and the extermination by the Forest Department of all game within these areas, making of unnecessary motor tracks through the forest and shooting from motor cars, absence of sanctuaries and the burning of the forests by the Forest Department and by villagers at a time when the forests are full of young life are all combining to one end – the extermination of our fauna. If we do not bestir ourselves now, it will be to our discredit that the fauna of our province was exterminated in our generation and under our very eyes, while we looked on and never raised a finger to prevent it.

2   Spellings vary. Sambhar are more commonly spelt as sambhur and neelgai as nilgai.

APPENDIX 3

EXTRACTS FROM LETTERS TO MAGGIE CONCERNING PHOTOGRAPHY

(The letters were written on photographic trips in 1933: Naya Gaon or Maldhan were villages in the *terai*, the former not very far from Kaladhungi and the latter between Kashipur and Ramnagar.)

MALDHAN: 21 MAY 1933

My cold is a thing of the past and I am fit as I can be. I got to Kathgodam with half an hour to spare, had a toast and a cup of tea and left at 8.15 in a through train for Ramnagar. I met several men at Kashipur whom I know and when they heard I wanted to leave the train at the cattle farm, one half squared up with the guard and the other half with the driver with the inevitable result that the train was brought to a stand at the wrong spot. However, after a lot of shouting we went on again and drew up at the level crossing opposite the farm. As I stood on the road and the train went on its way every head came out of a window and the whole train salaamed and re-salaamed. I had to be a bit careful when passing the farm for cows that are practically wild do not like strangers. A mile in the hot sun left nothing dry on me and when I came to the first stream I sat down to cool off under a convenient tree and to have something to eat. On the far side of the stream a couple of hundred cows were feeding and mixed up with them were a number of red animals. As the cows gradually fed down stream I saw that the red animals were Gond[1]. There were about 50 of them and they were sitting down or standing under three small dhank[2] trees. After I had fed and crossed the stream which was up to my knees, I passed within a hundred yards of the Gond and they paid no attention to me, with the rod over my shoulder and the scarf flourished in my left hand, they took me for a *gwala*[3]. Half a mile further on I saw a bunch of about 40 black buck. Ram Singh got to the bungalow a few minutes before I did and ten minutes later the cart rolled up and I had a much needed cup of tea. It was then about 2.30 pm. At about 4 I set out with Baktar to prospect the pool two miles north of the bungalow. I took the first track at the edge of the forest and by the time I got to the pool I had seen 38 Gond, about 30 pig and at

1 swamp deer.
2 'Flame of The Forest' trees.
3 a cowherd.

261

least 50 Cheatle. The pool has lots of water in it but there were not many deer prints round it. On the way back I saw more Gond and Cheatle and selected several likely trees to sit up in. The only crab is that the prevailing wind is blowing from the East i.e. towards the forest and until it changes there is no hope of my getting a picture anywhere along this fire track. I went to bed after an early dinner and Ram Singh had just salaamed and gone off when two bears started fighting. They appeared to have selected the same dingaras[4] hive and scrapped over their find the greater part of the night. Close to them were numbers of Gond, Cheatles, Sambhar and peafowl and the combined noise would have kept anyone less tired than I was awake all night. It was very stormy when I got up and after an early *chota hazri* I set off to look at the ground South of the bungalow. I saw plenty of tracks, found a small pool of water, but here again the wind was blowing from the wrong quarter. After tiffin Baktar and I set out to try and find a pool in the forest reported in the Ranger's letter to Bailey[5]. First we went and salted a lick I had found in the morning and then went up the *nala* in which Strathcona and Cator shot their tigers. We had only gone up the *nala* a few yards when we put up two big bunches of Gond and Cheatle. At the upper end of the *nala* we got to the Maldhan Jihrna(?) road and a mile further on we found the most beautiful place I have ever seen for jungle photography. An emerald green glade miles long and a hundred to three hundred yards wide, with a stream zig-zagging down the middle, and trees, some dhank in full bloom and other jaman in young leaf dotted about. The glade is bounded on either side by a wall of sal in bloom. I climbed a dhank tree and wish I could describe the view from the top of it. In the foreground were five para[6] one with horns in velvet; a little further on a sambhar stag; beyond him three hind Gond, beyond them about twenty Gond under a dhank tree. Further on 25 Gond and the same number of Cheatle, some sitting down and others feeding. Then a fringe of jaman trees and beyond them a long line, almost extending right across the glade, of Gond and Cheatle all mixed up and perfectly good friends. No place I have ever seen was better situated for photography. The glade was approximately East and West, light was just as it should be and the wind was right. Some of the animals were near enough for my camera but it was getting towards evening so I just sat and watched the view and listened to the Cheatle stag challenging each other. On the way back I saw a snow white animal in a big bunch of Gond and Cheatle. It may have been an albino Gond or Cheatle or possibly a Sambhar.

MALDHAN: 25 APRIL (no year given)

You would have been interested to watch me calling up a bunch of about 35 Gond today, take a picture of them and then dash towards them and send them

4   wild bees.
5   a forest officer.
6   a small forest deer.

flying for their lives. I had seen these particular Gond for three days and had not been able to do anything with them because they were lying out on a big maidan with short grass on it. Today I went out alone and found them as usual lying down in the shade of a tree. With a little care I got to a small dhank tree about five hundred yards from them without their seeing me. I climbed to the top of the tree and with a leap made the distress call of a young deer. When I saw they had heard me I got off the tree and walked on all fours round and round the tree calling like a leopard. As I did this the whole herd stood up and started barking. I let them bark for about five minutes and then went off on all fours to an ant hill about 100 yards away on some rising ground. I called repeatedly as I went and as soon as I reached the ant hill I stuck my shoulders out to one side and moved it up and down and did the same with my head on the other. This was too much for the Gond and the whole lot of them came down in line and when they were near enough to film (50 yards), I made them stop and exposed 30 feet on them.

NAYA GAON: 5 & 6 MAY 1933

This wretched weather has come just at the wrong time for me. After days of watching and planning I have got the animals in this forest just where I want them; and now the changing wind and clouds are preventing my getting any pictures. If the wind would only blow from one quarter I would be alright. I have arranged the water so that instead of a stream half a mile long, there are now only two pools in which all the animals including the tiger are drinking. And just as my labours are being rewarded, this wretched weather comes along with the wind blowing from all quarters and all I can see of the animals coming to drink are their hind legs as they dash off on getting a puff of tainted air.

Yesterday I sat over the upper pool, the one nearer the camp and to-day I am going to sit over the lower one, the one near the fire lines. At this lower pool all the birds for miles round come to drink and it would be worth a trip round the world just to sit on my *machan* for a day and watch them and hear them sing. Doves are the most numerous, the big kind we get in Naini. They come by ones and twos, and tens and thousands appear to quench their thirst in this pool in the course of a day. Next in number are bronze winged doves, Paradise fly catchers, Blue fly catchers, Bulbuls half a dozen kinds, Honey Suckers both scarlet and black. Three kinds of tree sparrow, three kinds of minahs, Bee-eaters both large and small, medium size Kingfishers (the kind that live mostly on frogs), Ring and Turtle Doves, Pied robin, Crested drongos, Woodpeckers, golden and green and numbers of tits, pipits and warblers. Every now and then there is great excitement among the birds as a Kestrel, Merlin Hawk or Eagle swoops down, lands light as a feather and then struts down to the water's edge to drink. The Goas also cause a little excitement as they drag themselves over the dead leaves and after a careful look round, waddle with great difficulty through the slush to the water. The pool is about 30 yards long and five yards broad and on the far side opposite my *machan* there are two runi and one simal tree with a big creeper looped over the former. In this creeper there is a small python about 12 feet long and as thick as my thigh. Yesterday about a hundred monkeys came to drink and the Boy Scouts among them discovered the python. Many suggestions were made but rejected and then one had a brain wave to shake the beastly thing down. The suggestion was immediately acted on and in a minute twenty scouts were shaking their hardest. The result was a failure. All the python did was to stiffen himself (it was lying in loops just like a huge coil of rope) and nothing short of cutting down the creeper would have brought it to the ground.

One is never dull at this pool for there is movement and sound at it all day long. It is one of the few places that has escaped the fire and life turns round it. A langar barks at the tiger every now and then and the alarm is taken up in turn by Cheatle, Sambhar, Karkar, peafowl and moorgis and all the time I have my finger on the trigger of the camera against the coming of the tiger.

NAYA GAON: UNDATED

I am writing this on a tree at the lower end of the Naya Gaon stream and close to the spot where we have tiffin on several occasions. I thought there was a good chance of getting a tiger picture here so did not move across to Haripura. The day I came over from Bidrampur I sat up where the water ends while the camp was being got ready. At about 2 p.m. three Cheatle came through the jungle on the far side of the pool, had a drink and then crossed the stream and came towards my tree. I exposed 20 feet of film on them. A little later a fine jarao[7] came up and went straight down to the pool and for half an hour stood behind the only bush on my bank cooling its feet and drinking. Eventually it went off without my being able to get an exposure. Next morning while I was having breakfast I sent Bahadur and Dhanban to cut down the bush and make up a *machan*. On my way down to join them I put up several pig, two of which went off in to the lantana in front of where I was going to sit up. Two hours later I heard a pig give one scream and carefully noted the direction. At 3 p.m. the men returned bringing tea with them. I had in the 6 hours sit-up not seen a single animal and after tea Bahadur, Dhanban and I set out to find the pig. The jungle was a bit thick and just as we got to the place where I had heard the pig both B and D said in a loud stage whisper 'Shair' ('Tiger'). The tiger was about 20 yards away drawing its breath in and out through its teeth and making a most unpleasant sound. We stood perfectly still for a minute or two then started walking backwards. It's not easy to walk backwards through thick scrub and keep your eyes fixed on a point ahead. We thought we were doing quite well but the

7   a sambhur (dialect name).

tiger was not pleased with our pace and came bounding out to tell us to hop it. She, of course, had no intention of doing us any harm and even if I had been armed with a heavy rifle and had seen more of her I would not have fired for I know she was shooing us away from her cubs. It was then too late to do anything with the camera so after an early breakfast next morning I brought along the goat and sat up in the *machan* near the stream where I had sat the previous day. Nothing happened up to about 2.30 or 3 p.m. and then five cheatle came through the jungle where I was expecting the tiger to come from and went down to the pool. Three of the cheatle were stags and as there was no sign of the tiger I thought I would take a picture of the cheatle; so I trained the camera on them and was waiting for them to come up into the open on my bank before pressing the trigger. One of the cheatle was uneasy and instead of drinking stood in the stream looking back in the direction in which they had come. Presently her tail went up and at the same moment I saw what I took to be a sixth and a very big Cheatle coming along the same track that the others had come. With one eye to the view-finder I was not able to see very well but my attention was attracted to this last arrival by the way it avoided a dead branch and when I looked more closely at it I saw it was the tiger. It was then about 20 feet from the Cheatle in an open patch of sunlight and just as I was getting it into the viewfinder it sprang forward and pulled up on the bank of the stream where it found there was no hope of getting a Cheatle. The Cheatle I had seen raising its tail appeared to me to be watching every movement of the tiger and when the tiger sprang the cheatle gave a yell and the whole lot dashed off under my tree. The tiger went back into the jungle and for the next two hours I expected any minute to see it come out to the goat. Nothing however happened and when the shadows came off the goat I called up the men.

After tea I went back to the place to select another tree for my *machan* and when I got up to the pool there was the tiger sitting on the edge of it having a drink. Bahadur and Peari were with me and I can't think why she did not hear us. Anyway she didn't and after having her drink she turned her head and looked right into my face. She did not appear to be at all put out and just kept her eyes on me for a bit and then walked up the stream.

INDEX

OXFORD

MORE OXFORD PAPERBACKS

Details of a selection of other Oxford Paperbacks follow. A complete list of Oxford Paperbacks, including The World's Classics, Twentieth-Century Classics, OPUS, Past Masters, Oxford Authors, Oxford Shakespeare, and Oxford Paperback Reference, is available in the UK from the General Publicity Department, Oxford University Press (RS), Walton Street, Oxford, OX2 6DP.

In the USA, complete lists are available from the Paperbacks Marketing Manager, Oxford University Press, 200 Madison Avenue, New York, NY 10016.

Oxford Paperbacks are available from all good bookshops. In case of difficulty, customers in the UK can order direct from Oxford University Press Bookshop, 116 High Street, Oxford, Freepost, OX1 4BR, enclosing full payment. Please add 10 per cent of the published price for postage and packing.

OXFORD LIVES

Biography at its best—this popular series offers authoritative accounts of the lives of famous men and women from all walks of life.

JOYCE CARY
Gentleman Rider
Alan Bishop

Joyce Cary is one of the great English novelists of the century, admired especially for his *First Trilogy—Herself Surprised, To be a Pilgrim,* and *The Horse's Mouth*—and perhaps his masterpiece, *Mister Johnson*. Alan Bishop, who has spent 10 years researching Cary's writing, has created a vivid portrait of the man behind the books, and brilliantly illuminated the works themselves, to give us the most complex view yet of this important but elusive literary figure.

'an admirably clear and fascinating portrait emerges of a complex and contradictory individual: a gentleman-bohemian, an artist-public servant, and a patrician-iconoclast' *William Boyd*

'A fine biography . . . increases my respect and admiration for Cary.' Paul Bailey, *Observer*

'excellent' John Bayley, *Sunday Telegraph*

Also available in Oxford Lives:

A Life of Chekhov   Ronald Hingley
R. V. W.: A Biography of Ralph Vaughan Williams
Ursula Vaughan Williams
Eliot's New Life   Lyndall Gordon
Keith Douglas 1920–1944   Desmond Graham

OXFORD LIVES

Biography at its best—this popular series offers authoritative accounts of the lives of famous men and women from the arts and sciences, politics and exploration.

'SUBTLE IS THE LORD'
The Science and the Life of Albert Einstein
Abraham Pais

Abraham Pais, an award-winning physicist who knew Einstein personally during the last nine years of his life, presents a guide to the life and the thought of the most famous scientist of our century. Using previously unpublished papers and personal recollections from their years of acquaintance, the narrative illuminates the man through his work with both liveliness and precision, making this *the* authoritative scientific biography of Einstein.

'The definitive life of Einstein.'
Brian Pippard, *Times Literary Supplement*

'By far the most important study of both the man and the scientist.' Paul Davies, *New Scientist*

'An outstanding biography of Albert Einstein that one finds oneself reading with sheer pleasure.' *Physics Today*

Also in the Oxford Lives series:

Peter Fleming: A Biography   Duff Hart-Davies
Gustav Holst: A Biography   Imogen Holst
T. H. White   Sylvia Townsend Warner
Joyce Cary: Gentleman Rider   Alan Bishop

OXFORD LETTERS AND MEMOIRS

Letters, memoirs, and journals offer a special insight into the private lives of public figures and vividly recreate the times in which they lived. This popular series makes available the best and most entertaining of these documents, bringing the past to life in a fresh and personal way.

MY LIFE

Marc Chagall

It is generally acknowledged that Marc Chagall is one of the greatest painters of the twentieth century, and his paintings, sketches, and gouaches hang in museums all over the world.

While in post-revolutionary Moscow in 1919, a time of great uncertainty for Chagall, he began to write his autobiography and later, back in Berlin, to prepare the illustrations that he eventually wove into the text. The result is a stunning literary and visual account of Chagall's formative years, and the key to the early influences which shaped his greatest masterpieces.

With characteristic humour and verve he describes his childhood in the provincial Russian town of Witebsk, his early adventures, his first meeting with his future wife Bella, and then his move from Russia to Paris where he joined the bohemian set of artists at work there, and where he eventually found fulfilment and recognition. When war broke out in 1914, Chagall and his family returned to Russia, and after the October Revolution of 1917 he was appointed Commissar for Fine Art at Witebsk by the Soviets, a post he was eminently unsuited to hold, his modern French techniques being incomprehensible to the authorities. The book ends with Chagall's decision to return to France.

Also in Oxford Letters and Memoirs:

OXFORD LETTERS & MEMOIRS

This popular series offers fascinating personal records of the lives of famous men and women from all walks of life.

JOURNEY CONTINUED

Alan Paton

'an extraordinary last testament, told in simple and pungent style . . . for anyone new to the period and to Paton, it will be a revelation' *Independent*

This concluding volume of autobiography (the sequel to *Towards the Mountain*) begins in 1948, the year in which Paton's bestselling novel, *Cry, the Beloved Country*, was published, and the Nationalist Party of South Africa came to power. Both events were to have a profound effect on Paton's life, and they represent two major themes in this book, literature and politics.

  With characteristic resonance and trenchancy, Paton describes his career as a writer of books, which were received with extreme hostility by his fellow South Africans, and also covers his political life, notably the founding—and later Chairmanship—of the Liberal Party of South Africa, the multi-racial centre party opposed to apartheid.

'required reading for anyone who wants to understand, compassionately, the full tragedy of South Africa' *Daily Express*

Also in Oxford Letters & Memoirs:

Memories and Adventures Arthur Conan Doyle
Echoes of the Great War Andrew Clark
A Local Habitation: Life and Times 1918–1940
Richard Hoggart
Pack My Bag Henry Green

HISTORY IN OXFORD PAPERBACKS

Oxford Paperbacks offers a comprehensive list of books on British history, ranging from Frank Stenton's *Anglo-Saxon England* to John Guy's *Tudor England*, and from Christopher Hill's *A Turbulent, Seditious, and Factious People* to Kenneth O. Morgan's *Labour in Power: 1945–1951*.

TUDOR ENGLAND

John Guy

Tudor England is a compelling account of political and religious developments from the advent of the Tudors in the 1460s to the death of Elizabeth I in 1603.

Following Henry VII's capture of the Crown at Bosworth in 1485, Tudor England witnessed far-reaching changes in government and the Reformation of the Church under Henry VIII, Edward VI, Mary, and Elizabeth; that story is enriched here with character studies of the monarchs and politicians that bring to life their personalities as well as their policies.

Authoritative, clearly argued, and crisply written, this comprehensive book will be indispensable to anyone interested in the Tudor Age.

'lucid, scholarly, remarkably accomplished . . . an excellent overview' *Sunday Times*

'the first comprehensive history of Tudor England for more than thirty years' Patrick Collinson, *Observer*

Also in Oxford Paperbacks:

John Calvin   William J. Bouwsma
Early Modern France 1515–1715   Robin Briggs
The Spanish Armada   Felipe Fernández-Armesto
Time in History   G. J. Whitrow

HISTORY IN OXFORD PAPERBACKS

Oxford Paperbacks' superb history list offers books on a wide range of topics from ancient to modern times, whether general period studies or assessments of particular events, movements, or personalities.

THE STRUGGLE FOR
THE MASTERY OF EUROPE 1848–1918

A. J. P. Taylor

The fall of Metternich in the revolutions of 1848 heralded an era of unprecedented nationalism in Europe, culminating in the collapse of the Hapsburg, Romanov, and Hohenzollern dynasties at the end of the First World War. In the intervening seventy years the boundaries of Europe changed dramatically from those established at Vienna in 1815. Cavour championed the cause of *Risorgimento* in Italy; Bismarck's three wars brought about the unification of Germany; Serbia and Bulgaria gained their independence courtesy of the decline of Turkey—'the sick man of Europe'; while the great powers scrambled for places in the sun in Africa. However, with America's entry into the war and President Wilson's adherence to idealistic internationalist principles, Europe ceased to be the centre of the world, although its problems, still primarily revolving around nationalist aspirations, were to smash the Treaty of Versailles and plunge the world into war once more.

A. J. P. Taylor has drawn the material for his account of this turbulent period from the many volumes of diplomatic documents which have been published in the five major European languages. By using vivid language and forceful characterization, he has produced a book that is as much a work of literature as a contribution to scientific history.

'One of the glories of twentieth-century writing.' *Observer*

Also in Oxford Paperbacks:

Portrait of an Age: Victorian England   G. M. Young
Germany 1866–1945   Gorden A. Craig
The Russian Revolution 1917–1932   Sheila Fitzpatrick
France 1848–1945   Theodore Zeldin

OPUS

General Editors: Christopher Butler,
Robert Evans, Alan Ryan

OPUS is a series of accessible introductions to a wide range of studies in the sciences and humanities.

METROPOLIS

Emrys Jones

Past civilizations have always expressed themselves in great cities, immense in size, wealth, and in their contribution to human progress. We are still enthralled by ancient cities like Babylon, Rome, and Constantinople. Today, giant cities abound, but some are pre-eminent. As always, they represent the greatest achievements of different cultures. But increasingly, they have also been drawn into a world economic system as communications have improved.

Metropolis explores the idea of a class of supercities in the past and in the present, and in the western and developing worlds. It analyses the characteristics they share as well as those that make them unique; the effect of technology on their form and function; and the problems that come with size—congestion, poverty and inequality, squalor—that are sobering contrasts to the inherent glamour and attraction of great cities throughout time.

Also available in OPUS:

The Medieval Expansion of Europe   J. R. S. Phillips
Metaphysics: The Logical Approach   José A. Bernadete
The Voice of the Past 2/e   Paul Thompson
Thinking About Peace and War   Martin Ceadel

POLITICS IN OXFORD PAPERBACKS

Oxford Paperbacks offers incisive and provocative studies of the political ideologies and institutions that have shaped the modern world since 1945.

GOD SAVE ULSTER!
The Religion and Politics of Paisleyism

Steve Bruce

Ian Paisley in the only modern Western leader to have founded his own Church and political party, and his enduring popularity and success mirror the complicated issues which continue to plague Northern Ireland. This book is the first serious analysis of his religious and political careers and a unique insight into Unionist politics and religion in Northern Ireland today.

Since it was founded in 1951, the Free Presbyterian Church of Ulster has grown steadily; it now comprises some 14,000 members in fifty congregations in Ulster and ten branches overseas. The Democratic Unionist Party, formed in 1971, now speaks for about half of the Unionist voters in Northern Ireland, and the personal standing of the man who leads both these movements was confirmed in 1979 when Ian R. K. Paisley received more votes than any other member of the European Parliament. While not neglecting Paisley's 'charismatic' qualities, Steve Bruce argues that the key to his success has been his ability to embody and represent traditional evangelical Protestantism and traditional Ulster Unionism.

'original and profound . . . I cannot praise this book too highly.'
Bernard Crick, *New Society*

Also in Oxford Paperbacks:

Freedom Under Thatcher   Keith Ewing and Conor Gearty
Strong Leadership   Graham Little
The Thatcher Effect   Dennis Kavanagh and Anthony Seldon

RELIGION AND THEOLOGY
IN OXFORD PAPERBACKS

Oxford Paperbacks offers incisive studies of the philosophies and ceremonies of the world's major religions, including Christianity, Judaism, Islam, Buddhism, and Hinduism.

A HISTORY OF HERESY

David Christie-Murray

'Heresy, a cynic might say, is the opinion held by a minority of men which the majority declares unacceptable and is strong enough to punish.'

What is heresy? Who were the great heretics and what did they believe? Why might those originally condemned as heretics come to be regarded as martyrs and cherished as saints?

Heretics, those who dissent from orthodox Christian belief, have existed at all times since the Christian Church was founded and the first Christians became themselves heretics within Judaism. From earliest times too, politics, orthodoxy, and heresy have been inextricably entwined—to be a heretic was often to be a traitor and punishable by death at the stake—and heresy deserves to be placed against the background of political and social developments which shaped it.

This book is a vivid combination of narrative and comment which succeeds in both re-creating historical events and elucidating the most important—and most disputed—doctrines and philosophies.

Also in Oxford Paperbacks:

Christianity in the West 1400–1700   John Bossy
John Henry Newman: A Biography   Ian Ker
Islam: The Straight Path   John L. Esposito

OXFORD REFERENCE

Oxford is famous for its superb range of dictionaries and reference books. The Oxford Reference series offers the most up-to-date and comprehensive paperbacks at the most competitive prices, across a broad spectrum of subjects.

THE CONCISE OXFORD COMPANION TO ENGLISH LITERATURE

Edited by Margaret Drabble and Jenny Stringer

Based on the immensely popular fifth edition of the *Oxford Companion to English Literature* this is an indispensable, compact guide to the central matter of English literature.

There are more than 5,000 entries on the lives and works of authors, poets, playwrights, essayists, philosophers, and historians; plot summaries of novels and plays; literary movements; fictional characters; legends; theatres; periodicals; and much more.

The book's sharpened focus on the English literature of the British Isles makes it especially convenient to use, but there is still generous coverage of the literature of other countries and of other disciplines which have influenced or been influenced by English literature.

From reviews of *The Oxford Companion to English Literature Fifth Edition:*

'a book which one turns to with constant pleasure . . . a book with much style and little prejudice' Iain Gilchrist, *TLS*

'it is quite difficult to imagine, in this genre, a more useful publication' Frank Kermode, *London Review of Books*

'incarnates a living sense of tradition . . . sensitive not to fashion merely but to the spirit of the age' Christopher Ricks, *Sunday Times*

Also available in Oxford Reference:

The Concise Oxford Dictionary of Art and Artists
edited by Ian Chilvers
A Concise Oxford Dictionary of Mathematics
Christopher Clapham
The Oxford Spelling Dictionary   compiled by R. E. Allen
A Concise Dictionary of Law   edited by Elizabeth A. Martin

ART AND ARCHITECTURE IN OXFORD PAPERBACKS

Oxford Paperbacks offers a growing list of art and architecture books, ranging from Michael Baxandall on Renaissance Italy to George Melly on pop art and from Anthony Blunt on art theory to Bram Dijkstra on fin-de-siècle 'erotic' art.

ENGLISH PARISH CHURCHES AS WORKS OF ART

Alec Clifton-Taylor

In the course of his life Alec Clifton-Taylor visited thousands of churches and recorded his observations and opinions on their merits. The result, in this book, is not a dry analysis of the chronological evolution of churches and their styles, but a revealing tour of the parish church with the greatest emphasis on aesthetic value.

As all those who got to know him through his television appearances will agree, Alec Clifton-Taylor was the ideal guide to architecture—deeply knowledgeable and enthusiastic in his responses. His first book, *The Pattern of English Building,* is regarded as a classic and his popular BBC television series, *Six English Towns,* and its sequels, claimed a wide audience.

'"What a church!" writes Alec Clifton-Taylor of Walpole St Peter in Norfolk . . . "an unforgettable experience" . . . [Mr Clifton-Taylor] was one of the most individual, civilized, and lovable historians I have ever met.' Patrick Nuttgens, *Times Higher Educational Supplement*

Also in Oxford Paperbacks:

Painting and Experience in 15th-century Italy
Michael Baxandall
American Buildings and their Architects: The Colonial and Neo-Classical Styles William H. Pierson
Vision and Design Roger Fry
Revolt into Style George Melly